THE FOREIGN POLICY OF LYNDON B. JOHNSON

The Foreign Policy of Lyndon B. Johnson

The United States and the World, 1963–1969

Jonathan Colman

EDINBURGH
University Press

To Tracy

© Jonathan Colman, 2010, 2012

First published in 2010 by
Edinburgh University Press Ltd
22 George Square, Edinburgh EH8 9LF
www.euppublishing.com

This paperback edition 2012

Typeset in Goudy by
Servis Filmsetting Ltd, Stockport, Cheshire, and
printed and bound in the United States of America

A CIP record for this book is available from the British Library

ISBN 978 0 7486 4013 3 (hardback)
ISBN 978 0 7486 4901 3 (paperback)

The right of Jonathan Colman to be identified as author of this work has been
asserted in accordance with the Copyright, Designs and Patents Act 1988.

Contents

Acknowledgments

The author would like to thank Martin Alexander, Gaynor Johnson, Andrew Priest, Len Scott, Michael O'Grady, Alaric Searle, Emma Whyte and Jake Widén for their helpful comments on portions of this book. Thanks are due to the anonymous referees for their comments on the proposal. My mother and late father helped to support my academic ambitions. The book is dedicated to Tracy, for her love and support. Any flaws of this work are entirely the author's own responsibility.

Jonathan Colman
Burnley, Lancashire, England
January 2010

Abbreviations

ABM: Anti-Ballistic Missile
ADST: Association of Diplomatic Studies and Training
AID: Agency for International Development
ARVN: Army of the Republic of Vietnam (South Vietnam)
BAOR: British Army of the Rhine
DCI: Director of Central Intelligence
DRV: Democratic Republic of Vietnam (North Vietnam)
EEC: European Economic Community
FO: Foreign Office
FOIA: US Freedom of Information Act
FRG: Federal Republic of Germany
FRUS: *Foreign Relations of the United States* series
GATT: General Agreement on Tariffs and Trade
IMF: International Monetary Fund
LBJL: Lyndon B. Johnson Presidential Library, Austin, Texas
MACV: Military Assistance Command, Vietnam
MLF: Multilateral Force
NARA: National Archives and Records Administration
NASA: National Aeronautics and Space Administration
NATO: North Atlantic Treaty Organization
NSA: National Security Agency
NSAM: National Security Action Memorandum
NSC: National Security Council
NVA: North Vietnamese Army
OAS: Organization of American States
OH: Oral history interview
PDB: President's Daily Brief
PFIAB: President's Foreign Intelligence Advisory Board
POL: Petrol, Oil, Lubricants

PRC:	People's Republic of China
SDR:	Special Drawing Rights
SEATO:	Southeast Asia Treaty Organization
SIGINT:	Signals intelligence
TNA:	The National Archives, Kew, Surrey
UK:	United Kingdom
UN:	United Nations
VC:	Viet Cong (Vietnamese communists)

Introduction

Writers have praised President Lyndon B. Johnson's 'Great Society' anti-poverty measures and his civil rights legislation,[1] but there has been much less enthusiasm for his handling of foreign affairs. This reticence is largely due to the Vietnam War.[2] Johnson sent American combat troops to support South Vietnam in 1965, but despite the presence of over half a million US soldiers by 1968 no victory was in sight. By the time the last American soldiers were withdrawn in 1973, some 58,000 American lives, plus countless times more Vietnamese ones, had been lost. South Vietnam collapsed in 1975. The military intervention generated powerful anti-war and countercultural movements, brought about the vilification of the political institutions and gave rise to an anti-interventionist 'syndrome' in US foreign policy. Philip Geyelin wrote in 1966 that Johnson was 'a swash-buckling master of the political midstream, but only in the crowded, well-traveled familiar inland waterways of domestic politics. He had no taste or preparation for the deep waters of foreign policy.' Johnson was 'king of the river and a stranger to the open sea'.[3] According to Robert Dallek, the expansion of the commitment in Vietnam rested on 'a combination of noble and ignoble motives that little serve' Johnson's 'historical reputation' and led to 'the worst foreign policy disaster' in American history.[4]

Thomas Alan Schwartz has noted that the debacle in Southeast Asia has led many historians to depict Johnson as the 'ugly American' – crude, provincial and lacking in subtlety in the conduct of foreign policy.[5] This view of Johnson was shared by some contemporaries, too, especially those associated with the Kennedy Administration. Lord Harlech, the British Ambassador to Washington and a close friend of John F. Kennedy, wrote in 1965 that President Johnson 'basically has no feeling for world affairs and no great interest in them except in so far as they come to disturb the domestic scene'. He had 'little sensitivity to the attitude of foreign-ers, as witness a statement of his that on the basis of his globe-trotting as

1

Vice-President he was convinced that every country he visited the people would prefer to be Americans'.[6]

Employing a bureaucratic politics perspective, in 1992 Paul Y. Hammond argued, among other things, that Johnson never became 'master in his foreign policy house', and that his relationship with advisers was both deferential and distrustful. Difficulties such as these contributed to poor decisions on issues such as Vietnam.[7] Other accounts of Johnson's foreign policies include a collection of essays edited by Warren I. Cohen and Nancy Bernkopf Tucker. While providing additional insights and nuance and drawing on newly released documents, the essays are generally critical of President Johnson. Waldo Heinrichs reiterates earlier views, stating that 'lacking a detached critical perspective', Johnson was 'culture bound and vulnerable to clichés and stereotypes about world affairs. Strangely, this master of domestic politics was . . . aware of change but slow to discard early Cold War assumptions and unsure how to deal with new realities.'[8] Nancy Bernkopf Tucker concludes that Johnson 'remained captive of Cold War illusions shaped by a Munich analogy where distinctions between communism and fascism blurred and a strong America always ready to counter aggression was essential'.[9]

Gradually, more and more scholars, especially those who consider issues 'beyond Vietnam', have been inclined to see Johnson in a more favourable light. In 1995 H. W. Brands drew mainly upon documents from the Lyndon B. Johnson Presidential Library in Austin, Texas, to argue in a general account of Johnson's foreign policies that although the President had 'too much determination' to defend South Vietnam 'and not enough judgement' about what the country was worth to American interests, he was on many other issues an effective manager of foreign affairs, dealing well with a complex international environment.[10] Brands' broad conclusion in a 1999 collection of 'beyond Vietnam' essays that he edited was that Johnson was intimately involved in the conduct of foreign affairs, and that 'his efforts to secure American interests in various parts of the world sometimes succeeded and sometimes failed'.[11]

Recent work also includes a number of single-author studies focusing exclusively on Johnson's policies 'beyond Vietnam'. These works confirm the general 'revisionist' tendency to evaluate Johnson's foreign policies more favourably as time goes on, as a result of the increased availability of archival evidence and a growing sense of detachment from the Vietnam War. Schwartz's exploration of Johnson's policies towards Europe examines matters such as how the President responded to various challenges to the NATO alliance and how he engaged in the pursuit of détente with the Soviet Union. Schwartz concluded that Johnson 'balanced the stability of the Western alliance with the need to stabilize the Cold War and reduce the nuclear danger'.[12]

Similarly, Andrew Priest has maintained that Johnson's foreign policies were 'broadly successful in dealing with NATO and European allies'.[13] John Dumbrell contended that Johnson's policies towards the Soviet Union were part of 'what went right' with the Johnson Presidency.[14] Michael Lumbers' account of US policy towards communist China noted that 'By refusing to take sides in China's domestic conflict or intervene in the country's political affairs', Johnson avoided 'the folly of adding fuel to the fire of Sino-American hostility and nourishing Mao's siege mentality'.[15] Although most authors are critical of Johnson's handling of the Vietnam War, American policy in Southeast Asia does have its defenders. Mark Moyar, for example, argued that the domino principle, a key reason behind the escalation in Vietnam, was valid in the light of communist China and North Vietnam's efforts to spread their influence.[16]

The present book seeks to provide a fresh, general account of the making and execution of Johnson's foreign policies, focusing largely on his own personal contributions but paying due attention to the input of key advisers. Although it takes advantage of existing research, including some of the very latest, the book is based mainly on primary documentation. This includes declassified State Department, White House, Pentagon and CIA documents, and transcripts of presidential telephone conversations, from the *Foreign Relations of the United States* series, the Johnson Library in Austin, Texas, the National Archives and Records Administration at College Park, Maryland, and the National Archives, Kew, England. Among other things, the British documents shed light on US policy towards the Cyprus question in 1964 as well as on the Anglo-American relationship. Memoirs, such as that by Johnson himself, are used, too, as is oral history testimony.

The first chapter provides a brief biography of Lyndon B. Johnson and introduces his White House. Chapters Two and Three explore the question of Vietnam. These are followed by an account of American bilateral ties with two European allies, Britain and France, and then – in Chapter Five – there is an exploration of two challenges to NATO connected with the Federal Republic of Germany. The next chapter considers American policies towards the Soviet Union and communist China, examining among other things the impact of the Sino-Soviet 'split'. Chapter Seven considers two crises in the Middle East. The following chapter examines several aspects of American policy in the Western Hemisphere, then there is coverage of Johnson's contribution to the foreign economic policies of the United States. The conclusion provides a summary of the preceding chapters and considers additional issues such as the nature of the international environment in the 1960s, the impact of Vietnam on US foreign policy in other parts of the world, and how far Johnson's foreign policy skills came to evolve.

The book is perhaps the most sympathetic general account to date of Johnson's foreign policies. It is argued that the escalation of the US commitment in Vietnam was a rational and well-considered policy, although it is also maintained that the war could have been waged more effectively even in the context of avoiding Chinese and Soviet intervention. There were some missteps on other issues, but overall Johnson handled American foreign and economic policy very capably, confounding the traditional image of him as maladroit in the realm of diplomacy and in keeping with the revisionist trend in historiography. Above all, Johnson dealt with successive challenges to the NATO alliance in a skilled and intelligent manner, leaving it politically stronger when he left office in 1969 than it had been in 1963.

Notes

1. Biographies of Johnson include Paul K. Conkin, *Big Daddy from the Pedernales: Lyndon Baines Johnson* (Boston: Twayne, 1986); Robert Dallek, *Flawed Giant: Lyndon Johnson and His Times, 1961–1971* (Oxford: Oxford University Press, 1998); Doris Kearns Goodwin, *Lyndon B. Johnson and the American Dream* (New York: Harper and Row, 1976); Randall B. Woods, *LBJ: Architect of American Ambition* (New York: Free Press, 2006). See Richard Dean Burns and Joseph M. Siracusa, *The Historical Dictionary of the Kennedy-Johnson Era* (Lanham, MD and Oxford: Scarecrow Press, 2007), pp. 363–90, for a general bibliography of the 1960s.
2. See David L. Anderson, 'The Vietnam War', in Robert D. Schulzinger (ed.), *A Companion to American Foreign Relations* (Malden and Oxford: Blackwell, 2006), pp. 309–29, and Randall B. Woods, 'Beyond Vietnam: The Foreign Policies of the Kennedy-Johnson Administrations', in ibid., pp. 330–74.
3. Philip Geyelin, *Lyndon B. Johnson and the World* (London: Pall Mall, 1966), p. 15.
4. Dallek, *Flawed Giant*, pp. 626, 627.
5. The phrase 'ugly American' is a reference to the 1958 novel of the same name by William J. Lederer and Eugene Burdick. Thomas Alan Schwartz, *Lyndon Johnson and Europe: In the Shadow of Vietnam* (Cambridge, MA: Harvard University Press, 2003), pp. 1–6.
6. The National Archives, Kew, Surrey, FO 371/179558, Lord Harlech's Valedictory Despatch, 15 March 1965.
7. Paul Y. Hammond, *LBJ and the Presidential Management of Foreign Relations* (Austin, TX: University of Texas Press, 1992), pp. 210–11.
8. Waldo Heinrichs, 'Lyndon B. Johnson: Change and Continuity', in Warren I. Cohen and Nancy Bernkopf Tucker (eds), *Lyndon Johnson Confronts the World: American Foreign Policy 1963–1968* (Cambridge: Cambridge University Press, 1994), p. 26.
9. Nancy Bernkopf Tucker, 'Lyndon B. Johnson: A Final Reckoning', in ibid., p. 313.

10. H. W. Brands, *The Wages of Globalism: Lyndon Johnson and the Limits of American Power* (New York: Oxford University Press, 1995), p. 259.
11. H. W. Brands, 'Introduction', in H. W. Brands (ed.), *The Foreign Policies of Lyndon B. Johnson: Beyond Vietnam* (College Station, TX: Texas A&M University Press, 1999), p. 5.
12. Thomas Alan Schwartz, *Lyndon Johnson and Europe: In the Shadow of Vietnam* (Cambridge, MA: Harvard University Press, 2003), p. 237.
13. Andrew Priest, *Kennedy, Johnson and NATO: Britain, America and the Dynamics of Alliance* (London: Routledge, 2006), p. 159.
14. John Dumbrell, *President Lyndon Johnson and Soviet Communism* (Manchester: Manchester University Press, 2004), p. 185.
15. Michael Lumbers, *Piercing the Bamboo Curtain: Tentative Bridge-building to China During the Johnson Years* (Manchester: Manchester University Press, 2008), p. 257.
16. Mark Moyar, *Triumph Forsaken: The Vietnam War, 1954–1965* (Cambridge: Cambridge University Press, 2006), p. xxi.

CHAPTER ONE

The Johnson White House and Foreign Policy

After the murder of John F. Kennedy, President Johnson, seeking to promote stability and preferring to focus on domestic issues, emphasised the theme of continuity in foreign affairs. The foreign policy advisory system he inherited was an informal, teamwork-based 'collegial' one, but it soon developed into what has been described as a 'collegial-formalistic hybrid' system. This was more structured than the Kennedy operation, as it involved greater reliance on the principal advisers and was more amenable to presidential control.[1] Among other things, this chapter will introduce Lyndon B. Johnson and his approach to foreign policy, and will outline the respective roles of the main foreign policy advisers, namely Dean Rusk, Secretary of State; McGeorge Bundy and Walt Rostow, successive National Security Advisers; and Robert S. McNamara, Secretary of Defense. The vexed question of the CIA's role in policymaking will be explored. Further discussion will cover the 'Tuesday lunch' as a forum for discussion, advice and decision-making, and Johnson's use of outside counsel such as the 'Wise Men'. Generally, the Johnson White House was a smooth-running operation that closely reflected the needs and proclivities of the President, including the provision of advice from a wide range of sources.

LYNDON B. JOHNSON

Johnson's modest Texas origins have been well covered by biographers.[2] His political career began when he served as secretary to Congressman Richard M. Kleberg (1931–5), and after a stint in the House of Representatives (1937–49) he was elected to the Senate in 1948. There he served as Democratic whip (1951–3), Minority Leader (1953–5) and Majority Leader (1955–61), when he was appointed Vice-President. As Majority Leader, Johnson was said to have 'controlled the Senate and dominated its actions as few legislators ever have'. Unlike most of his predecessors in the vice-presidency, Johnson had active political experience during his tenure there. He was Chairman of the Committee on Equal Employment, and he worked hard to further President Kennedy's campaign against segregation and poverty.[3] Johnson was no stranger to political scandal.[4] So far as his personality is concerned, one historian has written that he embodied 'intense physicality, intelligence, driving wilful ambition, coarseness, concern for the poor and excluded – above all, extreme emotional and personal complexity'.[5] He was famous for his intimidating 'treatment', delivering a cajoling, humouring, flattering or even bullying discourse close into the face of an individual he sought to influence. At well over six feet tall, Johnson was an intimidating presence in every sense. David Bruce, US Ambassador in London from 1961 to 1969, suggested that 'when he entered a room, particularly if you were the only person in it, somehow the room seemed to contract – this huge thing, it's almost like releasing a djinn from one of those Arabian nights bottles. The personality sort of fills the room.'[6]

Although wanting to prioritise domestic affairs, Johnson did bring significant foreign policy experience to the Presidency. While in Congress, he had served for almost twelve years on the House Naval Affairs and then on the Armed Services committees. He had chaired a preparedness subcommittee during the Korean War, participated in the Senate investigation of General Douglas Macarthur's dismissal by President Truman and shaped the legislation creating NASA and advancing the space programme. While serving in Congress he had travelled to Mexico, the southwest Pacific and Europe.[7] As Vice-President, he was Chairman of the Aeronautics and Space Council, and he attended most sessions of the National Security Council (NSC), went on diplomatic missions as a negotiator and visited some twenty-seven countries.[8] McGeorge Bundy suggested in 1964 that Johnson 'understands the world' and was fully 'aware of the danger to which he and the other holder of strategic power in the nuclear age have a shared responsibility'. Similarly, Walt Rostow noted that 'As the minority and majority leader of the Senate', Johnson had been 'in the middle of all the great foreign policy decisions of the 1950s . . . It's clear he knew a great deal about foreign policy.'[9]

Johnson and his principal advisers shared a common foreign policy outlook, centring on the belief that it was necessary to stand up to dictators and totalitarian states while avoiding nuclear war. They had all witnessed the failure of the appeasement of Hitler during the 1930s and then the spread of communism in Eastern and Central Europe after the Second World War. The Cuban Missile Crisis confirmed the need to stand up to

Moscow but not at the price of nuclear war.[10] Johnson's attitude to foreign affairs also included the assumption that allies should pull their weight. British Ambassador in Washington Patrick Dean suggested that Johnson had a pragmatic concern with relative power in both the domestic and international arenas.[11] Britain's international decline led Johnson to say after one of Harold Wilson's frequent visits to Washington that it was no longer worth spending two days with a British prime minister because Britain 'was not that important anymore'.[12] The President also felt a sense of compassion for the underprivileged of the world. He put himself firmly behind the 'Food for Peace' programme that made US agricultural surpluses available to poor nations, often personalising the plight of struggling farmers in developing countries, in what resembled the Great Society anti-poverty programme writ large. Food for Peace was also used to win support for American foreign policies in Vietnam and elsewhere.[13]

Despite a promising background, it has to be said that Johnson was not notably enthusiastic about foreign affairs, finding it remote and abstract compared to American politics.[14] Historian and diplomat Henry Kissinger has suggested that Johnson 'did not take naturally to international relations. One never had the impression that he would think about the topic spontaneously – while shaving for example.'[15] A journalist noted that Johnson disdained meetings with foreign representatives, feeling that little could be learned 'even from informal personal contact, that cannot be learned from reading diplomatic cables or the newspapers, both of which he spends a lot of time studying'. The President 'tends to grumble about any unnecessary visitor, comparing his presence with a visit from his mother-in-law just as he was trying to get to the ball game'.[16]

Although he once said humorously that 'Foreigners are not like the folks I am used to',[17] Johnson rued the lengthy preparation needed for meetings with foreign leaders and diplomats more than he did the meetings themselves. Seeking to be informed and responsive, he was always well prepared, often demonstrating a detailed understanding of his foreign visitors' respective situation at home as well as the foreign policy issues in question. His frequent meetings with Prime Minister Harold Wilson, for example, showed a President who was well versed about the British parliamentary situation. To be sure, Johnson could be diplomatically maladroit; Lord Harlech, British Ambassador in Washington from 1961 to 1965, found him egotistical,[18] and when Harlech's successor, Patrick Dean, was presenting his credentials to the White House in 1965 Johnson launched into an anguished monologue about Vietnam. He stated, in the words of Dean, that while his friends and allies should 'state their views they should not stab him in the back or slap him in the face'. Extraordinarily, Johnson then 'slapped his own face quite vigorously'.[19] Johnson's foreign interlocutors soon got the measure of him, though, and, perhaps more significantly, he matured in his role as diplomat-in-chief, rarely if ever demonstrating clumsy or inappropriate behaviour.[20]

Johnson was an indefatigable worker, with a working day that lasted from about 6:30 a.m. to 11:00 p.m., with further reading after bedtime. Early on in the Presidency, Bundy concluded that the 'best way to do business' with Johnson was mainly 'in writing rather than talking to him'. It was not only 'difficult to get to the President, but when one does it is usually at the end of the day when the President does not go into things thoroughly'. At night, though, Johnson 'works through his papers thoroughly', into the early hours.[21] Johnson's personal secretary, Juanita Roberts, explained in 1964 how she prepared the 'night reading'. She would 'sift, sort and shift' material received throughout the day, 'taking in some items . . . and giving them to the President in person or putting them in various spots on his desk (spots have meaning as to urgency) and into my "stack" for consideration at end of day for night reading'. Most of the night reading comprised various reports and papers with 'tedious detail' that needed 'uninterrupted time for reading and study'. Roberts would 'lighten the load' for the President by including 'thank-you notes, happy little items of information etc that are good to go to sleep on'.[22] The next day Johnson would communicate his thoughts and decisions to officials, such as the Secretary of State, so that the appropriate action could be taken.[23]

THE SECRETARY OF STATE

For Johnson, a Secretary of State should have a number of qualities:

> They ought to have been men that have travelled. If they could, it would be good if they had a language. If they didn't they ought to be good executives. They ought to be reasonably diplomatic, understanding people. They ought to have some grace and some culture and some background, and they ought to have some judgment. They should have been successes as business people or academic people or lawyers or bankers or something. I don't care whether they're Republicans or Democrats. I just want 'em to have integrity, to have judgment. Judgment's the most important thing a man can have.[24]

It was Dean Rusk who was supposed to embody these characteristics. He had been an army colonel in the China-Burma-India theatre in the Second World War, a staff officer in the Pentagon, Assistant Secretary of State for United Nations Affairs and then for the Far East. In 1952 he became head of the Rockefeller Foundation in New York, where he was working when Kennedy asked him to become Secretary of State. Under Kennedy, he worked tirelessly and without fanfare.[25]

In a paper about the organisation of the Department of State early in 1964, McGeorge Bundy suggested that Rusk had

> complete integrity and loyalty. He has discretion and experience. He is a master of exposition, both with diplomats and with Capitol Hill. He has the personal confidence of Committees of Congress and representatives of foreign government to a degree not matched since George Marshall, the man he most admires.[26]

But Rusk also had his limitations. He was

> not a manager. He has never been a good judge of men. His instincts are cautious and negative, and he has only a limited ability to draw the best out of those who work with him. His very discretion seems like secretiveness in his dealings with subordinates; it is a constant complaint in the bureaus that even quite high level officials cannot find out what the Secretary himself thinks and wants . . . The Secretary has little sense of effective operation. He does not move matters towards decision with promptness. He does not stimulate aggressive staff work. He does not coordinate conflicting forces within his own department.[27]

There were occasions when Rusk found his duties too onerous. He told Director of the CIA John McCone early in 1965 that he was 'tired and felt perhaps a new and fresh look at the frightening problems which face this country might be good'. He also indicated that he had problems 'working with the President, seemed to feel the President did not focus on issues of very great importance to the Department, and refused to receive foreign visitors except when subjected to great pressures'.[28]

As Johnson matured, though, Rusk found him easier to work with, and he remained in his post until 1969. This made Rusk the second-longest serving Secretary of State, after Cordell Hull (1933–44). Overall, he got along well with President Johnson. For a start, both men were both of modest, rural Southern backgrounds – Rusk joked that they used to argue 'over which of us was born in the smaller house'. For his part, Johnson valued his Secretary of State's discretion and loyalty, describing him as 'as loyal as a beagle'. (Discretion and loyalty were characteristics that Johnson felt strongly about in his advisers – he would 'rather have a one-eyed farmer as Secretary of State than, by God, a fellow that I can't write a memo to without having it on the front page of the [*New York*] *Times*'.[29]) Johnson always operated through Rusk rather than going through subordinates in the State Department, and he made a point of remaining conversant with Rusk's views. The Secretary built his influence with Johnson mainly in private meetings rather than through sending memoranda.[30]

Undersecretary of State George Ball would also play a notable role in Johnson's foreign policies, acting as a trouble-shooter for matters such as the Congo, Panama, Cyprus and NATO questions, as well as opposing the 'Americanisation' of the war in Vietnam – Ball's views became publicly known when some of his Vietnam memoranda were reproduced in the Pentagon Papers.[31] He had served as counsel to the Farm Credit Administration from 1933 to 1934, had helped to administer Lend-Lease aid in 1940 and had directed the US Strategic Bombing Survey. According to Bundy, Ball had some 'outstanding qualities'. He was a 'brilliant lawyer, a lucid and persuasive draftsman, and a formidable debater'. He served the President and the Secretary of State 'with zeal. He is a man of honour.'[32] But, like 'many lawyers'

> he is a lone wolf and does not use the departmental staff effectively. He spends an excessive amount of time with the press. His judgement is jumpy. He is self-confident to the point of breeziness, and he constantly reaches for more administrative authority than he knows how to use. Unable to administer the Department, he has consistently made it impossible for anyone else to do so.[33]

However, Johnson was less concerned with Ball's bureaucratic prowess than with his policy contributions. He regarded him favourably as a 'can-do' man and took seriously his views about Vietnam (see Chapter Two).[34] Ball resigned in September 1966, in part because of Vietnam. He was succeeded by the former Attorney General Nicholas Katzenbach, who remained in the post until 1969. Johnson respected Katzenbach's ability to handle Capitol Hill, once saying that 'he's the best I've seen in the government for Congress'.[35]

In late 1964, soon after the presidential election, Rusk sketched the work of the State Department, for the edification of a President now more inclined to address foreign policy questions. The Department dealt 'almost entirely with policy and negotiations . . . Its main responsibility is to recommend and administer foreign policy as the arm of the President.' It did this by 'daily contacts with foreign governments through 293 posts abroad (111 embassies, 66 consulates-general, 86 consulates, 17 consular agencies, 6 missions, 5 special offices, and 2 legations) and about 75 international organisations, and by constant discussions between 115 foreign embassies and legations and the Department in Washington'. Most of the Department's business with foreign governments was transacted through its posts abroad, but the most important decisions were made in Washington; only there was it 'possible to develop our policy toward a particular country in light of all the factors that may bear on it'. Much of the Department's business went through telegrams to and from the field. Some

1,000 or so telegrams were sent each day, and about 1,300 were received. There was also a regular flow of letters, airgrams, despatches and other communications.[36]

Johnson had little inherent interest in the functioning and organisation of government bureaucracies,[37] and when the State Department caught his attention as an institution it was usually for negative reasons. In 1965 he told Director of the FBI Edgar Hoover that the Department was full of 'sissy fellows' who were 'not worth a damn'.[38] Above all, he bitterly resented State's propensity to leaks, commenting in 1966 that it 'just nearly breaks my spirit every day'. He added, for good measure, that 'They just got no morale over there, and they got no imagination. They got no initiative. They got no ideas. You have to ask four or five times to get a report.'[39] Johnson was not the only one with reservations about the State Department – Bundy complained that although there were countless 'talented men' in State they did not fulfil their potential, because of:

> the cautious and slow-moving personnel policy of the Foreign Service, a premium which is placed on safety and the avoidance of error, the mindless proliferation of committees and clearance processes, the inhibitions imposed by Congressional Committees which have not been properly cultivated, the inescapable difficulties with other competitive departments, the tendency of all the rest of us to blame the State Department for the misbehaviour of 120 other countries, and the Department's own dangerous tendency to see other nations, not the USA, as its preferred clients.[40]

The State Department did change in the Johnson years, although probably more in the content than in the manner of its activities. As early as the summer of 1965, it was noted that the Department had 'learned to operate with long-sustained serious crises', mainly in Southeast Asia, 'which take a substantial percentage of the time and thoughts of top officials'. Vietnam also meant that military affairs had become much more prominent.[41]

THE NATIONAL SECURITY ADVISER

Between 1947, when it was established to coordinate national security affairs, and 1961, when Kennedy became President, the NSC had been an advisory body, and the role of the 'Special Assistant to the President for National Security Affairs', usually referred to as 'National Security Adviser', was essentially that of an administrator. The National Security Adviser became more significant in the Johnson years, in large part because of the high calibre of the men who fulfilled this role.[42] Johnson's first National Security Adviser was the well-starred McGeorge Bundy.

After performing brilliantly as an undergraduate at Yale, Bundy became a Junior Fellow at Harvard. He served in the Army during the Second World War, returned to Harvard to teach and became the youngest Dean of Faculty in the University's history. In 1961 Kennedy appointed him to head the NSC. Bundy saw his role as ensuring that the President was adequately briefed by the State and Defense departments and the intelligence agencies, but he did have his own input into policymaking. In the first few months after Kennedy's assassination, he counselled President Johnson on diverse topics such as 'how to deal with McNamara and Rusk, the press, Congressional leaders, foreign visitors, Panama, Cuba, Cyprus, Vietnam, Laos, the Soviet Union, NATO, and outer space'.[43]

Johnson sometimes found Bundy patronising,[44] while Johnson's idiosyncrasies often grated on Bundy.[45] Moreover, Bundy succumbed to growing doubts about Vietnam. Overall, though, the working relationship between him and Johnson was a constructive one. The President described him as 'a trusted aide' who after leaving the White House early in 1966 to head the Ford Foundation 'remained available to return whenever he could be helpful'.[46] Johnson called upon Bundy's services a number of times after 1966. For example, during the Six-Day War of June 1967 he brought him in to head a Special Committee of the NSC, to help coordinate the efforts of the NSC, State and Defense to deal with the simultaneous crises in the Middle East and Vietnam.[47]

Robert Komer occupied the post of National Security Adviser in an interim capacity for a few weeks after Bundy's departure. Komer had joined the CIA in 1947 and had, as Bundy wrote, been 'a career civil servant ever since'. He had various strengths, including 'extraordinary range, and a steadily growing mastery of the processes of international politics'. He was 'a tiger for work' with 'a temperament which allows him to bounce back easily when his advice is not taken'.[48] However, other of Komer's qualities were less agreeable. According to White House aide Jack Valenti, there was a 'petulance' about him that caused 'some concern with his co-workers', and he tended to live 'close to the surface of these problems and sometimes becomes emotional about them'.[49] Komer antagonised some senior diplomats in the State Department, and Johnson decided to send him to Vietnam to work on the pacification programme.[50]

Walt Rostow took over the NSC in October 1966. Rostow had studied at Yale, Oxford and the Massachusetts Institute of Technology. Of Russian parents, he was fiercely anti-communist and had prodigious intellectual self-confidence; his renowned *Stages of Economic Development: A Non-Communist Manifesto* (1960) was nothing less than an attempt to refute Karl Marx and to encourage postcolonial nations to adopt capitalist methods as a route to industrialisation. Rostow acted as an occasional adviser to the Eisenhower administration, but he made his presence felt more in the State Department Planning Council under Kennedy and then Johnson.[51] Johnson appointed Rostow to the post of National Security Adviser despite concerns about him being perceived as a 'hard-liner' on issues such as Vietnam.[52] Dean Rusk recalled that in the early phase of his career as National Security Adviser Rostow was 'a little prolific in his words, was not as succinct as McGeorge Bundy, but improved greatly . . . and got to be a very efficient special assistant in all respects'.[53] Rostow commended himself to the President because of his loyalty, his confident manner and his affability.

Johnson held the NSC in much higher regard than he did the State Department. It was less prone to cause him problems with 'leaks and sniping criticism',[54] and he was 'very happy with the memos, analyses, and recommendations coming from the [NSC] staff'.[55] The NSC was especially sensitive to the political needs of the President, perhaps because of its modest size. There were, as Bundy reported in August 1965, just seventeen 'professional officers with their secretaries'. Two of these officers were based in the White House with Bundy – Bromley Smith as executive manager and Gordon Chase, Bundy's assistant. The other fifteen were housed in the Executive Office Building. The three 'top men' were Francis Bator on Economics and Europe; Robert Komer on the Middle East and Africa; and Chester Cooper on the Far East.[56]

Despite Johnson's respect for the NSC, he never set much store by NSC meetings, which became little more than preliminaries to the smaller and more informal Tuesday lunch meetings (considered below). He convened meetings of the NSC mainly as a political gesture, often bringing leading Congressional figures for briefings about what the Administration was doing.[57] Clark Clifford, Secretary of Defense from 1968 to 1969, reflected that the meetings were held only 'because certain people expected them to be held. Subjects would be assigned to the National Security Council. They would be taken up. The subjects would be briefed. There would be some desultory discussion of the points. Then everybody would pick up and leave.'[58] By the summer of 1965 the NSC had become much less active. No longer did it 'initiate a variety of foreign policy demands and initiatives'.[59] It sat on the sidelines when the key decisions about Vietnam were taken. There were fewer National Security Action Memoranda (NSAM), a Kennedy innovation to notify agencies of presidential decisions and to order follow-up action. NSAM 322, the forty-sixth and last NSAM in 1964, was issued on 17 December. Sixteen NSAMs were issued in 1965, eighteen in 1966, ten in 1967 and just four in 1968.[60]

THE SECRETARY OF DEFENSE

As an Air Force officer during the Second World War, Robert S. McNamara had applied 'proven business methods to war'. In doing so, he secured a reputation for efficiency that later gained him a job with the Ford Motor Company, and he had become Ford's chief executive by 1961. Kennedy was impressed by McNamara's talent for running a large bureaucracy and offered him the leadership of the Pentagon. President Johnson found him to be hard-working, loyal and reliable.[61] McNamara was keenly aware of Johnson's outlook and priorities, as well as his own role as a channel of communication between the White House and the military establishment.[62] He was a major shaper of many aspects of foreign policy, but the task of exerting control over the sprawling Department of Defense was a challenging one. The Department employed 4.5 million personnel – 3.5 million in uniform and the rest civilian – and had a yearly budget of nearly $50 billion. The Department ran huge complexes of transportation, telecommunications, logistics and maintenance, along with armies, naval fleets and air forces, including the nuclear arsenal.[63] McNamara left the Administration early in 1968, in despair about Vietnam, and went on to head the World Bank. He was succeeded in February of that year by the urbane lawyer and Washington insider Clark M. Clifford. Johnson commented in 1967 that the working relationship between Secretaries Rusk and McNamara was 'good and they have no petty jealousies or quarrels'.[64] It has been suggested that the published transcripts of telephone conversations indicate a pecking order between the advisers, shown by the fact that Johnson spoke most to McNamara, then to Bundy, then to Rusk.[65] Such a ranking may simply suggest that McNamara was more inclined to telephone the President than were the other advisers, and little in the way of a pecking order is evident in the documentary record. Bundy, in fact, has commented that he, McNamara and Rusk were equals in the Johnson White House.[66] Rostow also worked well as part of the team. Although there were sometimes differences of opinion and emphasis, the advisers made a point of preserving a common front in the eyes of the President, understanding that any signs of conflict would erode their standing. According to Rusk, Johnson 'would always accept our common conclusion. He had views of his own, but he wanted to have the best effort of his colleagues invested in the problem before the President himself came to a final result.'[67]

Occasionally the relationship between the different agencies of foreign policy could be competitive, as in 1966 when the State Department tried to exploit the transition in NSC leadership from Bundy to Rostow to push a tough policy towards President de Gaulle of France (see Chapter Four). Generally, though, there were good relationships between the NSC, State and Defense. For one, the NSC's modest size made it less likely that it would antagonise other agencies, and for its part the State Department made efforts, as Dean Rusk noted, to encourage 'contacts at all levels' between it and Defense, 'between the majors and the desk officers, and the lieutenant colonels and the office directors, and people like that'. Therefore 'an inquisitive and suspicious press was not able to generate any impressions of a feud between the Department of State and the Department of Defense'.[68]

THE CIA

Presidential relationships with the CIA have sometimes been troubled. Presidents Eisenhower and Kennedy were diligent consumers of intelligence information while Richard Nixon tended to regard such material as being of little account or even biased. Johnson's relationship with the CIA was a difficult one, largely due to his own prejudices. He believed that the CIA had conspired against him in the 1960 Democratic Convention, helping him to lose the presidential nomination,[69] he had seen at first hand how covert actions such as the Bay of Pigs in 1961 could damage the standing of the White House and he believed that the CIA's sponsorship of assassination plots had led to Kennedy's own assassination.[70] He took the view that formulating foreign policies was difficult enough without the CIA complicating matters, not least because, unlike an intelligence organisation, a politician must consider the domestic dimension of foreign policy. On one occasion, Johnson outlined his reservations by means of a vivid anecdote:

> Let me tell you about these intelligence guys. When I was growing up in Texas, we had a cow named Bessie. I'd go out early and milk her. I'd get her in the stanchion, seat myself and squeeze out a pail of fresh milk. One day I'd worked hard and gotten a full pail of milk, but I wasn't paying attention, and old Bessie swung her shit-smeared tail through that pail of milk. Now, you know, that's what these intelligence guys do. You work hard and get a good program or policy going, and they swing a shit-smeared tail through it.[71]

Deputy Director of the CIA Ray Cline suggested that because the Agency was 'the bearer of bad tidings about the Vietnam War', it 'was not very happily received by any of the policymakers who tried to make the Vietnam intervention work'.[72] However, as noted earlier, Johnson's reservations towards the CIA went beyond Vietnam, and his openness to

George Ball's ideas about the war showed a willingness to consider pessimistic views. He probably felt that he had enough to deal with without the contributions of the CIA.

Johnson's desire to keep intelligence at a distance resulted in, among other things, frustration on the part of the President's Military Aide, General C. V. Clifton. Early in 1964 Clifton complained that Johnson 'was not getting a steady feed of intelligence on world situations'. The question was how to bring the President 'up-to-date on intelligence with a minimum of effort on his part'. After experimentation with the format of the intelligence material, it was decided late in 1964 to settle on what was dubbed the 'President's Daily Brief' (PDB).[73] The main virtue of the Brief from the President's perspective was indeed 'brevity' – typically, the PDB was just two to four pages long, plus maps and occasional photographs. However, the seemingly optimal format of the PDB did not eradicate concerns about Johnson's consumption of intelligence material. Deputy Director of the CIA Richard Helms reported in May 1965 that there was still 'quite a problem at the White House getting material to the President'. Undoubtedly, White House personnel knew of the President's attitude to intelligence documents and were reluctant to provide substantial amounts of this material. Therefore the issue was not, as Clifton once complained, that Johnson was 'a painfully slow reader'[74] (which was incorrect in any case), but Johnson's reservations towards intelligence reports. Later, after seeing Johnson, Henry Kissinger reflected upon the irony of 'the most powerful leader in the world, with instant access to all the information of our intelligence services, jumping up periodically to see what the news ticker was revealing'.[75]

Johnson's relationships with the various Directors of Central Intelligence (DCI) were at best ambivalent. The first of Johnson's DCIs was John McCone, who had worked for the US government in various capacities since 1948 and became DCI in November 1961. Soon after Kennedy's death, Johnson complained to McCone about the CIA's image of 'cloak and dagger' and suggested that 'every time' McCone or the CIA was mentioned 'it was associated with a dirty trick'.[76] The President tended to exclude his DCIs from policy deliberations. In April 1964, McCone lamented his limited contact with the President, pointing out that Johnson 'did not get direct intelligence briefings from me as was the custom with President Kennedy and had been the Eisenhower custom'. Johnson told the DCI that all he had to do was 'call up' whenever he wanted a meeting but McCone's response was that he rarely had success despite 'several "attempts"' to speak with the President. Later, Clark Clifford suggested as head of the President's Foreign Intelligence

Advisory Board, an oversight body, that Johnson should placate McCone by sharing a round of golf. The President did play golf with McCone, but only once.[77] McCone's complaints about the difficulties of seeing the President were in fact exaggerated, because by 25 April 1965 Johnson had seen McCone in as many as eighty-nine meetings and had spoken to him fourteen times over the telephone.[78] But the DCI's belief that Johnson was less than enthusiastic about spending time with him, especially alone, was accurate – the President complained that he was 'sick and tired of John McCone tugging at my shirttails'.[79]

McCone resigned in frustration in April 1965. His successor, Admiral William Raborn, a novice in the world of intelligence, did not fare much better. Raborn had managed the US Navy's adoption of the Polaris nuclear missile programme, and by the time he left the CIA in June 1966, he had a number of achievements to his credit, including the establishment of a 24-hour Operations Centre to deal with crises.[80] Generally, though, his leadership of the CIA left something to be desired – certainly in Johnson's view. In February 1966 the President suggested that Raborn had 'too much confidence in his people, and he's too complimentary of 'em, and he feels they're doing too well, and he is totally oblivious to the fact that he is not highly regarded and he is not doing a good job'.[81] As with McCone, Johnson felt little inclination to spend much time with the latest DCI, telling him bluntly that 'If I want to see you, Raborn, I'll telephone you!'[82]

Richard Helms was the next to run the CIA. He was an intelligence man to his fingertips, having worked for the Office of Strategic Services in the Second World War and for the CIA since its founding in 1947. However, he was not routinely invited to the Tuesday lunch meetings until the summer of 1967, after he had predicted the duration of the Arab–Israeli War.[83] The forecast had been very useful in helping Johnson to frame his policies, and was one of the few occasions when he and the intelligence community worked together well.

The Tuesday Lunch

The informal Tuesday lunch meeting was the most important forum for foreign policy discussion under Johnson. The first of these meetings was held on 4 February 1964. About 150 of the meetings were held.[84] Rostow commented in 1968 that the lunch was effectively 'a regular NSC meeting with carefully prepared staff work, plus the advantage of bringing together in a very human setting the President and his chief national security advisers'. Others, including the Vice-President, were invited 'when the

President decides that they can contribute'.[85] The Tuesday lunch gathering certainly had its admirers. Bromley Smith of the NSC said that the 'meetings were closely structured, highly valuable. The Tuesday luncheon was one of the most valuable pieces of machinery that I've encountered.'[86]

Late in 1968, after taking soundings in the Johnson White House, National Security Adviser Designate Henry Kissinger told President-elect Richard Nixon that the 'major strength' of the Tuesday lunch system was its 'flexibility and the speed with which decisions can be made', but 'the discussants are frequently inadequately briefed and often unfamiliar with the nuances of the issue before them'. In the absence of 'staff or previous staff study, there is no guarantee that all the relevant alternatives are considered, or that all the interested parties within the government have a chance to state their views'. As there was no 'systematic follow-up, it is often unclear exactly what has been decided or why. Nor is there any formal method for assuring that decisions are adequately implemented.'[87]

Other critics included Johnson's Undersecretary of State for the Far East William P. Bundy, who described the Tuesday lunch as 'an abomination', lacking both preparation and follow-up.[88] These comments cannot be ignored, but Kissinger had an axe to grind and Bundy was only an intermittent attendee. The Tuesday lunch was an important aspect of foreign policymaking in the Johnson White House, and it was something that suited the President's personal proclivities down to the ground. Johnson also – as Rostow has pointed out – made use of 'special ad hoc meetings on particular subjects', such as the 1966–7 offset negotiations over US troops in the Federal Republic of Germany (see Chapter Five).[89]

These, like the NSC meetings and Tuesday lunches, were formal meetings, but there was also an informal, 'shadow' side of the advisory process.[90] Rostow noted that Johnson talked frequently to erstwhile colleagues in the Senate. He consulted former Secretary of State Dean Acheson and other 'wise men'. He sought the views of old friends such as Abe Fortas, Arthur Krim, Ed Weisl, James Rowe and Tommy Corcoran.[91] The formal advisers were ambivalent to the role of outsiders, not least because of the question of accountability.[92] However, Johnson valued hearing from external sources because their views were from beyond official channels and were less influenced by bureaucratic politics and vested interests.[93]

Finally, as alluded to on a couple of occasions earlier, Johnson utterly loathed the widespread practice of leaks. He pointed out to the Joint Chiefs of Staff, for example, early in 1964 'how difficult and impossible it would have been for General Eisenhower to succeed if everything we were planning' for D-Day in 1944 'had been discussed by government officials, including State Department and military officials, before they even staged the landings'.[94] US Ambassador in London David Bruce felt that the President's 'hypersensitivity' to what appeared in newspapers was 'disturbing, unwise and undignified',[95] but the issue for Johnson was simply that leaks could complicate greatly the framing and implementation of policies.

According to an aide, a distinct Johnsonian advisory had emerged fully by the spring of 1966.[96] That system reflected the President's desire to keep his hand on the foreign policy helm, his desire to take advice from a wide range of inside and outside sources, the need to avoid leaks and his preference for informality. Johnson did not make many decisions in discussions and meetings. Instead, what tended to happen was that he would, according to Rostow, 'make up his mind while alone – after one final re-reading of a document, or one last telephone call'.[97] There was an element of inscrutability in this practice, but the precise mix of influences behind a decision can never be known with any certainty. Anyway, with Johnson, as Francis Bator put it, 'explaining his reasons to staff . . . was not in his nature'.[98] The thirty-sixth President rarely felt that there was much to be gained from showing his cards to subordinates, if anyone, but he established a White House operation that was, on the face of it, a very adequate foundation for the formulation of policy, with little evidence of the sort of internecine conflicts that would mar the making of foreign policy in later years. Johnson's precise choices and how they would play out was a different matter, though.

Notes

1. John Dumbrell, *Lyndon Johnson and Soviet Communism* (Manchester: Manchester University Press, 2004), p. 12.
2. See, for example, Randall B. Woods, *LBJ: Architect of American Ambition* (New York: Free Press, 2006), pp. 5–69.
3. The National Archives, Kew, Surrey (hereafter TNA), FO 371/168409, J. L. N. O'Loughlin, 'Lyndon Baines Johnson', 4 December 1963.
4. For a brief account, see Paul Johnson, *A History of the American People* (London: Weidenfeld and Nicolson, 1997), pp. 726–7.
5. Dumbrell, *Lyndon Johnson and Soviet Communism*, p. 5.
6. Quoted in Nelson K. Lankford, *The Last American Aristocrat: The Biography of Ambassador David K.E. Bruce* (New York: Little, Brown, 1996), pp. 326–7.
7. Robert Dallek, *Flawed Giant: Lyndon Johnson and his Times, 1961–1973* (Oxford and New York: Oxford University Press, 1998), p. 85.
8. TNA, FO 371/168409, J. L. N. O'Loughlin, 'Lyndon Baines Johnson', 4 December 1963.
9. Quoted in Dallek, *Flawed Giant*, p. 85.

10. Dumbrell, *Lyndon Johnson and Soviet Communism*, p. 14.
11. TNA, FO 371/179566, Dean to Paul Gore-Booth, 'Account of President Johnson's administration of US foreign policy', 5 June 1965.
12. Quoted in Henry Brandon, *Special Relationships: A Foreign Correspondent's Memoirs from Roosevelt to Reagan* (London and Basingstoke: Macmillan, 1988), p. 210.
13. See Kristin L. Ahlberg, *Transplanting the Great Society: Lyndon Johnson and Food for Peace* (Columbia, MO and London: University of Missouri Press, 2008).
14. Dallek, *Flawed Giant*, p. 87.
15. Henry A. Kissinger, *The White House Years* (London: Weidenfeld and Nicolson and Michael Joseph, 1979), p. 18.
16. *The Sunday Times*, 25 April 1965.
17. Quoted in Dallek, *Flawed Giant*, p. 86.
18. Michael F. Hopkins, 'David Ormsby-Gore, Lord Harlech, 1961–65', in Michael F. Hopkins, Saul Kelly and John W. Young (eds), *British Ambassadors to Washington, 1939–1977* (Basingstoke: Palgrave, 2009), p. 143.
19. Jonathan Colman, 'Patrick Dean, 1965–69', in ibid., p. 153.
20. See Elmer Plischke, 'Lyndon Johnson as diplomat-in-chief', in Bernard J. Firestone and Robert C. Vogt (eds), *Lyndon Baines Johnson and the Uses of Power* (New York: Greenwood Press, 1988), pp. 257–86.
21. Memorandum for the record, 28 February 1964, *Foreign Relations of the United States* (hereafter *FRUS*) *1964–1968 XXXIII Organization and Management of US Foreign Policy; United Nations* (Washington, DC: USGPO, 2004), p. 345.
22. Roberts to Reedy, 2 July 1964, *FRUS 1964–1968 XXXIII*, pp. 348–9.
23. W. W. Rostow, *The Diffusion of Power: An Essay in Recent History* (New York: Macmillan, 1972), p. 363.
24. Editorial note, *FRUS 1964–1968 XXXIII*, pp. 186–7.
25. Dallek, *Flawed Giant*, pp. 87–8.
26. Bundy to Johnson, 21 January 1964, *FRUS 1964–1968 XXXIII*, p. 34.
27. Ibid., pp. 34–5.
28. McCone to Johnson, 18 March 1965, *FRUS 1964–1968 XXXIII*, p. 69.
29. Michael Beschloss (ed.), *Reaching for Glory: Lyndon Johnson's Secret White House Tapes, 1964–1965* (New York: Simon and Schuster, 2001), p. 371.
30. Warren Cohen, *Dean Rusk* (Totowa, NJ: Cooper Square, 1980), p. 219; Dallek, *Flawed Giant*, pp. 87–8; Dumbrell, *Lyndon Johnson and Soviet Communism*, pp. 12–13; Dean Rusk, *As I Saw It: A Secretary of State's Memoirs* (New York: Norton, 1990), p. 281.
31. Neil Sheehan, Hedrick Smith, E. W. Kenworthy and Fox Butterfield (eds), *The Pentagon Papers: The Secret History of the Vietnam War: The Complete and Unabridged Series as published by the New York Times* (New York: Bantam Books, 1971).
32. Bundy to Johnson, 21 January 1965, *FRUS 1964–1968 XXXIII*, p. 35.
33. Ibid.
34. See James A. Bill, *George Ball: Behind the Scenes in US Foreign Policy* (New Haven, CT and London: Yale University Press, 1997) and David DiLeo, *George Ball, Vietnam and the Rethinking of Containment* (Chapel Hill, NC: University of North Carolina Press, 1991).
35. Johnson–Rusk telephone conversation, 16 September 1966, *FRUS 1964–1968 XXXIII*, p. 198.
36. Rusk to Johnson, 31 December 1964, *FRUS 1964–1968 XXXIII*, p. 31.

37. Bromley Smith Oral History Interview I, 29 July 1969, by Paige E. Mulhollan, Internet Copy, Lyndon B. Johnson Presidential Library, Austin, TX (hereafter LBJL).
38. Editorial note, 31 December 1964, *FRUS 1964–1968 XXXIII*, p. 190.
39. Dumbrell, *Lyndon Johnson and Soviet Communism*, pp. 12–13.
40. Bundy to Johnson, 21 January 1964, *FRUS 1964–1968 XXXIII*, p. 34.
41. State Department paper, undated, *FRUS 1964–1968 XXXIII*, p. 89.
42. Andrew Preston, *The War Council: McGeorge Bundy and the NSC* (Cambridge, MA and London: Harvard University Press, 2006), pp. 7–8.
43. Dallek, *Flawed Giant*, pp. 89–90.
44. Ibid.
45. Kai Bird, *The Color of Truth: McGeorge Bundy and William Bundy: Brothers in Arms* (New York: Touchstone, 1998), p. 342; McGeorge Bundy Oral History Special Interview I, 30 March 1993, by Robert Dallek, Internet Copy, LBJL.
46. Lyndon B. Johnson, *The Vantage Point: Perspectives on the Presidency, 1963–69* (New York: Holt, Rinehart, Winston, 1973), p. 21.
47. Rostow's Recollections of 5 June 1967, 17 November 1967, *FRUS 1964–1968 XIX Arab-Israeli Crisis and War, 1967* (2004), pp. 291–2.
48. Bundy to Johnson, 14 September 1965, *FRUS 1964–1968 XXXIII*, pp. 362–3.
49. Valenti to Johnson, 1 March 1966, *FRUS 1964–1968 XXXIII*, p. 374.
50. Dumbrell, *Lyndon Johnson and Soviet Communism*, p. 12.
51. See David Milne, *America's Rasputin: Walt Rostow and the Vietnam War* (New York: Hill and Wang, 2008).
52. Johnson–McNamara telephone conversation, 27 February 1966, *FRUS 1964–1968 XXXIII*, p. 372.
53. Dean Rusk Oral History Interview I, 28 July 1969, by Paige E. Mulhollan, Internet Copy, LBJL.
54. Memorandum for the record, 10 February 1964, *FRUS 1964–1968 XXXIII*, p. 344.
55. Editorial note, *FRUS 1964–1968 XXXIII*, p. 390.
56. Bundy to Johnson, 2 August 1965, *FRUS 1964–1968 XXXIII*, p. 360. The number remained steady – in late 1967 there were eighteen NSC staff members. Rostow to Johnson, 25 September 1967 *FRUS 1964–1968 XXXII*, p. 401.
57. H. W. Brands, *The Wages of Globalism: Lyndon Johnson and the Limits of American Power* (Oxford and New York: Oxford University Press, 1995), p. 21.
58. David C. Humphrey, 'NSC Meetings During the Johnson Presidency', *Diplomatic History*, 18, 1 (Winter 1994), pp. 33, 44.
59. State Department paper, undated, *FRUS 1964–1968 XXXIII*, p. 89.
60. Editorial note, *FRUS 1964–1968 XXXIII*, p. 356.
61. Dallek, *Flawed Giant*, pp. 88–9.
62. Summary, *FRUS 1964–1968 X National Security* (2002), http:www.state.gov/r/pa/ho/frus/johnsonlb/x/1278.htm
63. Robert S. McNamara, *In Retrospect: The Tragedy and Lessons of Vietnam* (New York: Times Books, 1995), p. 22.
64. Meeting with foreign policy advisers, *FRUS 1964–1968 V Vietnam 1967* (2002), p. 968.
65. John Prados, 'Feature Review: Looking for the Real Lyndon', *Diplomatic History*, 27, 5 (November 2003), pp. 754–5 (review of Beschloss (ed.), *Reaching for Glory*).
66. McGeorge Bundy Oral History Special Interview I, 30 March 1993, by Robert Dallek, Internet Copy, LBJL.

67. Dean Rusk Oral History Interview I, 28 July 1969, by Paige E. Mulhollan, Internet Copy, LBJL.
68. Ibid.
69. Christopher Andrew, *For the President's Eyes Only: Secret Intelligence and the American Presidency from Washington to Bush* (London: HarperCollins, 1995), p. 309.
70. Rhodri Jeffreys-Jones, *The CIA and American Democracy*, 3rd edition (New Haven, CT: Yale University Press, 2003), pp. 139–41.
71. Quoted in Andrew, *For the President's Eyes Only*, p. 323.
72. Ibid., p. 315.
73. Editorial note, *FRUS 1964–1968 XXXIII*, p. 416.
74. Editorial note, *FRUS 1964–1968 XXXIII*, pp. 473–4.
75. Kissinger, *The White House Years*, p. 18.
76. Editorial note, *FRUS 1964–1968 XXXIII*, p. 409.
77. Editorial note, *FRUS 1964–1968 XXXIII*, pp. 440–1.
78. Jeffreys-Jones, *CIA and American Democracy*, p. 146.
79. Quoted in Charles E. Lathrop (ed.), *The Literary Spy: The Ultimate Source for Quotations on Espionage and Intelligence* (New Haven, CT and London: Yale University Press, 2004), p. 339.
80. Raborn to Moyers, 14 February 1966, *FRUS 1964–1968 XXXIII*, pp. 533–5.
81. Editorial note, *FRUS 1964–1968 XXXIII*, p. 536.
82. Quoted in Lathrop (ed.), *Literary Spy*, p. 339.
83. Jeffreys-Jones, *CIA and American Democracy*, p. 166.
84. Editorial note, *FRUS 1964–1968 XXXIII*, p. 343. See David C. Humphrey, 'Tuesday Lunch at the White House: A Preliminary Assessment', *Diplomatic History*, 8, 1 (Winter 1984), pp. 81–102.
85. Bundy to Johnson, 5 December 1968, *FRUS 1964–1968 XXXIII*, p. 407.
86. Bromley Smith Oral History Interview I, 29 July 1969, by Paige E. Mulhollan, Internet Copy, LBJL.
87. Kissinger to Nixon, 27 December 1968, *FRUS 1969–1976 II Organization and Management of US Foreign Policy* (2006), pp. 2–3.
88. Humphrey, 'Tuesday Lunch at the White House', p. 92.
89. Rostow to Johnson, 11 May 1967, *FRUS 1964–1968 XXXIII*, p. 399.
90. Dumbrell, *Lyndon Johnson and Soviet Communism*, p. 13.
91. W. W. Rostow, *The Diffusion of Power: An Essay in Recent History* (New York: Macmillan, 1972), p. 362.
92. Cohen, *Dean Rusk*, p. 220.
93. Clark Clifford with Richard Holbrooke, *Counsel to the President: A Memoir* (New York: Random House, 1991), p. 394.
94. Memorandum for the record, 4 March 1964, *FRUS 1964–1968 XXXII*, p. 607.
95. Diary entry by David Bruce, 19 May 1966, *FRUS 1964–1968 XIII Western Europe Region* (1995), p. 392.
96. Saunders paper, 15 March 1968, *FRUS 1964–1968 XXXIII*, p. 403.
97. Rostow, *Diffusion of Power*, p. 361.
98. Francis M. Bator, 'Lyndon Johnson and Foreign Policy: The Case of Western Europe and the Soviet Union', in Aaron Lobel (ed.), *Presidential Judgment: Foreign Policy Decision Making in the White House* (Hollis, NH: Puritan Press, 2000), p. 59.

CHAPTER TWO

Vietnam: Going to War, 1963–5

The French had colonised Indochina in the nineteenth century, and after losing it to the Japanese during the Second World War were able to regain it in 1945 with Japan's defeat. France soon found its position in Indochina threatened by a communist-inspired uprising, and from 1950 to 1954 the United States, concerned, as one might expect, with preventing the spread of communism while also seeking indirectly to support France's position in Europe, provided $4 billion of aid to support the French war.[1] The Battle of Dien Bien Phu in 1954 brought an end to the French imperial presence in Indochina, which was then partitioned into North and South Vietnam, Cambodia and Laos. The North was under communist control, and, of course, the United States stepped up its presence considerably in support of South Vietnam. By 1965 American combat troops were fighting there in an anti-communist war.

This chapter explores the escalation of the American commitment under President Johnson from 1963 to 1965. Attention is given to key developments such as the Gulf of Tonkin Resolution in the summer of 1964, the initiation of a bombing campaign in Vietnam in February 1965 and the introduction of American combat troops throughout South Vietnam a few months later. There then follows an account of the various influences, potential or actual, upon the White House. These included concerns with international credibility; the 'domino theory'; the role of advisers; public opinion in the United States; the role of allies; the regime in Saigon; and the Sino-Soviet dimension to policymaking. Johnson escalated the US commitment in Vietnam with deep foreboding and reticence and only after seeking a range of opinions from both inside and outside the Administration. Cold War anxieties about the United States' international 'credibility' were the main motivation for intervention, a reasonable concern given that for years Washington had publicly upheld the importance of South Vietnam to American and 'Free World' interests.

The Gulf of Tonkin Resolution

By the time of John F. Kennedy's assassination on 22 November 1963, there were some 16,000 American advisers in South Vietnam.[2] National Security Action Memorandum (NSAM) 273 four days after Kennedy's death stated that 'all senior officers of the government will move energetically to insure the full unity of support for established US policy',[3] but apart from incremental increases in the number of advisers it was not until the late summer of 1964 that the next major development took place. Since 1962, US destroyers had conducted signals intelligence (SIGINT) missions in the Gulf under the cover-name DESOTO. Data was gathered on North Vietnamese radar installations in support of South Vietnamese commando raids on the North (OPLAN 34A). Although on 2 August the US destroyer *Maddox* was hit only by a single machine gun bullet in a North Vietnamese attack,[4] the incident was enough to provoke an outcry in Washington. The Administration condemned the 'unprovoked' assault on a US naval vessel operating supposedly on the high seas. Two days later, there were reports of engagements between North Vietnamese vessels and the *Maddox* and the *C. Turner Joy*, which Johnson had ordered to the Gulf after hearing of the initial attack on the *Maddox*. There is evidence of a minor engagement between the North Vietnamese and the *Joy* on 4 August, but knowledge of the contacts with the *Maddox* that day is fragmentary. According to the *Maddox*'s commander, the enemy's alleged use of torpedoes, for example, appeared 'doubtful'– the products of 'freak weather effects' on radar and of 'over-eager sonarmen'.[5]

In fact, the National Security Agency (NSA), the United States' chief SIGINT organisation, concluded in 2002 that no attacks took place on 4 August 1964. Through a compound of analytical errors, American SIGINT elements in the region and at NSA headquarters in the United States had reported Hanoi's plans to attack the DESOTO patrol. Additional errors of analysis and 'an obscuring of additional information led to the publication of more "evidence"'. The reality was that Hanoi's navy was engaged in nothing more than salvaging one of the ships damaged on 2 August. The NSA concluded that from the beginning of the crisis through to October 1964, SIGINT information was 'presented in such a manner as to preclude responsible decisionmakers in the Johnson Administration from having the complete and objective narrative of events of 4 August 1964'. Instead, the only SIGINT reports made available to Administration officials were those supporting the claim that the communists had attacked the two destroyers. The objective of the personnel who sifted and disseminated the material concerned was not, apparently, to mislead, but rather to support the Navy's claim that the DESOTO patrol had been attacked. An accurate conclusion would have been that the North Vietnamese 'did not attack but were even uncertain as to the location of the ships'. The small number of SIGINT reports suggesting that an attack had taken place contained 'severe analytic errors, unexplained translation changes, and the conjunction of two unrelated messages into one translation'. The latter product would become one of the Johnson Administration's 'main proof of the 4 August attack'.[6]

What is more significant than the NSA's poor performance in this affair is that Johnson and his colleagues knew that what had happened in the Gulf of Tonkin was not cut and dried, but nevertheless ordered a 'firm, swift retaliatory strike . . . against NVN [North Vietnamese] including actions against NVN naval craft . . . airstrikes against four torpedo boat bases on NVN coast, air cover for these operations which will engage any unfriendly aircraft'.[7] Johnson held a number of meetings with Congressional leaders to ensure their support, and Secretary of Defense Robert S. McNamara testified to Congress that the *Maddox* and the *C. Turner Joy* had been attacked while 'carrying out a routine patrol of the type we carry out all over the world at all times'.[8] This testimony was obviously disingenuous, but it is not surprising that McNamara kept quiet about the intelligence-gathering role of the US vessels as to do otherwise would have compromised American interests, as well as shedding unwanted light on the extremely secretive NSA. The White House succeeded in getting the Southeast Asia Resolution, also known as the Tonkin Gulf Resolution, through Congress on 10 August. There were no dissenting votes in the House and only two in the Senate. Johnson now had authorisation 'to take all necessary measures to repel any armed attack against the forces of the United States and to prevent further aggression'.[9]

Johnson reflected in his memoirs that he had been determined to seek from Congress full support for any major action he took.[10] He noted how President Truman had failed to obtain a comparable endorsement in relation to the Korean War, and felt that this failure was partly responsible for the declining public support. The punitive attacks upon the Vietnamese communists and the passage of the Resolution were also valuable as a way of neutralising the charge from the Republican presidential candidate Barry Goldwater that the Administration was soft on communism. Johnson's response to the Tonkin incidents certainly played well for him, winning considerable popular support – his popularity rating leapt from 42 per cent to 72 per cent overnight, helping to neutralise Goldwater on Vietnam.[11]

The Administration's disingenuousness over the Tonkin Gulf incidents and the profoundly divisive nature of the war in Vietnam meant that, unsurprisingly, the Resolution came to provoke a great deal of controversy. First, it should be understood that legally the Resolution was a conditional declaration of war. Such a declaration is, as one commentator has pointed out, 'an ultimatum permitting, but not requiring, the president the use of military force in certain circumstances'. Johnson had seen how President Eisenhower had gained conditional declarations of war in 1956 in relation to the Formosa crisis, and in 1957 in support of the 'Eisenhower Doctrine' against the spread of communism in the Middle East. In May 1964, Walt Rostow of the State Department used the Formosa Resolution as a model with which the President could gain 'discretionary authority to conduct war in Asia'.[12]

The dubious pretext notwithstanding, the Southeast Asia Resolution was a legitimate and sensible option, given the increasing threat to the security of the Saigon regime. The significance of the Resolution is less to be found in what went on in the Gulf of Tonkin than in the general point of providing the White House with freedom of action in Vietnam. The broad purpose of the Resolution was appreciated at the time by, among others, Senator J. William Fulbright, head of the Senate Foreign Relations Committee and the Resolution's sponsor. Fulbright stated during the Senate hearings in August 1964 that the Resolution would 'authorise whatever the Commander in Chief feels is necessary'.[13] He therefore had little to complain about later when Johnson expanded the war as he saw fit.

The use of the Gulf of Tonkin incidents – given their ambiguity – as a pretext for gaining Congressional support was not a wise move, though, because it ended up tainting both the Administration and the Resolution. However, the Resolution was always likely to face particular scrutiny as a result of the unsuccessful course of the war, and Henry Kissinger, for one, has commented that although the Resolution was 'not based on a full presentation of the facts, even allowing for the confusion of combat' it was not 'a major factor in America's commitment to ground combat in Vietnam'. More significant, he suggests, were 'the convictions of all the leading personalities' in bringing the United States 'to the same destination', that is, the various escalations of the US commitment in subsequent years.[14] With the Southeast Asia Resolution under his belt and with his electoral victory in November, President Johnson felt more secure politically and was in a better position to escalate the American commitment in Vietnam as his 'convictions' demanded.

TOWARDS ROLLING THUNDER

In November, Ambassador to Saigon General Maxwell Taylor noted the

> continuing political turmoil, irresponsibility and division within the armed
> forces of South Vietnam, lethargy in the pacification programme, some anti-
> US feeling which could grow, signs of mounting terrorism by VC [Viet Cong]
> directly at US personnel and deepening discouragement and loss of morale
> throughout SVN.[15]

The bombing of the US Army barracks at Pleiku on 6 February 1965, which killed eight Americans and injured many more, helped to put the decision to escalate into action. National Security Adviser McGeorge Bundy, who was in South Vietnam when the attacks occurred, argued in favour of a policy of 'sustained reprisal', in which air and naval policy against the North was 'justified and related to the whole Viet Cong campaign of violence and terror in the South'.[16] Advisers such as Secretary of State Dean Rusk and Robert S. McNamara also felt that an infusion of American military power was needed. For his part, Johnson stated memorably that

> he had kept the shotgun over the mantel and the bullets in the basement for a
> long time now, but that the enemy was killing his personnel and he could not
> expect them to continue their work if he did not authorise them to take steps
> to defend themselves.[17]

Flaming Dart air attack reprisals were soon underway against North Vietnamese targets, and Johnson announced the deployment to South Vietnam of a Hawk air defence battalion and that 'other reinforcements, in units and individuals, may follow'. These reinforcements, sent within a month, consisted of fully equipped ground combat units to protect US air bases.

Further attacks on American personnel led on 13 February to a more sustained air response, in the form of Rolling Thunder, the systematic and expanding bombing campaign against North Vietnamese targets. Above all, Johnson wanted to convey a clear signal of determination to both South and North Vietnam, and Rolling Thunder fitted the bill.[18] Rolling Thunder became the mainstay of the United States' military effort until President Johnson's resignation speech in March 1968 and a source of great devastation in Vietnam.[19] So in February 1965 Johnson had initiated what in retrospect was a major step in the escalation of the war, but it would be going too far to say that the United States was at war at this point – the introduction of combat troops was a more significant threshold to be crossed.

THE INTRODUCTION OF US COMBAT FORCES

The bombing failed to yield much success, in part because North Vietnam offered few industrial targets, while other targets such as bridges and roads could be repaired rapidly with Soviet and Chinese help. Nor did the air attacks do much to fortify the will of the South Vietnamese or to make the communists think twice about their actions. Director of Central Intelligence John McCone argued on 2 April 1965 that the airstrikes had done little to impede the North Vietnamese 'policy of directing Viet Cong insurgency, infiltrating cadres and supplying material. If anything, the strikes have hardened their attitude.' Moreover, the airstrikes' 'slowly ascending tempo' would generate 'increasing pressure to stop the bombing . . . from various elements of the American public, from the press, the United Nations, and world opinion'.[20]

General William C. Westmoreland, commander of US forces in Vietnam, noted a few weeks into the bombing how the VC still held the initiative throughout South Vietnam. The communists had experienced

> continuing success in their efforts to consolidate political gains in the rural areas; to increase their military strength by a combination of infiltrated cadre and levies on available manpower; and to improve their organisation, weaponry and logistic capability. Through the use of military action, intimidation, and propaganda, they are implanting a sense of inevitability of VC success.[21]

In contrast with the enemy, the South Vietnamese army was still ineffectual, lacking 'trained military, para-military and police manpower'.[22] Evidence emerged that North Vietnamese Army units were present in the South. Westmoreland's request that two battalion landing teams of Marines – 3,500 men – be assigned to guard the key air base at Da Nang ended up raising the total of US military personnel in Vietnam to 27,000. Within two weeks of the Marines' arrival, US Army Chief of Staff Harold K. Johnson requested an additional deployment to Vietnam of three divisions. In NSAM 328, dated 6 April, Johnson approved, among other things,

> an 18–20,000 man increase in US military support forces to fill out existing units and supply needed logistical personnel . . . the deployment of two additional Marine Battalions and one Marine Air Squadron and associated headquarters and support elements . . . a change of mission for all Marine Battalions deployed to Vietnam to permit their more active use under conditions to be established and approved by the Secretary of Defense in consultation with the Secretary of State.[23]

At this point there was little to suggest that a major war was on the horizon, as Johnson and his lieutenants were not aware that Hanoi had begun sending entire North Vietnamese Army regiments into the South.[24]

On 7 April Johnson made a speech at Johns Hopkins University to the effect that the United States would participate in 'unconditional negotiations' and was willing to spend a billion dollars for the development of the Mekong River Valley. The speech was intended to encourage Hanoi to stop waging war, and was also intended to assuage international and domestic critics of the escalation of the war. Johnson's affirmation of the American objective of South Vietnam's continued independence meant that there was little possibility of negotiations, given Hanoi's outright hostility to South Vietnam.[25] The offer of development also came to nothing.

By the time of the Honolulu conference about Vietnam early in May, McNamara, Taylor and Westmoreland had concluded that American forces had to undertake a fully-fledged combat role to prevent the Saigon regime from collapsing. The subsequent expansion of the American troop presence by another 40,000 was initially for the purpose of protecting American enclaves on the coast of Vietnam, but the enclave strategy proved ineffective and short-lived. Johnson did not give way to all of McNamara's demands for more troops to wage war throughout the South, but the increase of US forces in Vietnam from 75,000 to 125,000 – which the President announced at a low-key press conference on 28 July – was still substantial. Additional forces would be despatched as required and the draft call would be raised from 17,000 to 35,000 per month. The Joint Chiefs of Staff began implementing Johnson's decision by approving the deployment of the Air Mobile Division and the Marine Amphibious Brigade to South Vietnam.[26] The presence of US combat troops in an aggressive role now made this unequivocally an American war. US prestige was at stake as never before.

COLD WAR VERITIES

It is now time to say more about why, beyond South Vietnam's deteriorating security situation, the Johnson Administration felt it necessary to Americanise the war in Vietnam. Although Johnson bore the ultimate responsibility, and his decisions were never predetermined by the context in which he operated, the escalation was, in a sense, almost beyond him, a product of Cold War policies that had been in place for nearly twenty years. One historian refers to the 'deeply held ideological preconceptions' among most foreign-policymakers behind what had been a 'vigorous, global, anticommunist foreign policy' since the Truman doctrine of

1947.[27] Johnson had lent his support to President Truman's stand against the Soviet threat to Greece and Turkey in 1947, and he was part of the widely supported, non-partisan, anti-communist consensus that maintained that it was the role of the United States to lead the Free World in containing the forces of communism.[28] This is not to say that Johnson was a dogmatic, or 'locked-in', Cold Warrior; had he fitted this description he would hardly have been likely, for example, to pursue an arms control agenda with the Soviet Union.[29] However, Johnson, along with advisers such as Bundy, showed little or no inclination to question the assumptions of the Cold War, such as the 'expansive conception of national security' that had been in place since the late 1940s.[30]

Truman, Eisenhower and Kennedy had each proclaimed the importance of Vietnam to American security interests and had each taken actions to further those interests, with the result that by the time Johnson became President there was a long-standing institutional record of support for non-communist forces in Vietnam. Some of Johnson's colleagues – such as Undersecretary of State George Ball (considered below) – were willing to accept the loss of South Vietnam, but this was not something that Johnson would endorse. He felt that to give way would cast doubt upon the strength of US alliance commitments and public pledges: 'Wouldn't all those countries say Uncle Sam is a paper tiger – wouldn't we lose credibility breaking the word of three presidents?'[31] This concern with 'credibility' was not simply a Johnson idiosyncrasy, but a deeply rooted Cold War verity. Dean Rusk commented that 'If the Communist world finds out we will not pursue our commitment to the end, I don't know where they will stay their hand.'[32] Maxwell Taylor maintained that the loss of South Vietnam would damage the image of the United States in Africa and Latin America.[33] General Earle G. Wheeler, Chairman of the Joint Chiefs of Staff, argued that 'if we walk out of this one, we will just have to face others'.[34]

Cold War thinking also included the infamous domino principle, the notion that if one state succumbed to communism then so too would its neighbours in speedy succession (though the time scale was rarely if ever specified). In 1964 General Taylor argued that the loss of South Vietnam would mean that

> almost all of Southeast Asia will probably fall under Communist dominance (all of Vietnam, Laos, and Cambodia), accommodate to Communism so as to remove effective US and anti-Communist influence (Burma), or fall under the domination of forces not now explicitly Communist but likely then to do so (Indonesia taking over Malaysia). Thailand might hold for a period with our help, but would be under grave pressure. Even the Philippines would become

shaky, and the threat to India in the West, Australia and New Zealand in the South, and Taiwan, Korea, and Japan to the north and east would be greatly increased.[35]

The Chiefs of Staff thought along similar lines, but there were also those who questioned this outlook as being too mechanistic a way of understanding the international environment. In the summer of 1964, the CIA's top analyst, Sherman Kent, maintained that 'the loss of South Vietnam and Laos' would not lead to

> the rapid, successive communisation of the other states of the Far East . . . With the possible exception of Cambodia, it is likely that no nation in the area would quickly succumb to communism as a result of the fall of Laos and South Vietnam. Furthermore, a continuation of the spread of communism in the area would not be inexorable, and any spread which did occur would take time – time in which the total situation might change in any number of ways unfavourable to the Communist cause.[36]

John T. McNaughton, McNamara's deputy at the Pentagon, also doubted that the rest of Southeast Asia was going to fall like a row of dominos if the United States decided to leave it to its fate.[37]

While Francis Bator has suggested that President Johnson was 'much too empirical and contingent-minded to believe in some automatic theory of "dominoes"', it was Johnson who said, 'I don't believe I can walk out . . . If I did, they'd take Thailand . . . They'd take Cambodia . . . They'd take India . . . They'd come right back and take the Philippines.'[38] So Johnson did believe in the domino theory, at least enough to encourage him in the process of escalation. There is evidence in fact that the domino theory, as time-worn as it may seem some two decades after the end of the Cold War, had at least some validity – it has been argued that the United States' efforts to hold the line in Vietnam bolstered the anti-communist resolve of the generals of Indonesia, 'the domino of greatest strategic importance in Southeast Asia'.[39] The belief in falling dominos was a facet of the widespread general assumption among foreign policy decision-makers that one way or another the 'loss' of South Vietnam would be detrimental to American Cold War security interests.

ADVISERS

As noted in Chapter One, Johnson did not make much use of the formal machinery of the National Security Council, but the foreign affairs specialists in the White House could, and did, make their presence felt through memoranda, meetings and telephone conversations. Dean Rusk, Robert S.

McNamara and McGeorge Bundy were Johnson's most important foreign affairs counsellors. Generally, these men favoured prosecuting the war more vigorously, with McNamara and Bundy being especially influential in their advocacy of an expanded US commitment. One example of their counsel was the 'fork in the road' memorandum of 27 January 1965.[40] It was argued that 'both of us are now pretty well convinced that our current policy can lead only to disastrous defeat . . . Bob and I believe that the worst course of action is to continue in this essentially passive role which can only lead to eventual defeat and an invitation to get out in humiliating circumstances'. There were two alternatives: 'The first is to use our military power in the Far East and to force a change of Communist policy.' The second was 'to deploy all our resources along a track of negotiation, aimed at salvaging what little can be preserved with no major addition to our present military risks. Bob and I tend to favor the first course.'[41] The 'fork in the road' memo was effectively an ultimatum to Johnson to widen the war in Vietnam.[42]

The advocates of escalation were not always of one mind. For example, when McNamara argued in June 1965 in favour of sending 200,000 men to Vietnam, tripling the number of bombing raids and initiating a naval blockade of northern ports, Bundy argued that 'this program is rash to the extent of folly'. The communists would not fight the sort of war that the United States wanted.[43] Although Bundy had supported the sustained bombing of the North and, later, the sending of combat troops, he had in mind a smaller commitment, wanting, apparently, to see how matters progressed.

Johnson's informal advisers on Vietnam included Senator Richard Russell, Senator Michael Mansfield, Senator William Fulbright, former president Eisenhower, Vice-President Hubert Humphrey, Presidential aide Bill Moyers and the Senior Advisory Group, the so-called 'Wise Men'.[44] The composition of the Wise Men changed from gathering to gathering, but they included former Secretary of State Dean Acheson; General Omar Bradley, who had helped direct US forces during the Second World War; diplomat Arthur Dean, who had helped to negotiate the Korean armistice in 1953; Paul Hoffman, who had run the European Recovery Plan; plus several others from inside and outside the public sphere.[45] Generally, the Wise Men favoured taking a strong stand in Vietnam. Eisenhower, for example, told Johnson in February 1965 that 'When we say we will help other countries we must then be staunch.'[46]

Of course, there were those in important positions who doubted the wisdom of escalation; the most vigorous advocate of holding back or even pulling out was George Ball. Although he was always loyal to the

Administration, he pursued a memoranda campaign against escalation from October 1964 to July 1965.[47] Ball presented a range of military and political arguments against escalation on land. Militarily, 'the terrain in Vietnam could not be worse. Jungles and rice paddies are not designed for modern arms and, from a military point of view, this is clearly what General de Gaulle described to me as a "rotten country".' Politically, South Vietnam was 'a lost cause'. It had been 'bled white from twenty years of war and the people are sick of it'. It was a 'country with an army and no government'. By contrast, the Viet Cong was 'deeply committed', and the regime in Hanoi had 'a purpose and a discipline'. Overall, a 'deep commitment of United States forces in a land war in South Vietnam would be a catastrophic error. If ever there was an occasion for a tactical withdrawal, this is it.'[48]

Ball's hostility to the introduction of combat troops was heartfelt, rather than simply an intellectual exercise in devil's advocacy. Had he been simply a devil's advocate then it is unlikely that McNamara would have responded to one of Ball's memoranda as if it was a 'poisonous snake'.[49] Bundy, Rusk and McNamara convinced him not to send the first of his memos – a document consisting of sixty-seven single-typed pages – to Johnson, arguing the President would not want to be bothered until after the election. The supporters of escalation recognised that Ball's arguments were well-made,[50] and when he finally got through to Johnson, his ideas were taken seriously. For example, when in a meeting, the Undersecretary expressed 'serious doubt' about the chances of success for an 'army of westerners' fighting 'orientals in Asian jungle', the President responded, 'This is important – can Westerners, in absence of intelligence, successfully fight orientals in jungle rice-paddies? I want McNamara and Wheeler to seriously ponder this question.'[51]

Ball's position was weakened by the fact that he did not offer a practical policy prescription that might preserve South Vietnam as an independent, non-communist state. However, he did succeed in raising doubts in the minds of some other advisers about escalation. These included William P. Bundy and John McNaughton, contributors in the policy deliberations of late 1964, and the Washington insider Clark Clifford, who would become Secretary of Defense early in 1968.[52] Partly due to Ball's influence, Clifford argued in July 1965 that he did not 'believe we can win in SVN. If we send in 100,000 more, the NVN will meet us. If the NVN run out of men, the Chinese will send in volunteers. Russia and China don't intend for us to win the war. If we don't win, it is a catastrophe. If we lose 50,000, it will ruin us. Five years, billions of dollars, 50,000 men, it is not for us.'[53]

There were other 'insider' dissenters. These included Thomas Hughes, head of the Department of State Intelligence and Research Bureau, and

Vice-President Hubert Humphrey. Hughes was especially concerned about the possibility of Chinese and Soviet intervention, something that he believed McGeorge Bundy, for one, had tended to neglect. Nor in Hughes' view had the advocates of sustained reprisal paid much heed to intelligence assessments which had by early 1965 argued that any boost to South Vietnamese morale engendered by sustained bombing would be short-lived, and that allied support for American policy would be severely tested by sustained bombing. On 13 February, the day Johnson approved Rolling Thunder, Hughes and Hubert Humphrey wrote a powerful memorandum to the President which, among other things, outlined the likely domestic problems ensuing from escalating the commitment in Vietnam.[54]

Humphrey submitted another memorandum two weeks later, but he never received much of a hearing. He recollected that his participation in Vietnam discussions had ended by late February 1965, possibly because of Johnson's suspicion about leaks: 'in the brief span of my vice-presidency, I had spoken my mind on Vietnam only in the councils of government, yet the President . . . apparently thought I had leaked something about the meetings. I had not, but that became irrelevant.'[55] Johnson had long questioned Humphrey's discretion, complaining at the time of the Gulf of Tonkin affair that 'the damned fool . . . just ought to keep his god-damned big mouth shut on foreign affairs . . . he just yak-yak-yak'.[56] If the President did believe that Humphrey was responsible for another leak then it is understandable that he was excluded from policy deliberations on Vietnam, and Johnson may also have felt that it was enough for Ball to be making those sorts of arguments in the higher counsels of policymaking.

There were also some low-key efforts from a number of officials within the State Department who sought to restrain the Administration from bombing and land war in Vietnam. This group consisted of William Truehart, former deputy chief of mission in Saigon; Allen Whiting, deputy director of East Asia Research; Robert Johnson of the Policy Planning Council; and Carl Salans of the Legal Advisers' Office. However, there were several reasons why these officials had minimal impact: one, they were of relatively modest status within the bureaucracy; two, they tended to work individually rather than in concert; three, they did not seek allies in other agencies such as the CIA; and, four, career concerns inhibited them from pushing their views in a more forthright way.[57]

CONGRESSIONAL AND PUBLIC OPINION

Johnson saw a somewhat regrettable link between the future of his domestic programmes, which in the first part of 1965 were still winding their way through the legislature, and the war in Vietnam. He confided to a group of visitors to the White House late in 1964 that

> If we get into this war, I know what's going to happen. Those damn conservatives are going to sit in Congress and they're going to use this war as a way of opposing my Great Society legislation. People like [John] Stennis [senator from Alabama]. They hate this stuff, they don't want to help the poor and the negroes but they're afraid to be against it at a time like this when there's been all this prosperity. But the war, oh, they'll like the war. They'll take the war as their weapon . . . They'll say they're not against it, not against the poor, but we have this job to do, beating Communists. We beat the Communists first, then we can look around and maybe give something to the poor.[58]

Johnson's statement answers the question of whether he escalated the war at least partly out of fear that the failure to take a strong stand would precipitate a domestic right-wing attack that would destroy the Great Society. Had this motivation prevailed then it would have meant that he was willing to sacrifice American and Vietnamese lives largely for the sake of his domestic programme – morally, a deeply problematic scenario.[59] The 1964 statement indicates very clearly that Johnson escalated the war despite, and not because of, fears for the Great Society. Yet domestic concerns undoubtedly did influence the President. He feared that 'if we walked away from Vietnam and let Southeast Asia fall, there would follow a divisive and destructive debate in our country', as had happened when the communists took power in China in 1949.[60] Furthermore, Johnson's worries about 'credibility' probably related not only to the United States' international position but to his own personal reputation, and that of the Democratic Party.[61]

In Congress, there were a good number of Representatives and Senators who endorsed Johnson's Vietnam policies, although their motives probably had far more to do with Cold War national security thinking than with any intention to use the war as a weapon against the Administration's domestic initiatives. As Bundy noted in July 1965, Congressional support had been 'demonstrated in the 512-2 vote . . . on the Southeast Asia Resolution and in the votes approving the President's request for a supplemental Vietnam appropriation'.[62] Individual voices in support of escalating the war included the House Minority Leader, Gerald Ford, who agreed that 'We have to keep our commitment to the South Vietnamese.'[63]

Speaker of the House John McCormack thought there was no alternative to introducing US combat troops, reflecting, with the 1930s in mind, that 'the lesson of Hitler and Mussolini is clear'.[64] But Congressional support had its limits. Bundy noted that by the summer of 1965 the 'most vocal current comment on the Vietnam situation is coming from

Congress'. Senators Wayne Morse and Ernest Gruening, the two dissenters against the Southeast Asia Resolution, were 'convinced that we
should pull out'. There was 'another group, somewhat larger, which could
be termed "reluctant realists" whose viscera says get out but whose heads
tell them the present policy is unavoidable'. Congressmen in this group
included Senate Majority Leader Michael Mansfield, and Chairman of the
Senate Foreign Relations Committee J. William Fulbright. They had voted
in favour of the Southeast Asia Resolution and now struggled, said Bundy,
to offer 'a plausible alternative that would ensure the existence of a non-
Communist South Vietnam',[65] but at the same time their voices could not
be ignored. Both Mansfield and Fulbright would work strenuously against
the war, with the latter making the Foreign Relations Committee a forum
for criticism and debate.[66] Overall, the support of Congress for escalating
the war had distinct limits. This was something that Johnson recognised:
he said in July that before he 'went into the districts of the Congressmen
and Senators he would have done what [Generals] Westy [Westmoreland]
and Wheeler want done', that is, escalation on a much larger scale than he
was now prepared to countenance.[67]

Nor did public opinion offer any kind of consensus about the war.
For Bundy, the public response, as revealed by polls, to the initiation
of bombing raids in February 1965 revealed that 'we have an education
problem that bears close watching and more work'.[68] Johnson recognised
that public opinion would not always be consistent with an escalating
commitment in Vietnam. In conversation with his friend Senator Richard
Russell, he said, 'I don't think the people of the country know much about
Vietnam and I think they care a hell of a lot less.'[69] When Stanley Resor,
the Secretary of the Army, pointed to opinion polls showing strong public
support for the continuation of the Administration's Vietnam policy,
Johnson rebuked him by saying: 'if you make a commitment to jump off a
building, and you find out how high it is, you may withdraw that commitment'.[70] Of course, there have been few if any wars (except perhaps the
war with Japan after the surprise attack on Pearl Harbor in 1941) in which
the general public has been overwhelmingly supportive, so ambivalence
in this sphere was never likely to be a decisive influence on the President.
However, it did compound the considerable agonies of decision-making at
a critical time.

ALLIES

In a memorandum in February 1965, William P. Bundy noted that
Thailand, the Philippines, Australia, New Zealand, Taiwan, South Korea,

Laos and Germany were 'with us pretty strongly' on Vietnam. 'With us, but wobbly on negotiations' were the United Kingdom, Canada and India – these countries offered broad support for American objectives but sought an early negotiated settlement. Japan, Malaysia, Italy and other NATO allies were 'with us tepidly', Bundy noted in his February memorandum. France and Pakistan were 'sceptical or opposed'.[71] France urged the 'neutralisation' of Southeast Asia (see Chapter Four), but Robert S. McNamara, for one, maintained that any deal to 'neutralise' South Vietnam would inevitably mean 'a new government in Saigon that would in short order become Communist-dominated'.[72] (This view is borne out by recent evidence from the communist side, which indicates that in 1964 and 1965 North Vietnam would not have agreed to any settlement which did not enable them to take over the South rapidly.[73]) There were mixed feelings in Africa. There were also the 'neutralist Afro-Asian countries, such as Indonesia, most of which are opposed – some vehemently, but some also with an underlying appreciation of what we are doing'.[74]

Johnson was not impressed at the lack of support, especially among allies: 'we've got a treaty but, hell, everybody else's got a treaty out there and they're not doing anything about it'.[75] He wanted combat troops as well as diplomatic backing. London offered polite support but little else (see Chapter Four). The Federal Republic of Germany (FRG) was a supporter of the US dollar during the 1960s, helping in effect to finance the US war effort in Vietnam, and was one of the largest contributors to South Vietnam economically.[76] However, like London, Bonn's support – although 'strong', according to William P. Bundy – did not extend to providing soldiers even in a non-combat role. A German official stated in 1964 that 'Military adventures outside our own borders have characterised two disastrous world wars. People still remember and resent that all over the world. So please leave us out.'[77] Nearer to home, Canadian support had its limits, too. Prime Minister Lester Pearson feared 'escalation' and thought that the South Vietnamese were 'the first to want to get rid of the Americans' and that 'a compromise would have to be reached'. He told the Canadian House of Commons that the best solution was an international peace conference.[78] It is not unreasonable to suggest that any support for American policy from NATO countries was born in part from a desire not to upset an important ally, rather than from any major stake in Vietnam. For his part, President Charles de Gaulle of France had nothing good to say about American policy in Vietnam (see Chapter Four).

Australia and New Zealand provided combat troops, believing that, in the words of Paul Hasluck, the Australian Minister of External Affairs, 'if South Vietnam goes, then that is the end in Southeast Asia'.[79] Canberra

and Wellington were strongly committed to Cold War containment policies in Asia but abut also sought to strengthen their security links with
the United States in an era in which British power in Asia was declining.[80]
It has been argued that 'every country in Southeast Asia and the sur-
rounding area, aside from the few that were already on the Chinese side,
advocated US intervention in Vietnam, and most of them offered to assist
the South Vietnamese war effort'.[81] The Philippines, Thailand and the
Republic of Korea provided soldiers, but they needed substantial financial
inducements to do so. In 1966, for example, McNamara told Johnson that
Korean participation in Vietnam was definitely on the cards but would
come at a price. Seoul had requested 'about $600–$700 million worth of
cumshaw [gratuities or bribes] that they wanted from us in order to send
that division'.[82] So, overall, Free World support for the American position
in Vietnam was generally tepid. As with public opinion, the outlook of
allies was in itself never a decisive influence, but it was not an irrelevance
either – as shown by the Administration's courting of allies for troops (see
Chapter Three).

South Vietnam

The overthrow and murder of South Vietnamese leader Ngo Dinh Diem
in November 1963 was seen by many observers as favouring the construction of a new, more democratic and popular regime, but instead there was
a period of recurring coups with the Saigon government generating little
popular support. Johnson wondered 'How can we fight a war under a government that changes so frequently?'[83] Most Southerners were unwilling
to fight for the regime, believing that, as McGeorge Bundy and Robert
S. McNamara wrote early in 1965, 'the future is without hope for anti-
Communists. More and more the good men are covering their flanks and
avoiding executive responsibility for firm anti-Communist policy.'[84] This
was not surprising, given the communists' success in South Vietnam. In
1962–5, for example, there were over 6,000 assassinations among the
civilian population. Johnson reflected that in this situation 'A man thinks
twice about becoming chief of his village or a district official if two or three
of his predecessors have been murdered in their beds or disembowelled
in the village square. Even in Saigon it was easier, and safer to remain in
private life rather than work for the government.'[85]

The United States found itself in a Catch-22 situation: if the government and army of South Vietnam were strong enough to protect
themselves against the communists then American support would not
be needed. But if the South Vietnamese lacked unity or commitment

– fundamental ingredients of strength – then American forces would not be much good, in the words of one US government analysis, 'in the midst of an apathetic or hostile population'.[86] At one point Taylor pondered the idea that American officials might take over the operational control of the government of South Vietnam and that the United States 'might do better to carry forward the war on a purely unilateral basis' but this suggestion, as Short has suggested, seemed to be little more than a talking point and little came of it.[87] Ultimately, the consensus in the White House – that increased action was preferable to passivity or withdrawal – was such that the weakness of the Saigon regime ended up as a reason for deepening intervention rather than pulling out. Later, George Ball expressed his dismay at how

> ingenious men can, when they wish, turn logic upside down, and I was not surprised when my colleagues interpreted the crumbling of the South Vietnamese government, the Viet Cong's increasing success, and a series of defeats for South Vietnamese units not as proving that we should cut our losses and get out, but rather that we must promptly begin bombing to stiffen the resolve of the corrupt South Vietnamese government. It was classic bureaucratic casuistry.[88]

In fact, it is Ball's logic that is flawed here. Given that the consensus in the Administration was that US international interests would suffer gravely if South Vietnam collapsed, it was reasonable that South Vietnam's weakness led to a deepening of the US commitment rather than the cutting of losses.

THE SINO-SOVIET DIMENSION[89]

There were concerns in Washington that the People's Republic of China (PRC) was a militant and expansionist power that was fanning the fires of war in Vietnam. Johnson reflected in his memoirs that:

> In October 1964 the Chinese communists had set off their first nuclear explosion. Peking was promising Hanoi full support and was urging 'wars of national liberation' as the solution to all the problems of non-communist developed nations. The Chinese were training Thai guerrillas, and a 'liberation front' for Thailand was created with Chinese backing. There were reports that Red China's Foreign Minister, Chen Yi, had boasted at a New Year's Day diplomatic reception in 1965 that 'Thailand is next.'[90]

Fears of Chinese expansionism and the concern that Hanoi was a Chinese proxy were also reflected in contemporary documents. Robert S. McNamara maintained that the PRC 'looms as a major power threatening to undercut our importance and effectiveness in the world and, more remotely but more menacingly, to organize all of Asia against us'.[91] A May 1965 CIA analysis maintained that Beijing's foreign policy goals over the next two to three years were to eject the West, and above all the United States, from Asia and to diminish Western influence throughout the world, while increasing Chinese communist influence. Southeast Asia, and Vietnam in particular, was an opportunity for the Chinese to establish themselves as 'the champions and mentors of the underdeveloped nations'.[92]

Undoubtedly, the PRC had major interests in the war in Vietnam, as recent research has confirmed. First, there were worries about a large-scale American military presence in close vicinity (although the irony, as Qiang Zhai has pointed out, is that the growth of the American presence derived from concerns about Chinese actions). Second, support for North Vietnam was a way of demonstrating a commitment to national liberation struggles and a way of competing with Moscow for the leadership of communists across the world.[93] However, it has emerged that Chinese policy was fundamentally defensive; lacking military strength and preoccupied with ideological upheaval at home, Chinese leaders feared a direct confrontation with the United States. Another CIA report recognised that while China had built up its military strength in South China after the Southeast Asia Resolution and had taken measures to bolster Hanoi's air defences as defensive moves, the intention was to demonstrate solidarity with the North Vietnamese and to deter further US military action, while remaining out of the fray.[94]

Although many in Washington took the widely disseminated 1965 essay 'Long Live the Victory of People's War!' by the Chinese Defence Minister Lin Biao as confirmation of a predatory and aggressive foreign policy,[95] the underlying argument was that the PRC wanted to concentrate on its own internal development rather than engage in other wars of national liberation.[96] Moreover, the friendship between the North Vietnamese and the Chinese had distinct limits. Vietnamese nationalism had traditionally been aimed at the Chinese, and when Chinese troops went to Vietnam in 1965 there were a variety of tensions between them and their hosts.[97] But the defensive character of Chinese foreign policy and the strains in the Sino-North Vietnamese relationship were not widely appreciated in Washington. This meant that the Administration went to war in Vietnam in part to contain Chinese influence, while carrying out the escalation in a manner designed not to provoke Chinese intervention, as had occurred in Korea in 1950.[98]

Given that in 1961 Nikita Khrushchev had promised material support for revolutionaries waging 'wars of national liberation', one might think

41

that fears of Soviet expansionism played a role in encouraging the United States to Americanise the war in Vietnam. However, there is little evidence that Moscow's actions played much of a role in encouraging escalation – foreign policy analysts understood that despite Khrushchev's rhetoric in 1961, Moscow had soon 'virtually disengaged Soviet policy from the Indochina problem', because of the growing alignment between the North Vietnamese and Moscow's rival Beijing. After the post-Cuban Missile Crisis détente, the Soviet leader had also been reluctant to see 'a new increase in tensions in relations with the US develop from sharpening confrontation in Vietnam'. Khrushchev's joint successors from October 1964, Alexei Kosygin and Leonid Brezhnev, still wanted to improve relations with the United States, but at the same time they felt obliged to reject the 'virtual ceding of Chinese hegemony over the Communist movement in Asia'.[99] Kosygin was in Hanoi when the Viet Cong attacked the US base at Pleiku in February 1965 but Soviet surprise betrayed 'a clear lack of foreknowledge of this operation' – a further testimony to the limited ties between Moscow and Hanoi.[100]

Now the Soviet Union had to 'choose between giving North Vietnam military support' or desisting and 'opening itself to Chinese charges of capitulation to the imperialists'. Many Soviet officials suspected that the Chinese had 'inspired the Viet Cong raid in order to embarrass Kosygin and disrupt Soviet-US relations', and, in a further comment on the quality of the Sino-Soviet relationship, an anti-US demonstration in Moscow in March saw Chinese students turning against Soviet police, destroying 'what remained of the new leadership's attempts to maintain a façade of Communist unity'.[101] President Johnson, who was keen to pursue détente with Moscow, did not see the Soviets as implacable troublemakers who had to be faced down in Vietnam or anywhere else. Moscow, as well as its ideological tormentor Beijing, was firmly located in the 'great rear' of the Vietnam conflict rather than at the 'cutting edge'.[102] Johnson was wise to keep American troops out of North Vietnam, though. Evidence shows that the Chinese would have despatched ground troops to meet any US invasion of North Vietnam.[103]

One American official reflected of the escalations of 1965 that 'It was almost imperceptible, the way we got in. There was no one move that you could call decisive, or irreversible, not even very many actions that you could argue against in isolation. Yet when you put it all together, there we were in a war on the Asian mainland . . .'[104] The White House tried to maintain the impression throughout 1965 that policy had hardly changed, but ended up creating a damaging 'credibility gap' between official pronouncements and what was really going on. Johnson had no intention of misleading the American people but he had reservations about how far public opinion could be relied upon, and he felt in any case that his Constitutional status as the Commander-in-Chief entitled him to ample latitude in foreign policy without having to account for his actions.[105] Equally important, but trickier to execute, was the fact that while he sought to convey American commitment to South and North Vietnam, he did not want to arouse Moscow and above all Beijing, which had intervened against US troops in the Korean War in 1950, into expanding their support for Hanoi.[106] This was a justifiable concern in the circumstances.

One writer has suggested that Johnson was 'spoiling for war' in Vietnam in 1965.[107] This view of the President as a restless 'warmonger', seeking perhaps to bolster his domestic credentials by taking a tough stance in Southeast Asia, is at odds with the reality. Even though in 1964 he gained Congressional imprimatur for the use of armed force as he saw fit by means of the Southeast Asia Resolution, Johnson approached the possibility of expanding the US role with deep foreboding, cultivating and weighing seriously views from a spectrum of sources from both inside and outside the foreign policy establishment over a sustained period. He of course heard much from those such as Rusk, McNamara and Bundy who saw an infusion of American military power as probably the only realistic option if South Vietnam was going to survive, but he also listened carefully to, among others, George Ball and Clark Clifford who feared a long and indecisive war. Johnson had been facing up to the possibility of a land war for some time, and actions such as the Southeast Asia Resolution had their own momentum of escalation. However, the final decision to undertake a ground combat role only emerged in June 1965, based on changing realities in Vietnam rather than any preconceived agenda for escalation.[108]

In the light of the perceived stakes for the United States in South Vietnam, it was reasonable to put aside possible inhibitions such as the public and Congressional ambivalence and the tepid support of allies to take a firmer stand against the communist uprising. For Johnson, the war could be won, though probably not easily. He concluded, in an often-quoted statement, that having introduced ground troops, it would be over in a year or eighteen months; it would be like a 'filibuster – enormous resistance at first, then a steady whittling away, then Ho hurrying to get it over with'.[109] Few military interventions are risk free. As Charles de Gaulle once said, 'All policy involves risks. If it is a policy that does not involve risks there is no choice of policy.'[110] As will be seen, the US defeat in Vietnam was born of a different realm of decision-making and contingency than the question of whether or not to intervene in the first place. It was not inevitable.

NOTES

1. Ball to Johnson, 18 June 1965, *Foreign Relations of the United States* (hereafter *FRUS*) *1964–1968 III Vietnam June–December 1965* (Washington, DC: USGPO, 1996), p. 18.
2. For the view that Kennedy had planned to withdraw from Vietnam, see Robert S. McNamara with Brian VanDeMark, *In Retrospect: The Tragedy and Lessons of Vietnam* (New York: Times Books, 1995), p. 96. For the contrary view, see Lawrence J. Bassett and Stephen E. Pelz, 'The Failed Search for Victory: Vietnam and the Politics of War', in Thomas G. Paterson (ed.), *Kennedy's Quest for Victory: American Foreign Policy, 1961–1963* (New York: Oxford University Press, 1989), p. 252.
3. NSAM 273, 26 November 1963, in Neil Sheehan, Hedrick Smith, E. W. Kenworthy and Fox Butterfield (eds), *The Pentagon Papers: The Secret History of the Vietnam War: The Complete and Unabridged Series as published by the New York Times* (New York: Bantam Books, 1971), p. 233.
4. Historical Division, Joint Secretariat, Joint Chiefs of Staff, *The History of the Joint Chiefs of Staff: The Joint Chiefs of Staff and the War in Vietnam, 1960–68 Part I* (FOIA release, 1994), pp. 11–20; Robert D. Schulzinger, '"It's Easy to Win a War on Paper": The United States and Vietnam', in Diane B. Kunz (ed.), *The Diplomacy of the Crucial Decade: American Foreign Relations During the 1960s* (New York: Columbia University Press, 1994), p. 193.
5. Editorial note, *FRUS 1964–1968 I Vietnam 1964* (1992), p. 609.
6. Robert J. Hanyok, 'Spartans in Darkness: American SIGINT and the Indochina War, 1945–1975' (Center for Cryptologic History, National Security Agency, 2002), pp. 175–6. http://www.nsa.gov/public_info/_files/cryptologic_histories/spartans_in_darkness.pdf
7. State to Saigon Embassy, *FRUS 1964–1968 I*, p. 614.
8. Quoted in Schulzinger, '"It's Easy to Win a War on Paper"', p. 194.
9. Quoted in Robert D. Schulzinger, *A Time for War: The United States and Vietnam, 1945–1975* (New York and Oxford: Oxford University Press, 1997), p. 152.
10. Lyndon B. Johnson, *The Vantage Point: Perspectives of the Presidency 1963–1969* (New York: Holt, Rinehart, Winston, 1971), p. 115.
11. George C. Herring, *America's Longest War: The United States and Vietnam, 1950–1975*, 2nd edition (New York: McGraw Hill, 1986), p. 123.
12. Michael Lind, *The Necessary War: A Reinterpretation of America's Most Disastrous Military Conflict* (New York: Free Press, 1999), pp. 187–8.
13. Quoted in ibid., p. 190.
14. Henry A. Kissinger, *Diplomacy* (London and New York: Simon and Schuster, 1994), pp. 658–9.
15. Taylor (Saigon) to State, 6 January 1965, *FRUS 1964–1968 II Vietnam, January–June 1965* (1996), p. 13.
16. Bundy to Johnson, 'A Policy of Sustained Reprisal', 7 February 1965, in Sheehan et al. (eds), *The Pentagon Papers*, p. 423.
17. White House Meeting on Vietnam, 6 February 1965, *FRUS 1964–1968 II*, pp. 159–60; Johnson, *The Vantage Point*, p. 125.

18. Anthony Short, *The Origins of the Vietnam War* (London: Longman, 1989), p. 311.

19. Andrew Preston, *The War Council: McGeorge Bundy, the NSC and Vietnam* (Cambridge, MA: Harvard University Press, 2003), p. 180.

20. McCone to Rusk, McNamara, Bundy and Taylor, 2 April 1965, in Sheehan et al., *The Pentagon Papers*, p. 371.

21. Westmoreland to Wheeler, 6 March 1965, *FRUS 1964–1968 II*, p. 400.

22. Taylor to State, 7 March 1965, *FRUS 1964–1968 II*, p. 408.

23. NSAM 328, 6 April 1965, *FRUS 1964–1968 II*, p. 538.

24. Mark Moyar, *Triumph Forsaken: The Vietnam War, 1954–1965* (Cambridge: Cambridge University Press, 2006), p. xix.

25. James M. Carter, *Inventing Vietnam: The United States and State Building, 1954–1968* (Cambridge: Cambridge University Press, 2008), pp. 167–74.

26. Editorial note, *FRUS 1964–1968 III*, p. 273.

27. Preston, *War Council*, p. 4.

28. Randall B. Woods, 'The Politics of Idealism: Lyndon Johnson, Civil Rights, and Vietnam', *Diplomatic History*, 31, 1 (January 2007), p. 6.

29. Francis Bator, 'No Good Choices: LBJ and the Vietnam/Great Society Connection', *Diplomatic History*, 32, 3 (June 2008), p. 337.

30. Preston, *War Council*, p. 4.

31. Notes of meeting, 21 July 1965, *FRUS 1964–1968 III*, p. 195.

32. Ibid., p. 196.

33. Taylor to McNamara, 22 January 1964 in Sheehan et al., *The Pentagon Papers*, pp. 274–6.

34. Notes of meeting, 21 July 1965, *FRUS 1964–1968 III*, p. 204.

35. Taylor to McNamara, 22 January 1964 in Sheehan et al., *The Pentagon Papers*, pp. 274–6.

36. Board of National Estimates (Sherman Kent) to McCone, 9 June 1964, *FRUS 1964–1968 I*, p. 485. Although questioning the domino theory, Kent went on to argue that the loss of South Vietnam and Laos would still be damaging to US interests in the Far East, in large part due to the fact that Washington had 'committed itself persistently, emphatically, and publicly to preventing Communist takeover of the two countries'.

37. Benjamin T. Harrison and Christopher L. Mosher, 'John T. McNaughton and Vietnam: The Early Years as Assistant Secretary of Defense, 1964–1965', *History*, 92, 308 (October 2007), p. 504.

38. Bator, 'No Good Choices', p. 315; Johnson quotation from Mark Moyar's comment on Bator's article, same journal, *Diplomatic History*, 32, 3 (June 2008), p. 351.

39. Moyar, *Triumph Forsaken*, p. xxi.

40. Logevall, *Choosing War*, p. 389. See also Kai Bird, *The Color of Truth: McGeorge Bundy and William Bundy: Brothers in Arms* (New York: Touchstone, 1998), pp. 304–5; Johnson, *The Vantage Point*, pp. 121–2; McNamara with VanDeMark, *In Retrospect*, pp. 167–8.

41. Bundy to Johnson, 27 January 1965, *FRUS 1964–1968 II*, p. 96.

42. Preston, *War Council*, p. 167.

43. Bird, *The Color of Truth*, pp. 330–1.

44. David M. Barrett, *Uncertain Warriors: Lyndon Johnson and his Vietnam Advisers* (Lawrence, KS: University Press of Kansas, 1993), appendix.

45. McNamara with VanDeMark, *In Retrospect*, pp. 196–7.

46. Meeting with Johnson, 17 February 1965, *FRUS 1964–1968 II*, p. 308. Later, Eisenhower grew frustrated at what he regarded as the slow pace of escalation in Vietnam. David L. Anderson, 'A Question of Political Courage: Lyndon Johnson as War Leader', in Mitchell B. Lerner (ed.), *Looking Back at LBJ: White House Politics in a New Light* (Lawrence, KS: University Press of Kansas, 2005), p. 114.

47. James A. Bill, *George Ball: Behind the Scenes in US Foreign Policy* (New Haven, CT and London: Yale University Press, 1997), p. 159.

48. Ball, 'Cutting Our Losses in South Vietnam', undated, *FRUS 1964–1968 III*, p. 66. Also quoted in Bill, *Ball*, pp. 161–2.

49. Quoted in Bill, *Ball*, p. 160.

50. Preston, *War Council*, p. 158.

51. Notes of meeting, 21 July 1965, *FRUS 1964–1968 III*, p. 194. See also Ball to Johnson, 18 June 1965, pp. 16–21; Ball to Johnson, 23 June 1965, pp. 55–7; Ball, 'Cutting Our Losses in South Vietnam', undated, pp. 62–6, all ibid.

52. Logevall, *Choosing War*, p. 389; Bill, *Ball*, p. 166; Bird, *The Color of Truth*, pp. 291–3.

53. Notes of meeting, 25 July 1965, *FRUS 1964–1968 III*, p. 238.

54. Preston, *War Council*, pp. 180–1. The memo (Humphrey to Johnson, 17 February 1965) is reproduced in *FRUS 1964–1968 II*, pp. 309–13.

55. Hubert Humphrey, *The Education of a Public Man: My Life and Politics* (London: Weidenfeld and Nicolson, 1976), p. 325.

56. Michael R. Beschloss (ed.), *Taking Charge: The Johnson White House Tapes, 1963–1964* (New York: Simon and Schuster, 1997), p. 499.

57. Paul M. Kattenburg, *The Vietnam Trauma in American Foreign Policy, 1945–1975* (New Brunswick, NJ and London: Transaction, 1980), pp. 129–130.

58. Quoted in Woods, 'Politics of Idealism', p. 11.

59. Bator, 'No Good Choices', p. 332. See also the comments from Marilyn B. Young, pp. 347–50, Mark Moyar, p. 352, and Larry Berman, p. 362, in the same journal.

60. Johnson, *The Vantage Point*, pp. 151–2.

61. Fredrik Logevall comment on Francis Bator's 'No Good Choices', pp. 358–9.

62. Bundy to Johnson, 30 June 1965, *FRUS 1964–1968 III*, pp. 83–5. In early May Johnson had presented a supplemental appropriation request for extra support for South Vietnam. The bill passed 408–7 in the House and 88–3 in the Senate. Quotation from McNamara with VanDeMark, *In Retrospect*, pp. 183–4.

63. Johnson's meeting with Congressional leaders, 21 January 1965, *FRUS 1964–1968 II*, p. 68.

64. Schulzinger, '"It's Easy to Win a War on Paper"', p. 200.

65. Bundy to Johnson, 30 June 1965, *FRUS 1964–1968 III*, pp. 83–5.

66. See Joseph A. Fry, *Debating Vietnam: Fulbright, Stennis, and their Senate Hearings* (Lanham, MD: Rowman and Littlefield, 2008).

67. Meeting with Joint Congressional Leadership, 27 July 1965, *FRUS 1964–1968 III*, p. 264.

68. Michael H. Hunt, *Lyndon Johnson's War: America's Cold War Crusade in Vietnam, 1945–1968* (New York: Hill and Wang, 1996), p. 101.

69. Woods, 'The Politics of Idealism', pp. 10–11.

70. Quoted in Schulzinger, *A Time for War*, p. 176.

71. William P. Bundy to Johnson, 16 February 1965, *FRUS 1964–1968 II*, p. 292.

72. Fredrik Logevall, 'De Gaulle, Neutralization, and American Involvement in Vietnam, 1963–1964', *The Pacific Historical Review*, 61, 1 (February 1992), p. 82.

73. Moyar, *Triumph Forsaken*, p. xxi.
74. William P. Bundy to Johnson, 16 February 1965, *FRUS 1964–1968 II*, p. 292.
75. Woods, 'Politics of Idealism', p. 11.
76. From 1966 the FRG extended a modest amount of economic and humanitarian aid – equivalent to about $7.5 million per year – and provided a number of medical and technical personnel. Stanley Robert Larsen and James Lawton Collins Jr, *Allied Participation in Vietnam* (Washington, DC: USGPO, 1975), p. 164.
77. Lyndon B. Johnson Library, Austin, TX, NSF: Country File Vietnam, Box 7, Vietnam Memos Vol. XVI 8/16–31/64, Research Memorandum, Thomas L. Hughes (State Department Director of Intelligence and Research) to Dean Rusk, 28 August 1964. On the FRG's support for the dollar during the 1960s and the Vietnam War, see Hubert Zimmerman, 'Who paid for America's War? Vietnam and the International Monetary System, 1960–1975', in Andreas W. Daum, Lloyd C. Gardner, Wilfried Mausbach (eds), *America, the Vietnam War and the World: Comparative and International Perspectives* (Cambridge: Cambridge University Press, 2003), p. 170.
78. Quoted in Greg Donaghy, *Tolerant Allies: Canada and the United States, 1963–1968* (Montreal and Kingston: McGill-Queen's University Press, 2002), p. 128.
79. See, for example, memorandum of conversation, 16 July 1964, *FRUS 1964–1968 XXVII Mainland Southeast Asia; Regional Affairs* (2000), p. 5; memorandum of conversation, 22 October 1965, ibid.
80. Henry Brandon, *Anatomy of Error: The Secret History of the Vietnam War* (London: André Deutsch, 1970), p. 69. See also Andrea Benvenuti, 'The British Military Withdrawal from Southeast Asia and its Impact on Australia's Cold War Security Interests', *Cold War History*, 5, 2 (May 2005), pp. 189–210; and Saki Dockrill, *Britain's Retreat from East of Suez: The Choice between Europe and the World?* (Basingstoke: Palgrave, 2002), pp. 128–9.
81. Moyar, *Triumph Forsaken*, p. xxi.
82. Johnson–McNamara telephone conversation, 17 January 1966, *FRUS 1964–1968 IV Vietnam 1966* (1998), p. 79.
83. Notes of meeting, 21 July 1965, *FRUS 1964–1968 III*, p. 195.
84. Bundy to Johnson, 27 January 1965, *FRUS 1964–1968 II*, p. 96.
85. Johnson, *The Vantage Point*, p. 138.
86. Short, *Origins of the Vietnam War*, p. 249.
87. Ibid., p. 305.
88. Quoted in Bird, *The Color of Truth*, p. 303.
89. See Chapter six for US relations with the Soviet Union and the People's Republic of China.
90. Johnson, *The Vantage Point*, p. 134. See also Michael Lumbers, *Piercing the Bamboo Curtain: Tentative Bridge-Building to China During the Johnson Years* (Manchester: Manchester University Press, 2008), pp. 96–122.
91. McNamara to Johnson, 3 November 1965, *FRUS 1964–1968 III*, pp. 514–15.
92. Quoted in Matthew Jones, '"Groping toward coexistence": US China Policy During the Johnson Years', *Diplomacy and Statecraft*, 12, 3 (September 2001), p. 183.
93. Qiang Zhai, *China and the Vietnam Wars, 1950–1975* (Chapel Hill, NC and London: University of North Carolina Press, 2000), p. 139.
94. Lumbers, *Piercing the Bamboo Curtain*, p. 100.
95. Ibid., p. 89.

96. Robert Garson, 'Lyndon B. Johnson and the China Enigma', *Journal of Contemporary History*, 32, 1 (January 1997), p. 73. See also Kissinger, *Diplomacy*, pp. 644–5.
97. Zhai, *China and the Vietnam War*, p. 152; John Dumbrell, *Lyndon Johnson and Soviet Communism* (Manchester: Manchester University Press, 2004), p. 95.
98. Garson, 'Lyndon B. Johnson and the China Enigma', pp. 64, 77.
99. Policy Planning Council memorandum, 15 February 1965, *FRUS 1964–1968 XIV The Soviet Union* (2001), p. 245.
100. CIA report, 9 April 1965, *FRUS 1964–1968 XIV*, pp. 280–1.
101. Ibid.
102. Dumbrell, *President Lyndon Johnson and Soviet Communism*, p. 95.
103. Zhai, *China and the Vietnam Wars*, pp. 132, 139.
104. Quoted in Philip Geyelin, *Lyndon B. Johnson and the World* (London: Pall Mall, 1966), pp. 213–14.
105. Hunt, *Lyndon Johnson's War*, pp. 99–100.
106. Short, *Origins of the Vietnam War*, p. 311.
107. Kattenburg, *Vietnam Trauma*, p. 133.
108. Moyar, *Triumph Forsaken*, p. xix.
109. Quoted in Bird, *The Color of Truth*, pp. 310–11.
110. Ball to State, 6 June 1964, *FRUS 1964–1968 I*, p. 469.

Vietnam: Waging War, 1965–9

Lyndon Johnson's decision to Americanise the war in Vietnam in 1965 had been a deeply thought-out one, though not free of risk nor immune to contingencies. As will be seen, a particular presidential concern after the US combat intervention had begun was to enlist as many allies as possible to help legitimise the war. However, the results of the recruitment campaign fell short of what was desired; no NATO state, for example, provided combat assistance. The US military performed well in larger-scale engagements, although there was inadequate attention to 'pacification', that is, securing populated areas from communist influence. Rolling Thunder, the air campaign that had begun early in 1965 and continued to the end of 1968, played a modest role in minimising the infiltration of troops and material into the South, but large areas of North Vietnam remained untouched out of fear of Chinese intervention. The chapter then examines some of the third-party efforts to promote peace. Neither the United States nor the North Vietnamese were willing to make a significant compromise of their respective positions, and the involvement, though usually well-intentioned, of third parties was likely only to complicate matters without advancing the cause of peace. As such, the war went on. The United States and the South Vietnamese were able to defeat the communists' Tet Offensive in 1968 but the very fact that a large-scale assault could be launched in the first place shocked many observers and prompted a reappraisal of the war in Washington. The Administration duly found itself engaged in what proved to be fruitless negotiations with the North Vietnamese to secure peace terms. By 1968, American intervention had held the line while keeping the war limited, but no clear-cut victory was in sight.

COMMUNISM BEYOND VIETNAM

Initially, it is worth recognising that the American war in Vietnam was a facet of the broader anti-communist contest throughout Southeast Asia.[1] A 1968 CIA analysis reflected that communism had become a less potent force in Malaysia, Singapore, Indonesia and the Philippines than it had been two decades earlier. However, communist efforts to overthrow the Burmese, Thai and Cambodian governments had been 'stepped up in recent years, partly because of the war in Vietnam and partly because of the stimulus of Peking and Hanoi'. In Cambodia, guerrilla activity had revived and now posed a serious challenge to the Sihanouk regime. In parts of Cambodia, Vietnamese communists operated in support of the war effort in Vietnam. In Laos, the communists posed 'a major threat. They control about half the country and a third of its people, and the indigenous communists – the Pathet Lao – have an internationally recognized claim to a share in the national government.' The mainstay of the insurgency, however, was 'provided by regular North Vietnamese forces'. The assessment ended on a positive note. While most Southeast Asian nations suffered from a range of 'serious social, political and economic weaknesses', the governments concerned were generally 'buttressed by a sense of nationalism and a determination to preserve their independence'. All had experience in dealing with communist subversion, and had 'learned over the centuries to survive in the shadow of a powerful China'.[2] The examples of Malaysia, Singapore, Indonesia and the Philippines showed that Asian communism was not insuperable. But the challenge of communism in Vietnam would prove far less soluble, even with the application of hundreds of thousands of American and South Vietnamese troops, along with some soldiers from other nations.

THE SEARCH FOR ALLIES

From the outset Washington preferred to fight in Vietnam as part of a collective, largely as a means of furthering the international legitimacy of the war and 'selling' the conflict in the United States. The recruitment campaign began formally in April 1964, with the 'More Flags' or 'Many Flags' initiative. President Johnson stated in a press conference that 'we would like to see some other flags' in South Vietnam and that 'we would all unite in an attempt to stop the spread of . . . communism in that part of the world'.[3] Initially the programme was intended to elicit non-combat assistance such as medical, engineering and police support, but by the time of the bombing campaign and the introduction of American combat troops in 1965 this had given way to a desire to see third countries engaged in the fighting as well. Frederick Flott, a diplomat at the Saigon Embassy, noted that Johnson was

> personally very much interested in the program, and if he had a visiting head of state from a potential donor country coming in to see him in the Oval Office, he'd ask us, 'Just what should I ask this fellow for?' He was trying very hard to help.[4]

Johnson was soon 'leaning on all our embassies around the world to be supportive of this program and to try to find donors'.[5]

By 1969, there were almost 69,000 third-country combat personnel present in South Vietnam, alongside half a million American and 850,000 South Vietnamese troops.[6] Four countries – the Republic of Korea, Thailand, Australia and New Zealand – provided combat troops, while the Philippines contributed a 'civic action group' of medics and engineers with its own security force of infantry, armour and artillery. However, the number of contributor nations compared poorly with the Korean War of 1950–3, when there were combat forces from fourteen Free World countries, plus the United States.[7] Fewer countries felt as much of a stake in Vietnam as in Korea, and governments had to consider the unpopularity of the War in their respective countries.[8] American diplomats had wanted to mount the Vietnam coalition on the Southeast Asia Treaty Organization (SEATO), but this proved impossible in the absence of soldiers from SEATO members France, Pakistan and the United Kingdom, along with the fact that the main third-country troop contributor, the Republic of Korea, was not part of SEATO. The coalition was essentially an *ad hoc* grouping, and, as noted in Chapter Two, there was a recognition among Washington policymakers that American largesse featured among the motives of some of the troop-providing countries: the Koreans, the Thais and the Filipinos had their costs covered very generously.[9]

At the same time, third countries played a useful practical role. Early in 1966, Presidential adviser Jack Valenti commented that the cost of equipping two or more Korean divisions and sending them to Vietnam was 'cheap – equipping Koreans is at the ratio of 5–1 to 10–1 for the same equipment of the same number of Americans. Moreover, the Koreans are competent jungle fighters – and are ready to fight.'[10] On a fact-finding visit to Vietnam in June 1967, Presidential aide Harry McPherson noted that the Korean Marines and Tiger Troop were 'a tough bunch. They have a method of seal and search that is the epitome of war psychology; it is slow, harrowing, and effective.'[11] The Australians participated in as many as nineteen major operations, including one in 1966 when an Australian unit helped to uncover a vast complex of tunnels that turned out to be a Viet Cong headquarters.[12] In 1967 McPherson stated that he was 'stunned by the soldierly bearing of the Filipino soldiers'. They had 'an effective civic action project, a med cap [medical capabilities] program, and they are building a large and decent refugee camp'.[13]

With over 5,000 dead (mainly Korean) between them, third-country forces accepted a notable share of the losses.[14] This amounted to around a tenth of the total number of American casualties (58,000), and was proportional with the numbers of third-country troops in Vietnam. Stanley Robert Larsen and James Lawton Collins noted in 1975 that the Korean troops, for example, 'received almost no recognition in the American press and it is doubtful if many Americans fully appreciate their contributions in Vietnam'.[15] Decades later, third-country contributions have still not received much acknowledgment in the United States, either in the general literature of the War or in public perceptions.

THE SEARCH FOR VICTORY: THE GROUND WAR, 1965–7

As noted in the previous chapter, the American war in Vietnam was fought to bolster US international credibility and prestige by protecting South Vietnam in the face of the Northern-sponsored communist offensive. There was little dispensation among the war managers to authorise an invasion of the North and unify Vietnam under a pro-Western government, largely because of the fear of communist Chinese intervention. Similarly, there was no attack on the Ho Chi Minh trail – the umbilical cord of the Communist war effort – in Laos and Cambodia, largely because there were insufficient troops to do this while fighting across South Vietnam.[16] But there was a confidence among most senior American military and civilian officials that ultimately – though precisely when was rarely addressed – their material and technological strength would fend off the communists. In August 1965, the Joint Chiefs of Staff described their approach as the 'aggressive and sustained exploitation of superior military force'.[17] Military leaders sought a conventional war of attrition, albeit with some attention to 'pacification' efforts. This was the blanket term given to a range of military, political and economic programmes designed to prevent communism from gaining or preserving a foothold in populated areas.

The Chiefs of Staff tended to frame the war in favourable terms while, somewhat contradictorily, demanding more troops and urging heavier attacks against the North[18] – Harry McPherson referred aptly to the 'hungry optimism that is part of the military personality'.[19] Johnson reduced most of the requests, but troop numbers still expanded significantly. At the beginning of 1966, the United States had about 184,000 military personnel in Vietnam, reaching 385,000 at the end of the year and over half a million by the beginning of 1968.[20] Typically, about 80 per cent of those troops performed a support role, with the rest engaged in front-line activities. American forces were generally of high quality. According to McPherson, the officers he met while visiting South Vietnam in 1967 were, 'by and large, superb professionals, and some of them had a sense this war is far more complex, and its issues far more difficult, than could be addressed by military firepower alone'. Another informed observer suggested that 'there never has been an army like this. Our kids out here are the finest soldiers we ever put on a battlefield – and I went through World War II and Korea with some mighty good units. These boys don't wave the flag, but they do their job better than soldiers have ever done it.'[21] There was undoubtedly some hyperbole in this statement, but it cannot be dismissed entirely.

US soldiers did well in set-piece battles, which provided opportunities to bring helicopter-based mobility and superior firepower to bear on the communists. In the Ia Drang valley in November 1965, for example, American forces killed 2,000 soldiers of the North Vietnamese Army for 240 US deaths.[22] Despite his own growing doubts about the war (considered later), Secretary of Defense Robert McNamara conceded late in 1966 that the past twelve months had seen a 'large number of enemy killed-in-action resulting from the big military operations'. The communists were suffering losses of over 60,000 a year. The infiltration trails into South Vietnam were 'one way trails to death'.[23] The question of enemy numbers was a vexed one. Robert Komer, who ran the civilian component of the pacification programme, reported in August 1967 the conclusion of MACV's (Military Assistance Command, Vietnam) 'massive intelligence machine' that enemy strength numbered 298,000, while the CIA was then suggesting as many as 490,000.[24] Komer rejected the Agency's estimate because of the inclusion of

> some 120,000 so-called defense and secret defense forces, which are not organized military units at all but rather a shadowy, mostly unarmed hamlet defense element of women, children, and old men on which we have encountered little evidence and which is so inconsequential and rarely encountered by us as not to warrant inclusion in enemy strength.[25]

Komer, acknowledging that American public support for the war was not unlimited, feared that general knowledge of the Agency statistics would have 'a devastating impact' on perceptions, because 'despite our success in grinding down VC/NVA [Viet Cong/North Vietnamese Army] here, CIA figures are used to show that they are much stronger' than ever.[26]

The CIA estimate that finally emerged in this case proved more cautious than the initially stated maximum figure of 490,000, because DCI Richard Helms decided to exclude 'the self-defense force, the secret self-defense forces, and the youth combat organization'. The new estimate also omitted the non-combatant political cadres, which were thought to number 75,000–85,000. This meant an estimated maximum enemy strength of 248,000.[27] Helms reduced the assessment of enemy strength on analytical grounds, namely that the numbers of 'defense and secret defense forces' were too difficult to gauge, and of course there was also Komer's reasonable argument that these components of the communist military effort were only lightly armed. At the same time, Helms was also happy to convey a message that was more acceptable to President Johnson, who, as noted in Chapter One, tended to see intelligence as an unnecessary complication to the making of foreign policy.

Henry Kissinger, who was then a part-time adviser to the Administration, noted that even without the infiltration of about 4,500 men a month from the North, the Viet Cong could cover their losses by recruitment in the South.[28] The fact that about 200,000 North Vietnamese males reached draft age each year also made it hard to inflict upon the communists an unsustainable number of losses.[29] Although the United States and the South Vietnamese had the material advantage, the communists were more willing to wage 'total war', drawing on human and material resources from every element of society and economy. Despite the urgings of the US military, the reserves in the United States were never called up, and overall only a small fraction of American human resources was mobilised. Johnson's Great Society programmes were preserved, and, to minimise domestic controversy and dissent, the Administration sought to play down the war.[30]

Although US forces scored impressive results in larger-scale engagements, more than 96 per cent of all the engagements with the North Vietnamese and the Viet Cong occurred at company size strength (fewer than two hundred men).[31] Kissinger suggested that only the Marines, not MACV, understood that 'the war had to be won against the guerrillas and not against the main force units'.[32] Guerrilla soldiers were able to dictate the time and place of engagements and to disappear rapidly; their stealth and their ability to blend with the general population made them less susceptible to the 'search and destroy' methods of General William C. Westmoreland, head of MACV. But for the Army to have adopted the necessary small-unit tactics more extensively would have meant reversing MACV's reliance on technology and mobility in favour of foot patrols by small units.[33] One reason why this change did not come about was that effective pacification would take time. General Frederick Karch of the US Marines maintained that 'there was only one way that the war could be won, and it was going to take a force of 250,000 perhaps ten years of pacification to do it'.[34] The main burden of pacification was left to the South Vietnamese, who, although improving, were less competent in the more conventional operations. Success was hard to come by. In October 1966, Robert McNamara stated that compared with two years earlier,

> enemy full-time regional forces and part-time guerrilla forces are larger; attacks, terrorism and sabotage have increased in scope and intensity; more railroads and highways cut; the rice crop expected to come to market is smaller; we control little, if any, more of the population; the VC political infrastructure thrives in most of the country; continuing to give the enemy his enormous intelligence advantage; full security exists nowhere (not even behind the US Marines' lines and in Saigon); in the countryside, the enemy almost completely controls the night.[35]

Johnson, as well as MACV, was responsible for the lack of attention given to pacification. When, for example, General Victor H. Krulak of the Marines called upon him to advocate a greater commitment to pacification, the President, as Krulak put it, 'put his arm around my shoulder, and propelled me firmly to the door'.[36] But although Johnson always trimmed the frequent requests of General Westmoreland for more troops, he deferred to him on how the war should be fought. It is reasonable that civilian leaders should give their senior military personnel the leeway to fight as they see fit. However, at the Guam conference in March 1967, Johnson strove at last to boost the pacification programme, placing it under military command. Westmoreland proved supportive of this move, with Komer saying that they had had a 'good, workable meeting of minds' on the issue.[37] He reported a few months later that 'we [are] finally making some progress' in pacification, 'with every prospect [of it] doing better given [the] sizable and growing investment we [are] at long last putting into it'.[38]

THE SEARCH FOR VICTORY: THE AIR WAR

The Rolling Thunder bombing campaign began in February 1965 and, notwithstanding the sixteen bombing pauses or restrictions to encourage the communists to negotiate, continued until the end of October 1968. The campaign sought to reduce North Vietnam's ability to support the communist insurgencies in South Vietnam and Laos; to increase the pressure on North Vietnam to the point where the regime would decide that it was too costly to continue the war; and to enhance South Vietnamese morale and confidence.[39]

Walt Rostow, McGeorge Bundy's replacement as National Security Adviser in April 1966 and since the Second World War a keen advocate of air power, helped to bolster the arguments of the Joint Chiefs of Staff for more bombing.[40] The first nine months of 1966 saw 59,000 attack sorties, about 2.3 times the 1965 effort. This involved 90,000 tons of ordnance, 2.6 times that delivered the previous year. There were efficiency gains: average bomb load per attack sortie increased, and the rate of aircraft losses was just 42 per cent that of 1965.[41] The bombing of North Vietnam's POL (petrol, oil, lubricant) facilities might not have occurred as early as it did without the advent of Rostow. The first of the POL strikes took place in the Hanoi and Haiphong areas at the end of June 1966. There was intense protest in the United States and beyond at this example of American 'aggression', but the attacks were cleanly executed, killing few civilians and inflicting great damage on the POL facilities. In July, further attacks began against POL depots across the North. Most of the facilities were destroyed within months.[42]

Despite successes such as these, there were major critics of the bombing. In several intelligence reports in May 1967, for example, the CIA argued that Rolling Thunder was having little effect on the ability and will of the North Vietnamese to wage war. While an expansion of the war to include, for example, extensive mining of the sea and rivers around North Vietnam and increased bombing of North Vietnamese railroads would have 'serious economic consequences' on the country, it was unlikely to 'weaken the military establishment seriously or to prevent Hanoi from continuing its aggression in the South'.[43] The bombing had

> made only limited progress in meeting two of its current objectives: to limit or raise the cost of sending men and supplies to South Vietnam and to make North Vietnam pay a price for its aggression against the South. The damage to economic and military targets has not degraded North Vietnam's ability sufficiently to support current levels of combat in the South.[44]

As will be seen, views such as these influenced the growing doubts of Robert McNamara. However, the situation was not uniformly negative for the American air war; for one, North Vietnam had to expend a good deal of resources on the repair of roads and bridges and to prepare urban areas for possible attack.[45] An intelligence estimate from early 1966 suggested that 150,000–200,000 North Vietnamese were engaged in repairing bomb damage.[46] Although the communists overcame much of the impact of the POL strikes by importing more oil and dispersing their storage and distribution facilities,[47] the latter was a drain on resources and therefore had an indirect impact on the war effort.[48] President Johnson never expected the air campaign to be decisive,[49] but he did believe that it proved its worth by making the infiltration of soldiers and material into the South much more costly.[50]

There was even CIA evidence to support this claim. The Agency noted that of the enemy troops who began infiltration in 1966 about 20 per cent (10,000–15,000) never made it. As well as claiming lives directly, the bombing made infiltration longer and more arduous, generating high rates of desertion and disease.[51] Similarly, Maxwell Taylor pointed out in 1967 that photographic intelligence showed just 'what our bombing holds back. I do not see for the life of me how we could be justified in relaxing this brake which restrains the forces which can be brought against our men in the South.' Moreover, in the absence of sustained bombing, General Westmoreland's troop requirements would probably have been higher.[52] The idea of ending the bombing of the North gave him the 'shudders'. Rolling Thunder was 'our only trump card – our only pressure on the North'.[53]

Yet the bombing was never as extensive as the military would have liked, because of reasonable concerns about precipitating direct Chinese and Soviet involvement in the war. The CIA noted late in 1966 that 'the modern industrial sector of the North Vietnamese economy' was 'largely off-limits to air attack'.[54] Rolling Thunder remained essentially a tool of diplomatic persuasion rather than a serious effort to win the war.[55] However, while the uninhibited use of air power might have imposed greater damage on North Vietnam's war-waging abilities, the risk of Chinese involvement in particular justified the restraint. Edward Rice, the US Consul General in Hong Kong, noted in 1967 that the Chinese communists were 'publicly committed to sending their men if necessary and when requested'. Beijing was likely to 'honor this blank check should the Vietnamese present it', meaning that 'the war against North Vietnam is one in which winning could be more dangerous than failing to achieve decisive results'.[56]

THE SEARCH FOR PEACE: THE ROLE OF MEDIATORS

Johnson noted that there were more than seventy Vietnam peace initiatives during his time in office.[57] Most of these initiatives involved foreign governments, but private citizens played a role, too. On account of the

United Kingdom's role as convenor of the 1954 Geneva Conference and a member of the International Control Commission, the British government was one of the most active mediators. The most prominent of the nine British initiatives were the Commonwealth Peace Mission of June 1965 and the 'Phase A-Phase B' or 'Sunflower' (the American codename) affair in February 1967. In June 1965, Prime Minister Wilson and other leaders of the British Commonwealth, meeting in London, announced that a four-member mission (the Prime Ministers of the United Kingdom, Ghana, Nigeria, and Trinidad and Tobago) would speak to the governments chiefly concerned to try to bring about a peace settlement in Vietnam.[58] At one point, an unsympathetic Johnson noted privately that North Vietnam and China 'both have made statements on this Wilson mission, telling him to go to hell'.[59] Two days later, in a discussion in the White House, the President voiced:

> considerable concern about the Wilson mission and said that he saw no point in having the Prime Minister come to Washington if Washington and Saigon were the only capitals which would receive him. He expressed the view that a Wilson visit could be counterproductive, would achieve little in the interest of peace, and might turn out to be a further embarrassment to the United States' foreign policy.[60]

Nothing came of the British efforts, in large part because the communists thought that Wilson was little more than Johnson's 'errand-boy'.[61]

The British leader concluded after the British government's 'dissociation' from the POL bombings in June 1966 that he was now in a better position to act as an intermediary (see Chapter Four).[62] In February 1967, Wilson sought to use the visit to London of the Soviet premier, Alexei Kosygin, to initiate negotiations. He pursued this goal under the 'Phase A-Phase B' peace formula, which Johnson outlined to him at the end of January. The formula held that the United States would 'order a cessation of all bombing of North Vietnam the moment we are assured, privately or otherwise, that this step will be answered promptly by a corresponding and appropriate de-escalation on the other side'.[63] Yet the President had never felt enthusiastic about Phase A-Phase B, fearing that the North Vietnamese 'might use a bombing halt to improve its military position'.[64] On 8 February, he informed Ho Chi Minh that the United States would stop bombing 'only as soon as . . . infiltration into South Vietnam by land and sea *has stopped*'.[65] This was the opposite of the earlier formula. Johnson gave a broad outline to the Prime Minister of the letter to Ho, but declined to provide a copy of the letter on the grounds of secrecy on direct communications from Washington to Hanoi.[66]

Poor Anglo-American communication along with disorganisation in Washington meant that neither the White House nor the State Department tried to prevent the British from conveying the original peace formula to Kosygin during his visit to London. It was only later that Washington took action, when one night Walt Rostow told the British to substitute the new formula for the original one.[67] The new text was consistent with Johnson's letter to Ho: the United States would 'order a cessation of bombing of North Vietnam as soon as they were assured that infiltration from North Vietnam to South Vietnam *had stopped*'.[68] The change of tense was an embarrassment to the British, undercutting their status with the Russians, while the North Vietnamese proved unresponsive. Yet Johnson was blasé about the failure, claiming that he had never 'expected anything to come of probes at this phase; and his anxiety was to separate Kosygin and Wilson and avoid their heading for Hanoi; or Wilson's heading for Washington'.[69] This would be little more than a useless complication.

Private citizens as well as governments put themselves forward as intermediaries. At the Pugwash Conference of international scholars in Paris in June 1967, Herbert Marcovich, a French scientist, proposed to fellow conference attendee Henry Kissinger an unofficial visit to Hanoi to open peace negotiations. Marcovich intended to go with Raymond Aubrac, who worked for the United Nations Food and Agriculture Organization and had met Ho Chi Minh and Pham Van Dong, the North Vietnamese Premier. After discussions with Ambassador at Large Averell Harriman and his aide Chester Cooper, Kissinger briefed the two Frenchmen on the Administration's negotiating position and especially on the need for a concession from Hanoi in return for a partial bombing halt. The new peace channel was codenamed Pennsylvania. Marcovich and Aubrac were in North Vietnam from 21 to 26 July, meeting with Ho and Pham. The two intermediaries learned that the North Vietnamese wanted 'an unconditional end to the bombing and if that happens, there will be no further obstacle to negotiations'.[70] The halt did not have to be declared publicly, so long as it occurred. This was a modest concession.[71] In turn, the United States conceded that it would stop the bombing in return for an agreement to negotiate. Here too was a significant development in that Washington was no longer demanding an act of military reciprocity, although, in a vague formulation, the North Vietnamese must not 'take advantage' of the bombing halt.[72]

However, on 20 August, just before Marcovich and Aubrac were to leave for Hanoi again and four days before a planned bombing halt, the Administration intensified air attacks on North Vietnam. Johnson had wanted to strike authorised targets before the bombing halt came into force, to placate the hawks, and perhaps to soften up the communists for negotiations.[73] The intensification of bombing did not bode well for the Pennsylvania channel. By the time the bombing was resumed on 4 September, Hanoi had not responded either to the American message or to the request of the French intermediaries to return to North Vietnam for further discussions. Hanoi's representative in Paris asked the two Frenchmen to contact him again on 6 September for further word. The bombing halt was extended to 7 September, but nothing came of it. Richard Helms concluded that day that although in July Pham had shown greater interest in getting talks going than had previously been the case, this may have been little more than 'a tactical shift', because there was 'nothing in his private statements or in his recent public pronouncements indicating a significant change in Hanoi's position'.[74]

On 29 September, Johnson unveiled what became known as the 'San Antonio formula', named after the venue in which he presented it. This reiterated the formula first outlined privately through the Pennsylvania channel:

> The United States is willing to stop all aerial and naval bombardment of North Vietnam when this will lead promptly to productive discussion. We would, of course, assume that while discussions proceed, North Vietnam would not take advantage of the bombing cessation or limitation.[75]

Even though the United States had scaled back its bombing and had stated that it would stop it completely if the communists refrained from exploiting the pause (this still left them with ample room for manoeuvre), Hanoi's official newspaper asserted on 19 October that Johnson had no right to insist on North Vietnamese military restraint while the United States escalated the bombing over North Vietnam.[76] Pennsylvania had yielded an insubstantial concession from Hanoi in return for a major one from Washington, but otherwise it brought nothing constructive.

Clearly, for the Administration, going along with the numerous third-party peace initiatives had some public relations value, but none of them achieved anything of substance. In fairness, third-party intervention was probably little more than a complication, because if the principals ever had anything new to bring to a conference table then it could be conveyed directly to the opposite number. There were also qualms in the White House about the motivations of some of the third parties – for example, Wilson was regarded as driven in large part by a desire for publicity, while others, such as Raymond Aubrac, were unashamed sympathisers for Ho Chi Minh or were hostile to the United States.

THE TET OFFENSIVE

Some 84,000 communist troops launched their Tet (New Year) Offensive on nearly every major city and military base in South Vietnam on 31 January 1968, sustaining the assault until the end of February. The Offensive drew upon the use of both guerrilla forces and the North Vietnamese Army. While an offensive in the New Year had been expected, the range of the assault was a surprise. On 16 February, Helms met with the President's Foreign Intelligence Advisory Board (PFIAB). He explained that intelligence had not anticipated 'the precise times of the urban attacks, their widespread scale and their intensity', as a result of the limited number of agents in the Viet Cong, inadequate dissemination and analysis procedures within the CIA, and a weak performance by the South Vietnamese intelligence services. Further CIA investigations, culminating in a report to the PFIAB on 7 June, were generally more positive. It concluded that there had been no major intelligence failure, and that advance warnings of some of the attacks had been given to senior officials in Vietnam, thereby enabling the successful defence of the cities. It was also noted in the investigations that Communist security procedures were very efficient, often to the degree that they inhibited effective military coordination.[77]

So, intelligence sources provided sufficient warning to ensure that the United States and South Vietnam secured a military victory, albeit, in some areas, by a slender margin. US and South Vietnamese casualties were relatively light. In the first two weeks of the Offensive – the most intense period of the fighting – the United States lost 1,100 killed in action and South Vietnam 2,300.[78] According to Westmoreland, the Tet Offensive had in some respects been a blessing in disguise. It had woken up the South Vietnamese 'like nothing had before', creating 'a political atmosphere that permitted national mobilization, the drafting of 18 to 19 year old youngsters which traditionally not been done in Vietnamese society'. It helped to 'weed the men from the boys among the officer, non-commissioned officer ranks'. It bolstered the confidence of the South Vietnamese army because 'they fought bravely and well in general, and it gave them that confidence that they needed which has served them well since that time'. It also facilitated 'the modernization of our men with better weapons', such as the M16 semi-automatic rifle.[79]

To be sure, there was a touch of Westmoreland's inveterate optimism in some of his points. Secretary of Defense Clark Clifford reported a few months later that South Vietnamese troops were still not 'in a position to take over more of the war. Despite all the talk over the years, they are still are badly in need of better leadership, better training, additional equipment and an improvement of living conditions for them and their families.'[80] However, the South Vietnamese army had, to its credit, at least held up during Tet, something that might not have been the case had an assault on such a scale occurred a year or so earlier. Although, as will be seen, the impact of the Tet Offensive in the United States was a different matter, the communists fared poorly on a military level. They lost over 40,000 killed, 3,000 captured and perhaps 5,000 disabled or who died of their injuries.[81] Communist leaders had committed units with little heed to their combat effectiveness, and had forbidden withdrawal.[82] They did not fulfil their goals of precipitating a general uprising across South Vietnam or bringing about the collapse of the South Vietnamese army.

Reappraisal in Washington

Despite positive aspects of the US performance during the Tet Offensive, early 1968, as will be seen, saw a reappraisal of the war in Washington. The doubts of Robert McNamara about the war had already crystallised before then, however. McNamara had been a leading advocate of Americanising the war in Vietnam, but his tendency to take a statistical approach to matters had led him to overlook the moral and political dimensions of what was going on. The tenacity with which the communists fought and the vehemence of the growing anti-war movement in the United States shook him profoundly.[83] In a memorandum to President Johnson in October 1966, he noted that the United States had been successful in stalling 'the Communist military initiative' through 'emergency deployments and actions', and the 'program of bombing the North had exacted a price'. Despite high losses, enemy morale remained unbroken and 'he can more than replace his losses by infiltration from North Vietnam and recruitment in South Vietnam'. The prognosis was 'bad that the war can be brought to a satisfactory conclusion within the next two years', unless a variety of actions, such as 'enlivening the pacification program' began. Even here the prospects of success were less than even, given the patchy record since the days of the Kennedy Administration.[84]

The Secretary's doubts deepened. In May 1967, he informed Johnson that while the war between the United States and the regular North Vietnamese army units was going well, the effort against the Communist insurgents was less effective. He urged limiting additional troop deployments to 30,000, after which a ceiling should be imposed; and making more effort to seek a political settlement. The bombing campaign should focus on the main area of infiltration, just below the twentieth parallel.

All this would facilitate 'ending the war on satisfactory terms, of helping our general position with the Soviets, of improving our image in the eyes of international opinion, of reducing the danger of confrontation with China and the Soviet Union, and of reducing US losses'.[85]

On 1 November 1967, McNamara built on some of his previous arguments by suggesting to Johnson that the United States should begin a policy of stabilisation, involving the maintenance but not the expansion of the bombing and of troop numbers. He also recommended another bombing halt to encourage 'the suspension of overt enemy operations against the DMZ' (Demilitarised Zone between North and South Vietnam) and then bringing about talks with Hanoi. He also suggested making more effort to turn over responsibility for the war to South Vietnam.[86] Johnson did not reply to the memorandum, although he sought the views of Dean Rusk. He also asked Rostow to disclose the substance although not the author of the memorandum to Nicholas Katzenbach, Maxwell Taylor, William Westmoreland, Ellsworth Bunker and Abe Fortas. At one extreme was Katzenbach, who concurred with the arguments of the memorandum, and at the other extreme was Abe Fortas, who was vehemently opposed. Fortas felt that McNamara was proposing, in effect, 'a powerful tonic to Chinese Communist effectiveness in the world; and a profound retreat to the Asia dominoes'.[87] Clark Clifford was another who disliked what McNamara had said, responding that 'the course of action suggested . . . will retard the possibility of concluding the conflict rather than accelerating it'. It was essential, Clifford maintained, that no steps were taken that might suggest a weakening of will to the North Vietnamese. Instead, the Communists should face 'unremitting' pressure so that 'some day they will conclude that the game is not worth the candle'.[88]

Johnson met with the illustrious 'Wise Men', or 'Senior Advisory Group' of luminaries such as Dean Acheson, along with his regular foreign policy advisers, on 7 November. Even George Ball, who had striven in 1964–5 to discourage Johnson from Americanising the war, took the view that in the South 'the war of attrition and civil action is in competent hands and we are doing very well there'. Johnson summarised the meeting by saying that 'everyone agrees with our present course in the South', although there was 'general agreement that we should not extend the bombing' of the North.[89]

McNamara argued in his memoirs that the Wise Men had 'no clue' about the sort of arguments that he advanced in his 1 November memorandum, and that their views derived from their 'preconceived notions about the military and political situation in Vietnam'. But the meeting on 7 November provided him with an opportunity to enlighten the other attendees; instead, he merely outlined some of the latest technical measures to reduce infiltration into South Vietnam. Why he held back from expressing his concerns is not clear, but he may have felt that the meeting, involving as it did a number of 'outsiders', was not the best forum for dissent. Moreover, expressing that dissent would contradict the position with which he had been identified for some time. At the end of November, McNamara announced plans to leave the Administration to become President of the World Bank. Johnson continued to hold him in good personal regard, and he would remain Secretary of Defense until the end of February 1968.

Initially, the Tet Offensive had generated a 'rally around the flag' effect among the US public, with 70 per cent of Americans – compared to 63 per cent in December – indicating that they wanted a continuation of the bombing of North Vietnam. Fifty-three per cent favoured either a gradual broadening and intensifying of military operations or 'an all-out crash effort in the hope of winning the war quickly even at the risk of China or Russia entering the war'.[90] But this was too much for the President, and of course he could not ignore those who opposed the war. Public approval ratings for his handling of the war soon fell to 26 per cent.[91] Ellsworth Bunker, US Ambassador in Saigon, argued that although the Tet attacks were 'a failure within Vietnam', they were 'a brilliant success in America', given that they brought to a head many of the doubts about the running of the war.[92] By his own admission, one of Johnson's mistakes was his failure to use his State of the Union address on 17 January to warn of the possibility of intensified fighting.[93]

One of Clark Clifford's most pressing tasks after taking over the post of Secretary of Defense from McNamara in March 1968 was to investigate the likelihood of success in Vietnam. Shocked by the communists' ability to launch a major offensive, he reversed the arguments he had made some months earlier and concluded that the costs of the war had now begun to outstrip South Vietnam's inherent importance to the United States. He argued to Johnson that it would be enough to send only 22,000 troops rather than the 200,000 that Westmoreland had requested, to deal only with the immediate challenges. There were 'grave doubts that we have made the sort of progress we had hoped to have made by this time . . . We seem to have a sinkhole. We put in more – they match it. We put in more – they match it. I am not sure we can ever find our way out if we continue to shovel troops into Vietnam.'[94]

The Wise Men also began to question the value of continued escalation. On 25 March, Clifford opened a meeting with them by stating that the United States could either expand the war effort, 'muddl[e] along' with the present policy or reduce the bombing and ground operations. There was an optimistic briefing from General William DePuy, Special Assistant to the Joint Chiefs for Counterinsurgency and Special Activities, and a more pessimistic one from George Carver, an adviser to Richard Helms on the war. Deputy Assistant Secretary of State for East Asian and Pacific Affairs Philip Habib gave the most pessimistic briefing. Maintaining that the political situation was very poor and military victory could not be achieved, he advocated a bombing halt and peace negotiations. By the end of the meeting most of the attendees favoured a withdrawal from Vietnam,[95] although on what terms was a different matter. While the Wise Men had encouraged the intervention in 1965 and still supported the fundamentals of 'containment' policy, they felt, like McNamara and Clifford, that enough was enough. Now, among the senior civilian foreign policy advisers only Rusk and Rostow felt that the United States should continue to escalate in Vietnam.

On 31 March, Johnson announced a unilateral restriction of bombing, reaffirmed his desire for substantive peace talks and stated that he would not seek a second term in office. The arguments of Clifford and the Wise Men had shaken his confidence. There was also the growing public impatience with his handling of the war, shown by support for Senator Eugene McCarthy, who had made a strong showing in the New Hampshire primary on 12 March. McCarthy's only campaign issue was to seek an immediate settlement and withdrawal of American forces from Vietnam. Robert Kennedy, Johnson's arch-rival, had announced his candidacy for the Democratic nomination on 16 March. Kennedy's campaign platform included an early end to the Vietnam War. In the Republican camp, George Romney had withdrawn from the primary contest, leaving the field open for Richard Nixon, a stronger candidate;[96] Nixon said that he had a 'secret plan' to end the Vietnam War. Other factors behind Johnson's decision to run for the White House again may have included the reflection that President Eisenhower had secured peace terms in Korea in 1953 that were likely to have destroyed President Truman.[97] Johnson felt that he had suffered enough damage to his standing. However, the decision not to run for the Presidency was not solely a product of the circumstances of early 1968; for some months, he had wondered aloud about whether he should seek another term.[98]

THE SEARCH FOR PEACE: DIRECT TALKS

After the exertions of the Tet Offensive, the communist regime proved at least superficially receptive to Johnson's reiteration of his wish for talks. Albeit in the context of a lengthy anti-American diatribe, on 3 April Hanoi stated its readiness to 'send its representatives to make contact with US representatives to decide with the US side the unconditional cessation of bombing and all other war acts against the DRV [Democratic Republic of Vietnam – North Vietnam] so that talks could begin'.[99] After wrangling over a venue, preliminary talks began in Paris in May. Ambassador at Large Averell Harriman, Cyrus Vance, General Andrew Goodpaster of MACV, Philip Habib and William Jorden of the National Security Council represented the United States. The initial discussions dragged on, stumbling mainly on the North Vietnamese demand that the United States end the bombing before substantive talks could begin. Rusk and Rostow rejected this concession, while others, such as Clifford and Katzenbach, felt it worthwhile. Eventually, Johnson, who was torn between the need to secure peace and the possibility that the communists would exploit the pause for military advantage, took the middle ground, stipulating on 14 October that substantive talks must begin within 24 hours of the last bomb falling. However, the North Vietnamese responded that the bombing halt must be 'unconditional'. After further deliberations, the Rolling Thunder campaign ceased on 31 October.

During that month, the National Security Agency had intercepted a number of messages from the South Vietnamese Ambassador in Washington to President Nguyen Van Thieu, who, like many of his compatriots, rued the fact that the American commitment in Vietnam had limits and was therefore unenthusiastic about talks with the North Vietnamese.[100] The intelligence interceptions revealed that senior members of the Nixon entourage had intimated that South Vietnam would get a better deal from him than from an administration under Hubert Humphrey, who had emerged as the Democratic candidate.[101] South Vietnamese foot dragging was a setback, and after Nixon's victory in November the communists showed reluctance to deal with the lame-duck Johnson White House. The first substantive meeting was held on 25 January 1968, only days after Johnson had left Washington for good.[102] It was not until 1973 that there was a 'peace' agreement. Its merits became evident in 1975, when South Vietnam collapsed in the face of a North Vietnamese military assault.

Taking a wide perspective, Walt Rostow argued after retiring from Washington in 1969 that despite the failure to win in Vietnam, the American effort there had beneficial results for Southeast Asia more broadly. He noted, for example, that independent, non-communist nations in the region quadrupled their GNPs between 1960 and 1981 and he argued that this development would probably not have occurred had the United States withdrawn from Vietnam in 1963. According to Rostow's thesis, communism would have been greatly emboldened and would have spread much more widely had the United States not backed South Vietnam under President Johnson and held the line.[103] There are problems with such an argument. One, it is difficult to draw a direct connection between the future of Southeast Asia and the American effort in Vietnam, and, two, the basic aim of the war was to enable the survival of South Vietnam rather than to provide benefits for Southeast Asia in general. Any beneficial regional effects arising from the American war in Vietnam were at best very indirect, and would scarcely have justified the sacrifices of tens of thousands of soldiers had the regional effects been predictable.

However, although there were those in Washington who had argued against US military intervention on the grounds that the communist Chinese and the Soviet Union might undertake a direct combat role, Johnson had avoided a great power conflict. The United States had achieved the objective that had led to the commitment of combat troops in the first place, namely, preventing the North Vietnamese from taking over the South.[104] There had been no military collapse, and no precipitate and unilateral withdrawal of Allied forces in Vietnam, nor was there, in the words of the CIA, any 'negotiation involving political concessions so sweeping as to be tantamount to granting Hanoi outright achievement of its aims in the South'.[105]

It would also be easy to overlook the fact that there was a good deal of progress in Vietnam during Johnson's last year in office. The emergence of General Creighton Abrams as Westmoreland's successor was a positive development – Clifford described him as 'intelligent, experienced and resourceful. He appears to have the quality of flexibility which will be so necessary in the days ahead.'[106] An unnamed CIA source based in Saigon suggested at the end of 1968 that there was 'discernible and significant momentum in a forward direction on virtually all fronts'. There was a 'gathering confidence on the part of the South Vietnamese in their own capacity to govern, to fight, to talk, and ultimately to deal politically with the Communist organization in their midst'.[107] The realisation in Saigon that American support in Vietnam was finite inspired the Vietnamese, as Bunker described it, with 'greater determination, a greater willingness to sacrifice, a new confidence in their own government and armed forces'. By the beginning of 1969, South Vietnam faced Hanoi 'with a military machine greatly superior' to the one it had a year earlier.[108]

Yet by the time Johnson had left office, 29,000 American lives and countless more Vietnamese ones had been lost, hundreds of billions of dollars had been spent and no clear cut military and political victory was on the horizon. As 1968 concluded, Clifford made some damning comments about Johnson's management of the war, suggesting that he thought 'in terms of wars – like WWI and WWII'. Johnson, failing to understand 'the complexities of the situation', had urged the military to 'nail the coonskin to the wall'.[109] The Vietnam War was of course a mix of Hanoi-sponsored insurgency and more conventional military clashes with the North Vietnamese Army, and it was a conflict in which a decisive victory would be hard to gauge, short of North Vietnam ending its operations. Johnson did appreciate, quite correctly, that the US military could gain significant success even within the parameters of limited war, but he did little to foster a strategy that addressed the guerrilla element properly. As a result, the war went on with no decisive victory in sight.

Notes

1. See also Robert J. McMahon, *The Limits of Empire: The United States and Southeast Asia Since World War II* (New York: Columbia University Press, 1999).
2. National Intelligence Estimate, 14 November 1968, *Foreign Relations of the United States* (hereafter *FRUS*) *1964–1968 VII Vietnam September 1968–January 1969* (Washington, DC: USGPO, 2003), pp. 641–3.
3. Lyndon B. Johnson Presidential Library, Austin, TX (hereafter LBJL), NSF: Country File Vietnam, Box 7, Vietnam Memos Vol. XVI 8/16–31/64, Hughes to Dean Rusk, 28 August 1964.
4. Frederick W. Flott Oral History, interviewed 22 July 1984 by Ted Gittinger, LBJL/ Association for Diplomatic Studies and Training Foreign Affairs Oral History Project.
5. Ibid.
6. Troop numbers are from Stanley Robert Larsen and James Lawton Collins, *Allied Participation in Vietnam* (Washington, DC: USGPO, 1975) table, p. 23. Legally, the United States was a 'third country' in Vietnam, but given its role in backing first the French in Indochina from the end of the Second World War until 1954, then supporting South Vietnam, and given Washington's centrality in building the Free World coalition, the United States is considered integral to the conflict and as such distinct from other Free World participants.
7. See Stanley Sandler, *The Korean War: No Victors, No Vanquished* (Lexington, KY: University Press of Kentucky, 1999), pp. 149–69; and William Stueck, *The Korean War: An International History* (Princeton, NJ: Princeton University Press, 1995), pp. 167–203.
8. See Chapter Four for French and British attitudes towards Vietnam.
9. See Robert M. Blackburn, *Mercenaries and Lyndon Johnson's 'More Flags': The Hiring of Korean, Filipino and Thai Soldiers in the Vietnam War* (Jefferson, NC and London: McFarland, 1994).
10. Valenti to Johnson, 4 January 1966, *FRUS 1964–1968 XXVI Indonesia; Malaysia-Singapore; Philippines* (2001), p. 705.

11. McPherson to Johnson, 13 June 1967, *FRUS 1964–1968 V Vietnam 1967* (2002), p. 498.
12. Larsen and Collins, *Allied Participation in Vietnam*, p. 93.
13. McPherson to Johnson, 13 June 1967, *FRUS 1964–1968 V*, p. 497.
14. Blackburn, 'More Flags', p. xiii. The breakdown was as follows: Republic of Korea, 4,407; Australia and New Zealand, 475; Thailand, 350; and the Philippines, 9. Ibid.
15. Larsen and Collins, *Allied Participation*, p. 145.
16. Michael Lind, *The Necessary War: A Reinterpretation of America's Most Disastrous Military Conflict* (New York: Free Press, 1999), p. 94.
17. JCS to McNamara, 27 August 1965, *FRUS 1964–1968 III Vietnam June–December 1965* (1996), p. 357.
18. Robert S. McNamara with Brian VanDeMark, *In Retrospect: The Tragedy and Lessons of Vietnam* (New York: Times Books, 1995), p. 274–5.
19. McPherson to Johnson, 13 June 1967, *FRUS 1964–1968 V*, p. 500.
20. Robert D. Schulzinger, *A Time for War: The United States and Vietnam, 1945–1975* (New York and Oxford: Oxford University Press, 1997), p. 182.
21. McPherson to Johnson, 13 June 1967, *FRUS 1964–1968 V*, pp. 490, 491.
22. Robert Buzzanco, *Masters of War: Military Dissent and Politics in the Vietnam Era* (Cambridge: Cambridge University Press, 1997), p. 235.
23. McNamara to Johnson, 14 October 1966, *FRUS 1964–1968 IV Vietnam 1966* (1998), p. 728.
24. Komer to Rostow, 29 August 1967, *FRUS 1964–1968 V*, p. 732.
25. Ibid.
26. Ibid.
27. Special National Intelligence Estimate, 13 November 1967, *FRUS 1964–1968 V*, p. 1025.
28. Memorandum of conversation, 2 August 1966, *FRUS 1964–1968 IV*, p. 544.
29. McMahon, *The Limits of Empire*, p. 131.
30. Paul M. Kattenburg, *The Vietnam Trauma in American Foreign Policy, 1945–75* (New Brunswick, NJ: Transaction, 1980), p. 202.
31. Schulzinger, *A Time for War*, p. 200.
32. Memorandum of conversation, 2 August 1966, *FRUS 1964–1968 IV*, p. 544.
33. Schulzinger, *A Time for War*, p. 202.
34. Buzzanco, *Masters of War*, p. 248–9.
35. McNamara to Johnson, 14 October 1966, *FRUS 1964–1968 IV*, p. 728.
36. Quoted in Buzzanco, *Masters of War*, p. 261.
37. Komer to Johnson, 25 March 1967, *FRUS 1964–1968 V*, p. 286.
38. Komer to Johnson, 9 July 1967, *FRUS 1964–1968 V*, p. 586.
39. Intelligence report, 1 June 1966, *FRUS 1964–1968 IV*, p. 429.
40. David Milne, *America's Rasputin: Walt Rostow and the Vietnam War* (New York: Hill and Wang, 2008), p. 11.
41. Intelligence memorandum, November 1966, *FRUS 1964–1968 IV*, pp. 801–2.
42. Schulzinger, *A Time for War*, pp. 208–10.
43. Editorial note, *FRUS 1964–1968 V*, pp. 442–3.
44. Ibid., p. 443.
45. Sharp to JCS, 12 January 1966, *FRUS 1964–1968 IV*, p. 50.
46. Notes of meeting, 28 January 1966, *FRUS 1964–1968 IV*, p. 177.
47. Schulzinger, *A Time for War*, pp. 208–10.

48. Intelligence report, August 1966, *FRUS 1964–1968 IV*, p. 615.
49. Lind, *Vietnam*, p. 93.
50. Notes of meeting, undated, *FRUS 1964–1968 V*, pp. 923–4.
51. Rostow to Johnson, 9 August 1967, *FRUS 1964–1968 V*, pp. 678–9.
52. Taylor to Johnson, 11 May 1967, *FRUS 1964–1968 V*, pp. 410–11.
53. McNaughton to McNamara, *FRUS 1964–1968 IV*, p. 784.
54. Intelligence memorandum, November 1966, *FRUS 1964–1968 IV*, p. 803.
55. C. Dale Walton, *The Myth of Inevitable US Defeat in Vietnam* (London: Cass, 2002), p. 108.
56. Consulate Hong Kong to State, 1 May 1967, *FRUS 1964–1968 V*, p. 360.
57. Lyndon B. Johnson, *The Vantage Point: Perspectives of the Presidency, 1963–69* (New York: Holt, Rinehart, Winston, 1971), pp. 579–89.
58. Editorial note, *FRUS 1964–1968 III*, p. 15.
59. Quoted in Michael Beschloss (ed.), *Reaching for Glory: Lyndon Johnson's Secret White House Tapes, 1964–1965* (New York: Simon and Schuster, 2001), p. 366.
60. Cabinet meeting, 23 June 1965, *FRUS 1964–1968 III*, p. 40.
61. Cmnd. 2756, *Recent Exchanges Concerning Attempts to Promote a Negotiated Settlement of the Conflict in Vietnam* (London: HMSO, 1965), p. 94.
62. Chester L. Cooper, *The Lost Crusade: America in Vietnam* (New York: Dodd, Mead, 1970), p. 324. On the 1967 attempt by the British to open Vietnam negotiations, see John Dumbrell and Sylvia Ellis, 'British involvement in Vietnam peace initiatives, 1966–1967: Marigolds, Sunflowers, and "Kosygin Week"', *Diplomatic History*, 27, 1 (January 2003), pp. 113–49; and Geraint Hughes, 'A "Missed Opportunity" for Peace? Harold Wilson, British Diplomacy and the *Sunflower* Initiative to End the Vietnam War', *Diplomacy and Statecraft*, 4, 3 (2003), pp. 106–30.
63. Editorial note, *FRUS 1964–1968 IV*, p. 658.
64. Johnson, *The Vantage Point*, p. 252.
65. LBJL, NSF: Memos to the President, Box 13, Rostow Vol. 21 Feb. 12–28 1967 (2/2), Rostow to Johnson, 'For the President's Diary', 13 February 1967. Italics added.
66. Ibid.
67. Harold Wilson, *The Labour Government, 1964–1970: A Personal Record* (London: Weidenfeld and Nicolson, 1971), pp. 356–7.
68. National Archives and Records Administration, College Park, Maryland, Subject-Numeric 1967–69, POL 27-14 Viet/Sunflower 2.21.67, 2.21.67, 'Sunflower'.
69. LBJL, NSF: Memos to the President, Box 13, Rostow Vol. 21 Feb. 12–28 1967 (2/2), Rostow to Johnson, 'For the President's Diary', 13 February 1967.
70. Editorial note, *FRUS 1964–1968 V*, p. 654.
71. Robert K. Brigham and George C. Herring, 'The PENNSYLVANIA Peace Initiative, June October 1967', in Lloyd C. Gardner and Ted Gittinger (eds), *The Search for Peace in Vietnam 1964–1968* (College Station, TX: Texas A&M University Press, 2004), p. 62.
72. Cooper, *The Lost Crusade*, pp. 378–9.
73. Brigham and Herring, 'The PENNSYLVANIA Peace Initiative', in Gardner and Gittinger (eds), *The Search for Peace*, p. 64.
74. Helms to Johnson, 7 September 1967, *FRUS 1964–1968 V*, pp. 759–61.
75. Johnson, *The Vantage Point*, p. 267.
76. Editorial note, *FRUS 1964–1968 V*, p. 837.
77. Editorial note, *FRUS 1964–1968 VI Vietnam January–August 1968* (2002), pp. 240–1.

78. George C. Herring, *America's Longest War: The United States and Vietnam, 1950–1975*, 2nd edition (New York: McGraw Hill, 1986), p. 191.
79. Editorial note, *FRUS 1964–1968 VI*, p. 972.
80. Clifford to Johnson, 18 July 1968, *FRUS 1964–1968 VI*, p. 876.
81. Wheeler to Johnson, 27 February 1967, *Pentagon Papers*, p. 617.
82. *The History of the Joint Chiefs of Staff: The Joint Chiefs of Staff and the War in Vietnam 1960–1968 Part III* (unpublished manuscript), section 48, p. 13.
83. Benjamin T. Harrison and Christopher L. Mosher, 'John T. McNaughton and Vietnam: The Early Years as Assistant Secretary of Defense, 1964–1965', *History*, 92, 308 (October 2007), p. 497.
84. McNamara to Johnson, 14 October 1966, *FRUS 1964–1968 IV*, pp. 727–35.
85. McNamara to Johnson, 19 May 1967, *FRUS 1964–1968 V*, pp. 437–8.
86. McNamara to Johnson, 1 November 1967, *FRUS 1964–1968 V*, p. 950.
87. McNamara, *In Retrospect*, pp. 309–10.
88. Clifford to Johnson, 7 November 1967, *FRUS 1964–1968 V*, p. 993.
89. Meeting with foreign policy advisers, 2 November 1967, *FRUS 1964–1968 V*, pp. 963–4, 967.
90. Robert Dallek, *Flawed Giant: Lyndon Johnson and his Times, 1961–1973* (New York: Oxford University Press, 1998), p. 505.
91. Milne, *America's Rasputin*, p. 215.
92. Embassy Vietnam to State, 16 January 1968, *FRUS 1964–1968 VII*, pp. 823–4.
93. Walt W. Rostow, *The Diffusion of Power: An Essay in Recent History* (New York: Macmillan, 1972), p. 481.
94. Notes of meeting, 4 March 1968, *FRUS 1964–1968 VII*, pp. 316–27.
95. Editorial note, 16 January 1968, *FRUS 1964–1968 VII*, pp. 457–8.
96. Cooper, *The Lost Crusade*, pp. 393–4.
97. Brands, *The Wages of Globalism*, p. 253.
98. Woods, *LBJ*, p. 837.
99. Herbert Y. Schandler, 'The Pentagon and Peace Negotiations after March 31, 1968', in Gardner and Gittinger (eds), *The Search for Peace in Vietnam*, pp. 322, 337, 351.
100. In January 1968, Averell Harriman stated that it should be pointed out to Foreign Minister Thanh, in particular, that 'he should stop seeing ghosts and . . . realize that we are embarking on serious and sober discussions here. Difficulties are created by fertile, devious and terrified imaginations.' Note 2, *FRUS 1964–1968 VII*, p. 829.
101. Matthew M. Aid, *The Secret Sentry: The Untold History of the National Security Agency* (New York: Bloomsbury, 2009), pp. 145–6.
102. Johnson, *The Vantage Point*, p. 510.
103. Walt W. Rostow, 'The Case for the War', *Times Literary Supplement*, 9 June 1995; Walt W. Rostow, *The United States and the Regional Organization of Asia and the Pacific, 1965–1985* (Austin, TX: University of Texas Press, 1986); Walt W. Rostow, 'Vietnam and Asia', *Diplomatic History*, 20 (Summer 1996), pp. 467–71. For a critique of Rostow's views, see Milne, *America's Rasputin*, pp. 250–4.
104. Harriman memorandum, 14 December 1968, *FRUS 1964–1968 VII*, p. 760.
105. National Intelligence Estimate, 14 November 1968, *FRUS 1964–1968 VII*, p. 643.
106. Clifford to Johnson, 18 July 1968, *FRUS 1964–1968 VI*, p. 876.
107. Memorandum for the record, 24 December 1968, *FRUS 1964–1968 VII*, pp. 779–80.
108. Embassy Vietnam to State, 16 January 1968, *FRUS 1964–1968 VII*, p. 824.
109. Notes of meeting, 5 November 1968, *FRUS 1964–1968 VII*, p. 566.

CHAPTER FOUR

Two Allies: Britain and France

The Johnson Presidency saw particular strain in the bilateral connections between the United States and two of its chief European allies, Britain and France. The relationship with Britain had, by and large, been unusually close since the cooperation against the Axis powers during the Second World War. The ties rested on institutional collaboration on diplomatic, nuclear and intelligence matters. Most conspicuously, it also featured some high-profile friendships between presidents and prime ministers, such as that between John F. Kennedy and Harold Macmillan.[1] Lyndon Johnson believed, though, that the British gave little in return for the vaunted 'special relationship' with Washington. Vietnam proved to be a particular problem. The Labour government (1964–70) of Harold Wilson extended diplomatic support for US policy in Vietnam, but at the same time it had to accommodate the growing hostility in Britain towards the war. The British would not fulfil American requests for combat troops, and 'dissociated' themselves in 1966 from the bombing of petrol and oil facilities near Hanoi and Haiphong. There was the further difficulty of Britain's declining international status, reflected in economic problems and an inability to preserve the long-standing military presence in Asia – the 'East of Suez' presence. Despite the Prime Minister's personal pledges to Johnson, announcements were made in 1967 and 1968 for plans to withdraw from East of Suez. There was a sense of betrayal in Washington that the United States had been left to man the ramparts in Asia alone, and a view that Britain was no longer a reliable or important ally.

France had already liquidated most of its extra-European connections by 1963 but, like Britain, was a major player in NATO, which had been established in 1949 and which institutionalised the American commitment to the security of Western Europe. Since 1958 President Charles de Gaulle had been pursuing a foreign policy of 'grandeur' designed to boost France's international status and freedom of diplomatic manoeuvre, in part by reducing US influence in Europe.[2] In 1966 he announced that France was withdrawing from the integrated command structure of NATO, feeling that such integration was inessential in what was an improving climate of East–West relations. The French move sparked a debate in the Administration about whether or not to punish France in some way for damaging an organisation that was the foundation of US policy in Europe, but President Johnson's view that a tough response would merely exacerbate French nationalism came to prevail. In a demonstration that on occasions the Anglo-American relationship could be a very constructive one, Washington and London used the French demarche as an opportunity for NATO reform. France's policy on Vietnam, in contrast to Britain's qualified support, was one of outright opposition. Paris wanted the United States to announce plans to leave South Vietnam, then an international conference to bring about the 'neutralisation' of Southeast Asia. Washington rued the French approach, feeling that neutralisation would merely lead to rapid communisation and defeat for American interests.

APPROACHES TO THE ANGLO-AMERICAN RELATIONSHIP

The British recognised that President Johnson's primary political interests were domestic, and concluded shortly after John F. Kennedy's assassination in 1963 that 'We cannot expect United Kingdom views to obtain the ready hearing and almost automatic acceptance that the late President gave them.'[3] Johnson had admired the wartime leadership of Winston Churchill, but no subsequent prime minister seemed to gain his respect. The visit of Conservative Prime Minister Alec Douglas-Home in February 1964 left the President with a particular distaste towards close Anglo-American ties and the frequent summit meetings that the bonds entailed. Douglas-Home had intended to address US objections to British exports of buses to communist Cuba, but he did not get round to raising the topic. Later, outside the White House, he gave the impression to journalists that he had asserted himself forcefully on the issue.[4] The 'Douglas-Home episode' was long remembered. As late as 1968, a British official suggested that Johnson was still 'obsessional about Cuban buses and in any conversation with anybody about Britain they always came up'.[5] In contrast to Johnson, Labour Prime Minister Harold Wilson (elected in October 1964 by a narrow margin) was a keen advocate of close Anglo-American bonds, seeing them as a way of magnifying British influence and of bolstering his image as a statesman. In 1964 the Labour MP Anthony Wedgwood Benn noted Wilson's belief that a Labour government 'would be able to establish a much more informal relationship with the American President than Home has been able to do'.[6] Wilson was a great personal admirer of the President. White House adviser Richard Neustadt commented in 1965 that he felt a strong 'emotional commitment to the US', which he 'personified . . . in LBJ'.[7]

STRAINS OVER VIETNAM[8]

The issue of Vietnam helped to confound Wilson's hopes for a close relationship. As the war intensified, he worried about the effects on the East–West détente that had developed after the Cuban Missile Crisis, and feared the escalation of the conflict. At the same time, he did not want a withdrawal by American forces, because pulling out would damage the credibility of American foreign policy pledges not only in Asia but in Western Europe.[9] Therefore the Labour government was willing to extend diplomatic support to Washington over Vietnam, but not to provide troops.[10] Wilson noted that, beginning with the Washington summit conference of December 1964, 'From time to time . . . [Johnson] would ask me if we could not just put in a platoon of Highlanders in their kilts with bagpipes, despite their relatively limited military value.'[11] But there was no support in Britain for sending soldiers. Even the normally pro-American Foreign Office had no desire to see British troops in Vietnam, feeling that the growing American presence helped the communists win support.[12] In fact, the President always made his requests for troops more in hope than in expectation, and he and his colleagues valued British public support in Vietnam and appreciated British efforts in Malaysia, where the British were engaged in a counterinsurgency campaign until 1966.[13]

Wilson's concerns about the Vietnam situation getting out of hand were heightened on 10 February 1965, when he heard of an 'extremely vicious attack by the Vietcong in the Saigon area, involving the destruction of a club largely used by US servicemen'. He claimed to be worried about 'the pressures on the President to escalate the war, if need be by the use of nuclear weapons'.[14] In fact, there was little pressure to drop the bomb, but Wilson was influenced by Prime Minister Clement Attlee's transatlantic odyssey during the Korean War in 1950, which took place for similar reasons. Wilson's late-night telephone call to the White House to arrange a visit did not go well: Johnson replied that there was nothing 'to be gained by flapping around the Atlantic with our coattails out . . . Why don't you run Malaysia and let me run Vietnam?'[15] Johnson was already under strain over Vietnam, and felt it impertinent that allies who would not provide troops should still want to come over to Washington telling him what to do. The response to Wilson's telephone call also seemed to demonstrate a preference for pressuring allies for troops rather than taking advice from them.[16]

The British general election of March 1966 brought a sizable increase in the number of left-wingers in Parliament, and their hostility to the United States' position in Vietnam was especially difficult for Wilson to ignore. In late May that year, the Johnson Administration informed London that the bombing of POL (petrol, oil, lubricants) facilities in the North Vietnamese cities of Hanoi and Haiphong was under consideration. The risk of civilian casualties meant that this was not something that 10 Downing Street would condone. Walt Rostow saw British reticence towards the planned bombings as nothing short of cowardly: 'an attitude of mind which, in effect, prefers that we take losses in the Free World rather than the risks of sharp confrontation'.[17] While Johnson resented the subsequent public statement 'disassociating' the British government from the raids in the Hanoi-Haiphong areas, the Labour government had at least reaffirmed its basic support for US policy in Vietnam at the same time.[18] Moreover, the bombing was a tactical success. In July, at the next summit meeting in Washington, Johnson heaped lavish, if slightly sarcastic, praise on Wilson's leadership and his stringent domestic economic policies. However, the 'dissociation' episode had done little to erode the President's reservations about British policy towards Vietnam. Johnson also ascribed self-seeking motivations to the numerous British efforts to bring peace in Vietnam (see Chapter Three for more details).

Vietnam, the Pound and 'East of Suez'

There was concern among American policymakers about British defence policy East of Suez, because of the situation in Vietnam, the weakness of the British economy and the Defence Review, which Labour had introduced to try to bring its commitments more into line with its capabilities.[19] Since the late 1950s, growth in the British economy had fallen behind relative to that of countries such as France and West Germany, whose defence responsibilities were confined largely to Europe. Heavy military spending abroad contributed significantly to Britain's chronic balance of payments difficulties – there was an £800 million deficit when Labour entered office in October 1964 – and frequent speculative attacks on sterling. Deflecting these attacks without devaluation sterling required foreign – mainly American – support. Wilson did want to devalue, fearing that it would damage perceptions of the Labour Party – the Attlee government had devalued the pound in 1948, when Wilson was a junior minister. For his part, Johnson feared that the devaluation of sterling might 'easily throw the world economy into the kind of vicious cycle that had been so disastrous between 1929 and 1933', and undermine the status of the dollar, itself in a weakening position as a result of heavy defence spending in Vietnam and in Western Europe.[20] (See Chapter Nine.)

The US Treasury orchestrated several multilateral bailouts for the pound. Some of Johnson's advisers saw a chance to link London's need for economic support with the nature of British defence policy. In July 1965, Francis Bator of the National Security Council, Secretary of the Treasury Henry Fowler, Secretary of Defense Robert McNamara and Undersecretary of State George Ball agreed terms for supporting the pound: 'East of Suez and BAOR [British Army of the Rhine] are sacrosanct (by and large) . . . $2.80 [the parity of the pound with the dollar] is sacrosanct', and 'UK troops in Vietnam, while not strictly a necessary condition for us to be forthcoming on sterling, would greatly improve the odds'.[21] McGeorge Bundy was especially keen on pursuing the link with Vietnam: it made 'no sense for us to rescue the pound in a situation in which there is no British flag in Vietnam, and a threatened British thin-out in both east of Suez and in Germany . . . a British brigade in Vietnam would be worth a billion dollars at the moment of truth for sterling'.[22] However, his views generated some opposition: Ball believed that any demand for British soldiers presented in the context of 'balance of payments help' would lead the British to think that they were being asked to provide mercenaries.[23]

Francis Bator noted Johnson's belief that anything 'which could be regarded as even a partial British withdrawal from overseas responsibilities is bound to lead to an agonising reappraisal' of US support for sterling.[24] The President was happy with an implicit link between supporting the pound and the British maintaining their commitments East of Suez, but he did not want to use British economic weakness to get UK troops in Vietnam. He realised that if the Prime Minister agreed to send soldiers only under economic pressure then the controversy over American policy in Southeast Asia might be exacerbated.[25] He vetoed any efforts to try to force the British to commit troops to Vietnam.[26] Wilson and Johnson did not therefore strike any formal 'deal', but the British leader did realise that if Britain began to abrogate its status as a world power, then the Americans might well think twice about providing further financial support. In effect, any American pressure was superfluous; as noted, Wilson already had no wish to devalue the pound, and, because he relished Britain's role on the world stage, he also had little personal desire to oversee deep cuts in defence spending. Moreover, the US stake in international economic stability meant that there was a fair likelihood of supporting sterling regardless of Britain's defence posture.

The announcement in July 1966 of a cut of £100 million in overseas spending, much of it from the military establishment, meant that Britain's commitment to a world defence role had now declined. There was also a growing belief in London that Britain's economic and political future was to be found in Europe. Shortly after the Nassau agreement of 1962 – when the United States agreed to provide Britain with Polaris missiles – France had rejected the first British application to join the European Economic Community (EEC) on the grounds that Britain would be a 'Trojan horse' for American influence in Europe. However, in November 1966 the Wilson government, seeking to reinvigorate the British economy, announced the decision to seek EEC membership once more. Johnson claimed that he was 'immensely heartened' by the decision, feeling that British membership would help to 'strengthen and unify the West'.[27]

While the President supported the European unity movement, he was never an ideologue on the matter. It was East of Suez that concerned him more, and he was deeply worried when in spring 1967 the British Cabinet, reflecting the need to reduce spending and in keeping with the new European vocation, decided to cut British strength East of Suez substantially. In June, Johnson warned Wilson of a possible 'chain reaction' that any plans to withdraw from East of Suez would 'almost inevitably provoke – a reaction which could extend to the American troops in Germany'.[28] His concern was that the British actions would lead to intensified Congressional pressures for cuts in American commitments in the Federal Republic of Germany (FRG) (see Chapter Five). In July, Johnson told Wilson that the situation in Vietnam meant that this was the wrong time 'for Britain to make or to announce a decision that it is sharply reducing its presence in Southeast Asia'.[29] However, the British were well along the road to a formal decision to withdraw from East of Suez. London announced plans to cut by half the forces deployed in Singapore and Malaysia during 1970–1.

There was no US bailout when in November 1967 another financial crisis struck Britain, because the Administration had reconciled itself to the devaluation of sterling, and British defence policy had begun to move away from the East of Suez commitment. Feeling that it could no longer delay the inevitable, the Wilson government devalued the pound, from $2.82 to $2.40. This was a smaller reduction than some had feared, but the change in parity added £50,000,000 immediately to annual defence costs.[30] Johnson worked hard to dissuade the British from further cuts East of Suez,[31] but in January 1968 London announced plans to accelerate the withdrawal from East of Suez and the Persian Gulf. The planned withdrawals, plus President de Gaulle's veto in December 1967 of the British application to join the EEC, meant that by early 1968 Britain lacked a distinct role in world affairs. In common with the thinking behind his 1962 veto, de Gaulle alleged that Britain's close connections with the United States would mean 'continued US domination of Europe'.[32]

However, the relationship between London and Washington had declined. Secretary of Defense Clark Clifford asserted in 1968 that 'the British do not have the resources, the back-up, or the hardware to deal with any big world problem . . . they are no longer a powerful ally of ours because they cannot afford the cost of an adequate defence effort'.[33] Johnson told a journalist that although Britain and America would 'always remain friends . . . when our common interests shrink, the flow of communications and common business shrinks, too'.[34] Yet the British still had much to offer the United States. The State Department noted that Britain was 'still the third largest nuclear power in the world', with 'a small but high quality naval and air nuclear capability', plus a 'not inconsiderable 55,000 man British Army of the Rhine . . . the third largest national force that is unquestionably committed to NATO'.[35] The Anglo-American relationship had weakened due to British decline but it was still a relationship that offered much to Washington.

De Gaulle and Franco-American Relations

President de Gaulle's announcement in February 1966 that France was withdrawing from NATO's integrated command structure came after various measures that had also caused concern in Washington. Upon returning to power in September 1958 de Gaulle initiated a foreign policy of 'grandeur' designed to boost the self-confidence and international status of a country that had lost much of its youth in the First World War and had collapsed ignominiously in 1940. France's woes also came to include defeat in colonial wars in Indochina in 1954 and in Algeria in 1962.[36] In 1958 de Gaulle suggested the creation of a political directorate within NATO comprising France, the United States and Britain. The Directorate would formulate joint strategy, especially in relation to crises outside the NATO theatre. However, Washington had no wish to boost French status at the expense of other members of the Alliance, and the British were unwilling to dilute their bilateral connections with the United States.[37] As if to emphasise that there were other options, the French then withdrew their Mediterranean fleet from the NATO command. As well as vetoing successive British attempts to join the EEC, de Gaulle strove to inhibit the growth of supranationalism within the EEC.[38] In 1963 France signed a treaty of friendship with the FRG, in order to boost French influence in Europe. Washington saw bilateral diplomacy of this kind as corrosive to NATO unity (see Chapter Five).

The French President professed doubt about whether in an era of 'flexible response' Washington would use nuclear weapons to defend Western Europe, given the risk of devastation in North America. For de Gaulle, this made the French independent nuclear deterrent all the more necessary. Early in 1958 the French had begun efforts to develop an independent nuclear arsenal; an atomic bomb was tested in 1960 and a hydrogen bomb in 1968. There is evidence that the French would have been willing to authorise a nuclear first strike in the event of the Soviet Union launching a conventional attack on Western Europe. De Gaulle hoped this would then lead to the American use of long-range missiles.[39] Of course, American diplomats denied the idea that the United States would leave Western Europe undefended in the event of Soviet aggression. According to US Ambassador in France Charles Bohlen, 'the stationing of troops in Europe, the presence of US nuclear weapons on the soil of Europe, provisions of the [NATO] Treaty', along with 'the fundamental considerations which led the United States to sign the Treaty in the first place' all meant that de Gaulle's thesis was nonsense.[40]

Washington was willing to preserve a 'special' nuclear relationship with Britain, which had detonated its first bomb in 1952, but was unwilling to support the ambitions of newcomers on the nuclear scene. Concerns about nuclear proliferation led in Washington in 1964 to NSAM 294, which affirmed US policy 'not to contribute to or assist in the development of a French nuclear warhead capability or a French national strategic nuclear delivery capacity'.[41] France's nationalist policies and its dislike of integrated alliance structures meant that Paris opposed the Multilateral Force scheme for nuclear-sharing within NATO (see Chapter Five). De Gaulle had long envisaged the emergence of a Europe 'from the Atlantic to the Urals' as a third power centre in world affairs to match the United States and the Soviet Union.[42] France would dominate this new Europe. Although loathing communism, de Gaulle had an essentially non-ideological conception of international affairs, and saw opportunities for détente in the Sino-Soviet dispute (see Chapter Six), restiveness in Eastern Europe and American involvement in Vietnam.[43] In June 1966, soon after his NATO demarche, de Gaulle visited Moscow. Dean Rusk suggested that the challenge to NATO was based partly on the view that 'acting alone' de Gaulle 'can do more to promote European détente than can NATO and that NATO in fact . . . is an obstacle to the promotion of more favorable East–West relations'. But, for Rusk, NATO's strength and unity were essential for improvements in the East–West relationship.[44] However, while the Soviets were open to improved relations with France, little of substance came from de Gaulle's overtures to the Soviet Union.[45]

Paris's international monetary policies were another nuisance for the American government – in 1966 France began exchanging US dollars for gold and demanding a return for an international gold standard (see Chapter Nine). According to Charles Bohlen, de Gaulle's international monetary policies reflected his wish to 'strike [a] new blow for "independence" from the United States'.[46] It should be emphasised that although policies such as these were problematic for Washington, de Gaulle was not inherently anti-American. He accorded unequivocal support for the United States during the Cuban Missile Crisis of 1962, for example, and opposed various schemes for disengagement in Central Europe, feeling that they would leave American troops too far away and Soviet troops too close.[47] De Gaulle sought to enhance France's international status and freedom of action, but not an American disengagement from Western Europe. After all, the Cold War was not over. President Johnson was right to believe that 'in any crisis that threatened the American people, France would always be with us'.[48]

RESPONDING TO DE GAULLE'S NATO OVERTURE

Soon after France's withdrawal from the integrated elements of NATO, it was agreed that the North Atlantic Command would move to Brussels, SHAPE (Supreme Headquarters, Allied Powers, Europe) to Casteau in Belgium and AFCENT (Allied Air Forces, Central Europe) to Maastricht in the Netherlands.[49] Moves such as these were carried out with despatch and efficiency, but it was an expensive process and there was damage to NATO's operational strength. A 1967 analysis stated that uncertainty about 'French cooperation in the event of war in Europe, and the denial of the use of French territory and facilities in peacetime' undermined 'the readiness and capabilities of NATO to respond to Warsaw Pact aggression'. The loss of French territory and airspace divided 'NATO territory and mutual defense into two principal regions, making mutual support far more difficult than in the past'.[50] It would not be until after the end of the Cold War that the French took steps towards reintegration in NATO. As well as undermining the physical coherence of the Alliance, there was the political danger that the French move in 1966 would reduce support among the European and American public and legislatures for an integrated NATO. Countries such as Italy and Denmark might move towards more detached positions, and the FRG might adopt bilateral policies in relation both to France and the United States.[51] All these developments would damage the transatlantic alliance.

There was some debate in the Administration over whether or not to respond aggressively to de Gaulle, either in a war of words, by seeking to strengthen the remaining integrated elements of NATO or even by depriving France of NATO protection. While Dean Rusk urged American diplomats not to 'get too excited and show too much public concern . . . since this only helps achieve France's aims',[52] privately he was furious at de Gaulle's action; he, George Ball and Dean Acheson felt that the United States should take a hard line.[53] Charles Bohlen maintained that the French withdrawal amounted to 'a complete destruction from the French point of view of the entire NATO organization and cooperative defence efforts'. For Washington merely to 'accede gracefully' would, for one thing, undermine the considerable opposition to de Gaulle in France.[54] During the interregnum between the departure of McGeorge Bundy and the arrival of Walt Rostow as National Security Adviser, the State Department seemed to be looking for opportunities to strengthen its influence over foreign policy.[55] Within the Senate, Henry Jackson, head of the Governmental Operation Committee, pushed for an aggressive response.[56]

At the same time, there were those, especially the White House foreign policy advisers, of a more restrained outlook. They thought that a confrontation with de Gaulle would achieve little and were especially sensitive to President Johnson's political need to avoid a crisis. Francis Bator noted that while it might be possible to deprive France of NATO protection, this was 'at best barely credible, and at worst just plain silly'. The defence of France was integral to defending Western Europe as a whole. The best approach would be to 'reaffirm our continuing commitment to an integrated NATO, and to do what is necessary to make good on that commitment – with an empty chair always waiting'.[57] Similarly, Robert Komer argued that the Administration should 'stop, look and listen before flinging down the gauntlet to de Gaulle'.[58] For his part, Robert McNamara had little desire to argue with de Gaulle and wanted to get on with strengthening NATO in the absence of France.[59]

The most important perspective was of course that of President Johnson. Johnson had serious reservations about de Gaulle, who he felt 'let high rhetoric and big issues take the place of accomplishments'.[60] He complained that 'We can't get the American people to support our NATO policy when they see the actions taken by the French.'[61] Johnson preferred to accede gracefully, however. A belligerent response would merely inflame de Gaulle's nationalism, and it would also be 'bad manners to speak harshly of de Gaulle or engage in an acrimonious exchange with him'.[62] After delivering a mild admonition about the value of mutual organisation and planning as a foundation of NATO's strength, the President told de Gaulle that 'As our old friend and ally her place will await France whenever she decides to resume her leading role' in the Alliance.[63] The conciliatory note reflected the influence of Francis Bator as well as Johnson's own inclinations.[64] Evidently, and to his great credit, Johnson did not succumb to any temptation to exploit de Gaulle's move – though he might have done so to draw attention away from the crisis in Vietnam and to play upon the considerable popular hostility in the United States to French policy.[65] Rusk noted in June 1964 that in a recent poll 76 per cent of the American people supported NATO, while 74 per cent opposed the policies of de Gaulle.[66]

Johnson did not want to antagonise de Gaulle, but he understood that how far US diplomats adopted a conciliatory line was not quite the same thing. He was willing to assert himself on the matter. In a meeting on 19 May 1966 the President launched what US Ambassador in London David Bruce described as a 'wholly intemperate attack on United States officials who had assailed de Gaulle for his NATO stance'. Dean Acheson replied that he 'resented the President's inferences about his own statements, as well as what he had said about George Ball. Acheson was furious, so was the President.' Ball asked Johnson whether he had even read his recent speech about NATO. No, replied Johnson, 'but . . . no-one in the Administration should contravene his orders about being scrupulously polite in references to the General.' The atmosphere was tense: 'The fat sizzled in the fire for quite some time . . . Acheson visibly seethed in silence; LBJ looked like a human thundercloud.'[67]

THE QUESTION OF FRENCH TROOPS IN THE FRG

A particular concern of Acheson was the presence of around 76,000 French military personnel in the FRG.[68] For the French, stationing troops in the FRG was of strategic value and a symbol of France's position as one of the victors of the Second World War.[69] Legally, France's right to maintain forces in the FRG derived from various agreements dating back to 1945 rather than from the North Atlantic Treaty, so continued adherence to the Treaty did not automatically mean a continued troop presence in the FRG. Paris stated that the assignment to NATO of 'the French ground and air forces stationed in Germany' would end on 1 July 1966, but also said that French forces would stay if the Bonn government preferred. By

American standards, the French troops were poorly trained, manned and equipped, so the issue was mainly of political rather than military significance.[70] As Francis Bator and Walt Rostow suggested, a continued French presence 'without a new agreement is unacceptable as a matter of German politics – it would smell of occupation'.[71]

If Bonn insisted that the troops remained only under NATO auspices, there would be a French withdrawal from the FRG and a rift in Franco-German relations. However, permitting the continued presence of French troops under a new arrangement would seem to condone French policy toward NATO.[72] Ultimately the question of French troops in the FRG could only be resolved by Paris and Bonn. In April, Rusk, McNamara, Ball and Acheson decided that if the Germans insisted that French troops could stay only under existing arrangements and would have 'to withdraw if the French proceed[ed] to decommit these forces from NATO', then 'the US should fully support the Germans and do nothing to dissuade them'. But if the Germans decided to find a new arrangement to keep the French troops in the FRG, Washington should push Bonn to obtain 'effective safeguards' assuring the use of the troops 'in accordance with NATO requirements'. The French should also provide 'an adequate quid pro quo giving to other allies in Germany facilities in France such as transit and overflight rights'.[73] Rusk et al knew that Paris would find these options unattractive and would find its position compromised. It was intended that the terms would inform instructions to John McCloy, President Johnson's envoy, in talks with Chancellor Ludwig Erhard.[74]

However, Francis Bator, for one, objected to the tough line, thinking that it could cause domestic difficulties for Erhard and would contravene Johnson's desire for a restrained response to de Gaulle's policies. Moreover, if the American position led to the eviction of French troops from the FRG, then the United States would be partly responsible for damaging Franco-German relations.[75] Johnson endorsed Bator's advice, and John McCloy duly advised Erhard that the United States would 'support any position taken by the FRG that recognized the seriousness of the situation and provided an adequate response to the French'.[76]

Despite an initial preference for a tough position, Bonn softened its stance, mainly for domestic reasons. By September, according to Ambassador George McGhee in Bonn, the FRG had come to see 'the continued presence of the [French] forces . . . as a symbol of close Franco-German cooperation'. The German government had decided against a confrontation with France. Although Washington might still be able to stiffen the German position, there was still the danger, noted by Bator some time earlier, of precipitating a Franco-German rift. So the United

States, according to McGhee, 'should not get in front of the Germans on the issue of French troops'.[77] By December 1966 the Franco-German talks had finished. It was agreed that the French troops would stay, although France dissolved some missile units and withdrew its air forces. The connection between French troops and the NATO defence system was upheld only with large qualifications and only in the event of war.[78] Dean Acheson resented this outcome, condemning the 'irresolution' and 'feeble counsels' of the Johnson Administration.[79] Yet Johnson's concilia-tory strategy was a wise one, because in doing so he minimised the strain in Franco-American relations and avoided a crisis in the Franco-German relationship, too. Moreover, NATO was already undergoing a process of reform and renewal, as will be seen below, that would help to compensate for some of the damage caused by de Gaulle.

ANGLO-AMERICAN COOPERATION AGAINST DE GAULLE

NATO was as important to British security interests as to American ones, especially when the cost of the commitments outside Europe was increasingly prohibitive.[80] In the months before the French demarche, the British sought to prepare Washington for a French move to destabilise NATO, but little came of it: George Ball feared the 'appearance of an Anglo-American cabal in NATO'.[81] Once de Gaulle had acted, though, Anglo-American cooperation came into play. On 7 March, Ambassador Patrick Dean gave Dean Rusk a draft declaration by the fourteen (exclud-ing France) NATO governments affirming the continuing integrity and validity of the organisation.[82] The next day, Rusk expressed a 'strong desire to let the British take the lead on this question'.[83] The draft declara-tion was discussed at meetings of the fourteen on 11, 12 and 13 March.[84] The final version of the declaration reflected Anglo-American agreement not by referring to the French or the crisis they had created but by affirm-ing NATO's purpose, achievements and strength.[85]

Although the British opposed de Gaulle's move, they did feel that in some ways NATO would benefit from reform. Ambassador Patrick Dean, for example, suggested to Rusk and Ball that the NATO staff could be made more efficient and streamlined.[86] Later, Wilson suggested to Johnson that there was scope for reform on the question of foreign exchange costs for troops in the FRG, and that establishing a consultative mechanism would satisfy the question of nuclear sharing.[87] British as well as American diplomacy in the wake of de Gaulle's NATO demarche contributed to the resolution of the troop 'offset' question, and to the establishment of the

Nuclear Planning Group in 1966–7 (see Chapter Five). Moreover, the military restructuring mentioned earlier was organised successfully at the NATO ministerial meeting in December 1966. The December meeting also saw the establishment of the Nuclear Defense Affairs Committee and the NPG.[88] One effect for the British of helping to reform NATO was strengthening their relations with prospective partners in the EEC.[89] Although de Gaulle's veto of the British EEC application late in 1967 was obviously a setback for European unity, it was around this time that NATO accepted the findings of the Harmel Report. Named after the Belgian Foreign Minister Pierre Harmel, the Report maintained that the Alliance had two aims: détente and deterrence. Détente could be pursued multilaterally, a riposte to the French view that NATO was an obstacle to improved East–West relations.[90]

FRANCE AND VIETNAM

Although, as noted in Chapter One, the United States provided billions of dollars worth of support for the French war effort in Indochina from 1950 to 1954, by the 1960s the French had now come to have grave doubts about US policy.[91] In 1964 Foreign Minister Maurice Couve de Murville compared the Vietnamese situation to that which France had faced in Algeria. In 1962, when Algeria gained its independence, France had 'almost complete physical control . . . but in spite of that we still lost the battle. You can't win without the people.'[92] Later, de Gaulle told George Ball that the United States could not win in Vietnam 'even though you have more aircraft, cannons, and arms of various kinds'. The problem was essentially 'political and psychological'. Vietnam was 'a rotten territory in which to fight'.[93]

De Gaulle took the view that only a political rather than military solution was possible in Vietnam. First of all, though, the United States had to announce plans 'to withdraw from Vietnam and to end all intervention in the internal affairs of the country'.[94] Southeast Asia would then be 'neutralised'. Although de Gaulle was vague about precisely what this would entail, it involved the Vietnamese people being able to make their own political choices free of foreign interference.[95] Most foreign policy specialists in Washington were not impressed by such ideas. Dean Rusk explained in 1964 that a political solution had been reached through the 1954 and 1962 accords over Indochina and Laos respectively, but there the communists still used force to seek more ground. There was no political answer 'which would not be much worse for the interests of the West'. Only when the North left South Vietnam alone would American troops be withdrawn. The terms 'neutralization' and 'political solution' were 'merely words, not a policy'.[96] For his part, President Johnson thought that 'Old Man de Gaulle is puffing through his hat'.[97] He complained to Couve de Murville that while he had greatly valued de Gaulle's support during the Cuban Missile Crisis, French opposition in Vietnam made it very difficult to 'explain our alliances to the American people'.[98]

One feature of de Gaulle's Vietnam diplomacy after the Americanisation of the war in 1965 was his castigation of the United States for its stubbornness. In September 1966, he told a large audience in Phnom Penh that 'while your country succeeded in maintaining its body and soul because it remained its own master, the political and military authority of the United States was seen installed in its turn in South Vietnam and, simultaneously, the war gained new strength there in the form of national resistance'.[99] De Gaulle was 'totally confident that the United States will not be able to bring about a military solution' in Vietnam.[100] The address caused consternation among American observers. For Charles Bohlen, the speech was 'a further example' of the French leader 'ignoring facts in favour of his favorite position'. It was 'extraordinary' how 'an alleged ally of the US would present right on the spot within a few kilometers of the battle line so erroneous a picture of cause and effect'.[101]

THE FRENCH RECOGNITION OF THE PEOPLE'S REPUBLIC OF CHINA

Negotiations over the future of Vietnam would, according to Paris, have to include the communist People's Republic of China (PRC) (see Chapter Six). De Gaulle stated at a press conference that there was 'not a war or peace imaginable' in Asia 'without China's being implicated in it'.[102] He saw the PRC's policy as primarily defensive because Beijing had the Cultural Revolution and economic modernisation to contend with: the PRC 'needs rest, it needs help, it needs commerce and technical assistance from other countries'. Externally, the Chinese were also preoccupied with their dispute with Moscow. According to de Gaulle, the Americans misunderstood the PRC, believing incorrectly that it was 'like Russia in 1917 – intransigent, warlike, and expansive'.[103] In January 1964, France took the controversial step of extending diplomatic recognition to Beijing. It was the first time since 1950 that a major power had recognised the regime.[104] Chinese support of the rebel Front de Libération Nationale in Algeria had made it impossible for France to recognise the PRC until the Algerian War had ended, but the fact that Paris waited until 1964 to extend recognition was due largely to Asian developments and the desire to achieve a political solution in Vietnam with France at the forefront.[105]

For Rusk, President de Gaulle's recognition of the regime in Beijing was 'almost intolerable for many reasons, but particularly in [the] light of ChiCom [Chinese communist] involvement in South Vietnam where US troops were incurring almost daily casualties'.[106] President Johnson had a similar view, although he felt it best to 'play it . . . low key and just make a little protest for the record'.[107] Nevertheless, the strains in the Franco-American relationship were such that the French Ambassador in Washington Hervé Alphand felt obliged to explain that France was not engaged in a conspiracy in Southeast Asia, that France remained firmly anti-communist, and that it had no wish to see the military effort in South Vietnam fail.[108] It was not long, though, before Dean Rusk attempted to make use of Paris's connections with Beijing, albeit more in hope than in expectation. He asked the French to try to persuade Beijing and Hanoi to cease waging war. Paris rejected the request, on the basis that such an attempt at mediation would not succeed unless Washington acceded to the neutralisation plan.[109]

It was anticipated that the wave of demonstrations and strikes that hit France in May 1968 would, according to Sargent Shriver, Bohlen's successor as Ambassador in Paris, encourage de Gaulle to 'ease off his anti-American posture'.[110] However, there were no basic changes in French foreign policy. Later, it was expected that the Soviet invasion of Czechoslovakia in August 1968 might also encourage the French leader to 'consider closer military and political cooperation for the sake of Western collective security', but 'this demonstration of raw Soviet power apparently confirmed the General even more in his determination to work against Western political and military unity and "against blocs"'.[111] The difficulties posed by France boosted Britain's standing in Washington, despite the plans to withdraw from East of Suez. Patrick Dean suggested that the UK's 'manifest support for NATO is a real encouragement at a time when voices are raised in Congress for the withdrawal of troops from Europe', and stated that British society appeared to be a 'rock of stability by comparison with France today'.[112] De Gaulle resigned from office in 1969 after the defeat of a referendum for political reform.

Though there was an asymmetry in material power between Britain and the United States – as shown by British financial dependence on the United States – the relationship was one of political interdependence. Washington needed British support over Vietnam, preferably to include a contingent of troops, and sought a continued British presence East of

Suez as much for its symbolic value as for anything else. Both Britain and the United States were experiencing relative decline. Evidence of this was quite obvious in the British case, but the United States was losing its first war and, partly due to the cost of that war, was struggling to maintain its global economic preponderance. So there was a negative backdrop to the Anglo-American relationship, but this is not to say that the relationship itself was entirely negative. Wilson and Johnson consulted one another regularly and, more often than not, effectively, about their policies. The joint response to de Gaulle's action on NATO was a model of cooperation. The British leader gave ample warning of the dissociation from the bombing of Hanoi and Haiphong, thereby enabling the White House to influence the terms of 10 Downing Street's statement.[113] Although Vietnam, British economic troubles and the withdrawal from East of Suez damaged the high-level Anglo-American relationship, it still had the potential to blossom in future years.

The Johnson Administration believed that France was a disloyal ally acting out of narrow self-interest rather than concern for the Atlantic Alliance.[114] Dean Rusk considered that de Gaulle's policies derived from a 'messianic belief in the glory and importance of France, and thus are not subject to reasoned argument'.[115] De Gaulle was undoubtedly a difficult leader to understand, not least because he played his cards very close to his chest and engaged in what Charles Bohlen described as the 'deliberate utilisation of "Ruse" (one of his favourite gambits in international affairs)', to worry and disarm allies and adversaries alike.[116] However, the view that French policy was informed by some kind of mysticism indicates a limited understanding of French policy. For one, de Gaulle's approach to Vietnam was closely connected with European affairs and was quite rational. In pursuing his goal of neutralising Southeast Asia, he sought to avoid a run-down of the American commitment in Europe as the Asian theatre took priority. This was not an implausible scenario, and indeed as the war in Vietnam intensified there was growing pressure from Congress to reduce American commitments abroad (see Chapter Five). However much he might have resented it, de Gaulle knew that French security was dependent in large part on American military power.[117] There were limits to the coherence of French policy, though, because withdrawing from NATO gave succour to those in the United States who believed that American commitments abroad were excessive and felt that if France could scale back its NATO commitments then so too could the United States.

It should be emphasised that there was a good deal of common ground between the United States and France in the Johnson years. Both countries believed in the continued necessity of NATO, although they did have different visions for the organisation. Shared views over Vietnam included the belief that Hanoi was the main agent of communist operations in the South.[118] Although the French were more inclined to put ideological issues to one side when framing their policies, neither the United States nor France had any sympathy for communism. There was limited consultation between Washington and Paris, but there was no shortage of communication. Most of this communication was entirely congenial and polite. Late in 1965, for example, de Gaulle noted Washington's 'extreme courtesy in advising him privately and promptly' about 'the moves President Johnson was taking in regard to the Vietnam conflict'.[119] Although little of substance was addressed, the meeting of de Gaulle and Johnson at the funeral of Konrad Adenauer in Bonn in April 1967 was good-natured and courteous.[120] Johnson's restraint and courtesy towards de Gaulle was a credit to him, and minimised the strains in the Franco-American relationship.

Notes

1. Surveys of Anglo-American relations include Kathleen Burk, *New World, Old World: The Story of Britain and America* (London: Little, Brown, 2007); Alan P. Dobson, *Anglo-American Relations in the Twentieth Century* (London: Routledge, 1995); John Dumbrell, *A Special Relationship: Anglo-American Relations in the Cold War and After*, 2nd edition (Basingstoke: Macmillan, 2006). See also Michael F. Hopkins, Saul Kelly and John W. Young (eds), *The Washington Embassy: British Ambassadors to the United States 1939–1977* (Basingstoke: Palgrave, 2009).

2. On Franco-American relations see Charles G. Cogan, *Forced to Choose: France, the Atlantic Alliance, and NATO: Then and Now* (Westport, CT: Praeger, 1997); Frank Costigliola, *France and the United States: The Cold Alliance since 1945* (New York: Twayne, 1992); and Robert O. Paxton and Nicholas Wahl (eds), *De Gaulle and the United States: A Centennial Reappraisal* (Oxford: Berg, 1994).

3. The National Archives, Kew, Surrey (hereafter TNA), FO 371/168409, J. L. N. O'Loughlin, 'Lyndon Baines Johnson', 4 December 1963.

4. Philip Geyelin, *Lyndon B. Johnson and the World* (London: Pall Mall, 1966), pp. 90–1.

5. TNA, PREM 13/2445, Palliser to Wilson, 26 February 1968.

6. Tony Benn, *Out of the Wilderness: Diaries 1963–1967* (London: Hutchinson, 1987), p. 108; Saki Dockrill, *Britain's Retreat from East of Suez: The Choice Between Europe and the World?* (Basingstoke: Palgrave, 2002), p. 44.

7. Lyndon B. Johnson Presidential Library, Austin, TX (hereafter LBJL), NSF: Name File, Neustadt Memos Box 7, Neustadt to Bundy, 7 August 1965.

8. For a comprehensive account of British policy towards the Vietnam War, see Sylvia Ellis, *Britain, America and the Vietnam War* (Westport, CT: Praeger, 2004).

9. Bodleian Library, Oxford, Harold Wilson Papers, C. 1127, L-2 1963–66, House of Commons speech, undated.

10. On the effort to recruit allies, see Jonathan Colman and J. J. Widén, 'The Johnson Administration and the Recruitment of Allies in Vietnam, 1964–68', *History*, 94, 4 (December 2009), pp. 483–504.

11. Harold Wilson, 'How a Prime Minister and an Ambassador almost stopped the Vietnam War', *The Diplomatist*, 35, 4 (April 1979), p. 31.

12. See John Young, 'Britain and "LBJ's War", 1964–68', *Cold War History*, 2, 3 (2002), pp. 71–2.

13. Bundy to Johnson, 3 June 1965, *Foreign Relations of the United States* (hereafter FRUS) *1964–1968 II Vietnam, January–June 1965* (Washington, DC: USGPO, 1996), pp. 716–17.

14. Harold Wilson, *The Labour Government, 1964–1970: A Personal Record* (London: Weidenfeld and Nicolson, 1971), p. 80.

15. Wilson–Johnson telephone conversation, 10 February 1965, *FRUS 1964–1968 II*, pp. 229–32.

16. Fredrik Logevall, *Choosing War: The Lost Chance for Peace and the Escalation of War in Vietnam* (Berkeley, CA: University of California Press, 1999), p. 183.

17. LBJL, NSF: Memos to the President, Box 9, Rostow Vol. 9 July 16–31, Rostow to Johnson, 28 July 1966.

18. National Archives and Records Administration, College Park, Maryland, Subject-Numeric 1964–66, POL 2-1 UK, Joint Weekas UK 4.14.66, Embassy to State, 1 July 1966.

19. See Jeremy Fielding, 'Coping with Decline: US Policy towards the British Defence Reviews of 1966', *Diplomatic History*, 22, 4 (Fall 1999), pp. 633–56.

20. Lyndon B. Johnson, *The Vantage Point: Perspectives of the Presidency, 1963–1969* (New York: Holt, Rinehart, Winston, 1971), p. 316.

21. LBJL, Francis Bator Papers, Box 2, Chron. File NSC 4/1/65-8/31/65, Bator to Bundy, 'The UK problem, and "Thinking about the Unthinkable"', 29 July 1965.

22. LBJL, NSF: Memos to the President, Box 4, Bundy Vol. 12 (1/3), Bundy to Johnson, 28 July 1965.

23. LBJL, George Ball Papers, Box 1, The United Kingdom III (11/24/64-12/31/56), 'Telcon, Bundy-Ball', 29 July 1965.

24. LBJL, Francis Bator Papers, Box 2, Chron. File NSC 1/1/65-6/30/65, 'Agenda: Preparation for Trend', 28 July 1965.

25. Clive Ponting, *Breach of Promise: Labour in Power 1964–1970* (London: Hamish Hamilton, 1989), p. 51.

26. LBJL, NSF: Memos to the President, Box 4, Bundy Vol. 14 (2/3), Bundy to Johnson, 'Report from George Ball', 10 September 1965.

27. LBJL, Francis Bator Papers, Box 19, Trilateral/British Bailout, Johnson to Wilson, 13 November 1966.

28. TNA, PREM 13/1906, 'Visit of the Prime Minister to Canada and the United States', 1–3 June 1967.

29. TNA, PREM 13/1457, Johnson to Wilson, 6 July 1967.

30. Jeffrey Pickering, *Britain's Withdrawal from East of Suez: The Politics of Retrenchment* (London: Macmillan, 1998), p. 164. See also Rajarshi Roy, 'The Battle for Bretton Woods: America, Britain and the International Financial Crisis of October 1967–March 1968', *Cold War History*, 2, 2 (January 2002), pp. 33–60.

31. Johnson to Wilson, 11 January 1968, *FRUS 1964–1968 XII Western Europe* (2001), pp. 608–9.

32. Bowie to Rusk, 20 July 1967, *FRUS 1964–1968 XIII Western Europe Region* (1995), pp. 597–8.
33. NSC meeting, 5 June 1968, *FRUS 1964–1968 XII*, p. 625.
34. Quoted in Henry Brandon, *Special Relationships: A Foreign Correspondent's Memoirs from Roosevelt to Reagan* (London: Macmillan, 1988), p. 231.
35. Jonathan Colman, '"What Now for Britain?" The State Department's Intelligence Assessment of the "Special Relationship", 7 February 1968', *Diplomacy and Statecraft*, 19 (June 2008), p. 360.
36. Henry A. Kissinger, *Diplomacy* (New York: Simon and Schuster, 1994), pp. 602–3.
37. Ibid., pp. 610–11.
38. Geir Lundestad, *The United States and Western Europe Since 1945* (Oxford: Oxford University Press, 2003), pp. 111–41.
39. See Jeffrey W. Vanke, 'De Gaulle's Atomic Defence Policy in 1963', *Cold War History*, 1, 2 (January 2001), pp. 119–26.
40. Bohlen to Tyler, 14 September 1964, *FRUS 1964–1968 XIII*, p. 72.
41. NSAM 294, 20 April 1964, *FRUS 1964–1968 XII*, p. 50.
42. Bohlen to Rusk, 3 June 1966, *FRUS 1964–1968 XIII*, p. 404.
43. Thomas Alan Schwartz, *Lyndon Johnson and Europe: In the Shadow of Vietnam* (Cambridge, MA: Harvard university Press, 2003), pp. 99–100.
44. State to Embassy Germany, 23 May 1966, *FRUS 1964–1968 XIII*, p. 399.
45. Frédéric Bozo, *Two Strategies for Europe: De Gaulle, the United States and the Atlantic Alliance* (Lanham, MD: Rowman and Littlefield, 2001), p. 178.
46. Embassy France to State, 11 March 1965, *FRUS 1964–1968 XII*, pp. 91–2.
47. Kissinger, *Diplomacy*, pp. 605–6.
48. Memorandum of conversation, 11 October 1968, *FRUS 1964–1968 XII*, p. 165.
49. State to Embassy France, 28 October 1966, *FRUS 1964–1968 XIII*, p. 488.
50. Paper prepared by Joint Chiefs of Staff, undated, *FRUS 1964–1968 X National Security Policy* (2002), p. 576.
51. Rostow and Bator to Johnson, 18 May 1966, *FRUS 1964–1968 XIII*, p. 387.
52. Notes of Rusk's Special Staff Meeting, 24 April 1964, *FRUS 1964–1968 XII*, p. 52.
53. Rostow and Bator to Johnson, 18 May 1966, *FRUS 1964–1968 XIII*, p. 387.
54. Embassy France to State, 3 March 1966, *FRUS 1964–1968 XII*, pp. 113–14.
55. Schwartz, *Lyndon Johnson and Europe*, p. 104.
56. Ibid., p. 103.
57. Bator to Johnson, 7 March 1966, *FRUS 1964–1968 XIII*, p. 327.
58. Komer to Johnson, 16 March 1966, *FRUS 1964–1968 XIII*, p. 337.
59. Rostow and Bator to Johnson, 18 May 1965, *FRUS 1964–1968 XIII*, p. 387.
60. Quoted in Doris Kearns, *Lyndon Johnson and the American Dream* (London: André Deutsch, 1976), p. 195.
61. 566th NSC meeting, 13 December 1966, *FRUS 1964–1968 XIII*, p. 387.
62. Memorandum of conversation, 20 May 1965, *FRUS 1964–1968 XIII*, p. 394.
63. Johnson to de Gaulle, 22 March 1966, *FRUS 1964–1968 XIII*, p. 44.
64. Andreas Wenger, 'Crisis and Opportunity: NATO's Transformation and the Multilateralization of Détente, 1966–1968', *Journal of Cold War Studies*, 6, 1 (Winter 2004), p. 37.
65. Schwartz, *Lyndon Johnson and Europe*, p. 104.
66. Memorandum of conversation, 9 June 1966, *FRUS 1964–1968 XIII*, p. 413.
67. Diary entry by David Bruce, 19 May 1966, *FRUS 1964–1968 XIII*, pp. 391–2.

68. Memorandum, 9 April 1966, *FRUS 1964–1968 XIII*, p. 359.
69. Helga Haftendorn, *NATO and the Nuclear Revolution: A Crisis of Credibility. 1966–67* (Oxford: Clarendon Press, 1996), pp. 234–5.
70. Memorandum, 9 April 1966, *FRUS 1964–1968 XIII*, pp. 357–9.
71. Rostow and Bator to Johnson, 18 May 1965, *FRUS 1964–1968 XIII*, p. 388.
72. Schwartz, *Lyndon Johnson and Europe*, p. 106.
73. Memorandum of conversation, 4 April 1966, *FRUS 1964–1968 XIII*, p. 354.
74. Schwartz, *Lyndon Johnson and Europe*, p. 107.
75. Ibid., pp. 107–8.
76. Embassy in Germany to State, 17 April 1966, *FRUS 1964–1968 XIII*, p. 367.
77. Embassy in Germany to State, 3 September 1966, *FRUS 1964–1968 XIII*, pp. 462, 463.
78. Haftendorn, *NATO and the Nuclear Revolution*, p. 239.
79. Quoted in Schwartz, *Lyndon Johnson and Europe*, p. 109.
80. Geraint Hughes, *Harold Wilson's Cold War: The Labour Government and East-West Relations, 1964–1970* (Woodbridge and Rochester, NY: Boydell, 2009), p. 85.
81. Quoted in James Ellison, 'Defeating the General: Anglo-American Relations, Europe and the NATO Crisis of 1966', *Cold War History*, 6, 1 (February 2006), pp. 92–3.
82. Note 5, *FRUS 1964–1968 XIII*, p. 330.
83. State to Mission to NATO and European Regional Organisations, 8 March 1966, *FRUS 1964–1968 XIII*, p. 330.
84. Note 5, *FRUS 1964–1968 XIII*, p. 330.
85. Ellison, 'Defeating the General', p. 95.
86. Memorandum of conversation, 17 March 1966, *FRUS 1964–1968 XIII*, p. 340.
87. Ellison, 'Defeating the General', p. 95.
88. Wenger, 'Crisis and Opportunity', p. 31.
89. Ellison, 'Defeating the General', p. 103.
90. Washington had its doubts, in fact, about what NATO could do to hasten détente but that does not detract from the point that NATO's acceptance of the Harmel Report was a victory over de Gaulle. See James Ellison, *The United States, Britain and the Transatlantic Crisis: Rising to the Gaullist Challenge, 1963–1968* (Basingstoke: Palgrave, 2007), pp. 111–12. Also see ibid., pp. 174–83 for the Anglo-American dimension to Harmel.
91. On Franco-American relations and Vietnam, see, for example, Charles G. Cogan, '"How fuzzy can one be?" The American Reaction to de Gaulle's Proposal for the Neutralization of (South) Vietnam', in Lloyd C. Gardner and Ted Gittinger (eds), *The Search for Peace in Vietnam* (College Station, TX: Texas A&M University Press, 2004), pp. 144–61; Fredrik Logevall, 'De Gaulle, Neutralization and American Involvement in Vietnam, 1963–1965', *The Pacific Historical Review*, 61, 1 (February 1992), pp. 69–102; Youko Torikata, 'Reexamining de Gaulle's Peace Initiative on the Vietnam War', *Diplomatic History*, 31, 5 (November 2007), pp. 909–38.
92. Memorandum of conversation, 12 April 1964, *FRUS 1964–1968 I Vietnam 1964* (1992), p. 235.
93. Ball to State, 6 June 1964, Ibid., p. 467.
94. Bundy to Johnson and Rusk, enclosing de Gaulle letter to Johnson, 5 February 1966, *FRUS 1964–1968 IV Vietnam 1966* (1998), p. 213.
95. Torikata, 'Reexamining de Gaulle's Peace Initiative on the Vietnam War', p. 918.
96. Memorandum of conversation, 1 July 1964, *FRUS 1964–1968 I*, pp. 533–6.

97. Michael Beschloss (ed.), *Taking Charge: The Johnson White House Tapes, 1963–64* (New York: Simon and Schuster, 1997), p. 214.
98. Memorandum of conversation, 19 February 1965, *FRUS 1964–1968 XII*, p. 84.
99. Note 2, *FRUS 1964–1968 XII*, p. 130.
100. Quoted in Torikata, 'Reexamining de Gaulle's Peace Initiative on the Vietnam War', p. 935.
101. 101. Embassy France to State, 1 September 1966, *FRUS 1964–1968 XII*, p. 130, and n. 2.
102. Editorial note, *FRUS 1964–1968 I*, p. 49.
103. Ball to State, 6 June 1964, Ibid., p. 468.
104. Garrett Martin, 'Playing the China Card? Revisiting France's Recognition of Communist China', *Journal of Cold War Studies*, 10, 1 (Winter 2008), p. 52.
105. See Ibid., pp. 52–80.
106. State to Embassy Republic of China, 18 January 1964, *FRUS 1964–1968 XXX China* (1998), p. 8.
107. Editorial note, *FRUS 1964–1968 XXX*, p. 3.
108. State to Embassy in Vietnam, 29 February 1964, *FRUS 1964–1968 I*, pp. 107–8.
109. Torikata, 'Reexamining de Gaulle's Peace Initiative on the Vietnam War', p. 920.
110. Embassy France to State, 28 May 1968, *FRUS 1964–1968 XII*, p. 152.
111. Embassy France to State, 10 October 1968, ibid., p. 163.
112. TNA, PRO, FCO 7/742, Dean to Gore-Booth, 1 July 1968.
113. Johnson to Wilson, 14 June 1966, *FRUS 1964–1968 IV*, pp. 426–7.
114. Torikata, 'Reexamining de Gaulle's Peace Initiative on the Vietnam War', p. 910.
115. State to All NATO Missions, 2 March 1966, *FRUS 1964–1968 XII*, pp. 111–12.
116. Embassy France to State, 31 March 1966, *FRUS 1964–1968 XIII*, p. 351.
117. Torikata, 'Reexamining de Gaulle's Peace Initiative on the Vietnam War', p. 912.
118. Ball to State, 6 June 1964, *FRUS 1964–1968 I*, p. 465.
119. Embassy France to State, 31 December 1965, *FRUS 1964–1968 III Vietnam June–December 1965* (1996), pp. 757, 760.
120. Memorandum of conversation, 25 April 1967, *FRUS 1964–1968 XII*, p. 141.

CHAPTER FIVE

NATO Nuclear Sharing and Troop Offset

As well as the challenge posed by France's withdrawal from the NATO command structure in 1966 (see Chapter Four), the Johnson years saw other threats to the unity of NATO.[1] These were centred on the Federal Republic of Germany (FRG). One of the challenges was to give the FRG a greater say in the Alliance's nuclear affairs. This question found expression in the Multilateral Force (MLF), an ambitious American scheme for a nuclear-equipped NATO fleet operating under a US veto. The MLF concept had been around for several years but had not come to fruition when Johnson became President. Initially, he let his advisers pursue the project while he concentrated on domestic issues and on the election of November 1964, after which, having concluded that the project was more trouble than it was worth, he put the onus onto the Europeans to take things further. With no agreement on a hardware solution emerging, gradually the MLF lost momentum. Fortunately, its demise enabled various constructive developments that had a number of benefits for American interests and the transatlantic alliance, including the NATO Nuclear Planning Group (NPG).[2]

The second issue to be explored is the question of the Bonn government's 'offset' of the foreign exchange costs for American troops in the FRG. The American troops issue was related to the nuclear question, because those troops were part of an implicit bargain to prevent, among other things, Bonn from pursuing nationalistic policies that might include seeking an independent nuclear capability.[3] Although the question had emerged under Kennedy, it arose in a more acute form in summer 1966 when the Ludwig Erhard government decided that it could no longer adhere to the agreement whereby the FRG was supposed to buy military equipment from the United States sufficient to 'offset' the balance of payments deficit caused by the presence of troops in the FRG. The Johnson Administration feared that if the costs were not met then isolationist pressure from the Senate would force a major withdrawal of troops, which might encourage other countries, especially Britain, to remove troops from the FRG. For its part, the Bonn government was suffering from economic problems and was reluctant to be seen yielding to American pressure. A series of 'trilateral' negotiations led to a satisfactory if short-term offset formula. President Johnson made a significant personal contribution to resolving both the MLF and the offset questions, and as such helped to maintain NATO's unity in a challenging period.

THE ORIGINS OF THE MLF

The proposal for a NATO nuclear fleet dated from the end of the last Eisenhower Administration. The scheme was designed mainly to ease Western European concerns that the United States would be less likely to defend Western Europe with nuclear weapons now that the Soviets had intercontinental ballistic missiles and thereby the ability to strike American cities.[4] The naval force concept evolved in various ways after its inception, and by 1962 it had taken the form of a fleet of surface ships armed with Polaris nuclear missiles. The project had also gained political momentum, with discussions involving politicians, foreign ministries and defence ministries having taken place in various capitals. However, most policymakers in the Kennedy Administration saw no need for an immediate decision from the governments concerned about whether or not they would participate. This would change. The UK's own Blue Streak project, then the US Skybolt system, which Britain was to purchase, had both been cancelled on cost, technical and strategic grounds, and the British wanted an alternative. An agreement was made at the Anglo-American conference at Nassau in December 1962 to provide the British with Polaris nuclear missiles, thereby keeping Britain in the nuclear club.[5]

The post-Nassau veto by France of British membership of the European Economic Community on the grounds that Britain was too close an ally with the United States created a crisis of Western unity which the MLF, it was hoped, might help to overcome. However, although the British had agreed under Nassau to deploy their Polaris submarines under NATO command, they much preferred the vessels to remain under national control.[6] As discussed in Chapter Four, an increasingly assertive France under Charles de Gaulle was also determined to keep its nuclear arsenal under national control, and so opposed the MLF on the grounds that the project would tie its members to a transatlantic nuclear policy rather than a European one.[7] The MLF was far more appealing to Bonn than it was to London and Paris, because it would give the FRG political equality with

Britain and France in the Atlantic Alliance.[8] In the absence of the MLF, aspirations of this nature might seek an outlet in a quest for a national deterrent. President Johnson recognised that a German deterrent would be abhorrent to East and West alike.[9] US Ambassador in Bonn George C. McGhee noted that if the Germans took steps towards an independent deterrent there were would be serious consequences: one, 'we would withdraw forces and support for the FRG first'; two, the 'other NATO allies would . . . probably move to dissociate themselves from Germany in NATO'; and, three, any German efforts to acquire a national deterrent would lead to a Soviet pre-emptive strike.[10]

From Washington's perspective, the signing of a Franco-German Treaty of Friendship and Co-operation in January 1963 highlighted the need for greater transatlantic unity. The Treaty provided for frequent consultations between the heads of state, foreign ministers and defence ministers to help coordinate foreign policy decisions and to develop common military doctrines. The reaction in Washington was one of profound shock, with concern about the possibility of a Bonn–Paris deal with Moscow, leading towards a Soviet withdrawal from East Germany to be followed by some sort of confederation between the two parts of that divided country. This would mean the end of NATO and the advent of a neutral Germany that might try to play East against West. There were also concerns that Germany might cooperate with France in the nuclear field.[11]

The Treaty galvanised the MLF advocates within the State Department to act with renewed vigour in pushing the project forward. The supporters of the MLF included George Ball, Thomas Finletter, Henry Owen, Walt Rostow, Henry Rowan, Gerard Smith and William Tyler.[12] These officials saw the MLF not only as a means of mitigating some of the Atlantic Community's immediate difficulties, but as a step towards their ultimate vision of a politically unified Europe. There were others in Washington who supported the MLF in principle but felt that pushing it onto reluctant Europeans would weaken, not strengthen, the transatlantic relationship. In June 1963, for example, National Security Adviser McGeorge Bundy urged Kennedy to ease the pressure on the Europeans to create an MLF and instead recommended broadening the discussion of the nuclear problem to include 'more people' (above all, the French), and 'more problems', such as consultation, alternative weapons systems and non-proliferation. Kennedy favoured this approach and the project soon faded into the background again,[13] although in October 1963 the Working Groups were established to explore how in practice the MLF would work.

THE MEETING OF 10 APRIL 1964

Lyndon Johnson had had little exposure to the issue of the MLF when he was Kennedy's Vice-President. When in November 1963 Johnson became President, backers of the MLF saw a chance to push the project once more. In order to plan a negotiation schedule and set a deadline, MLF supporters had to consider the impact of several elections. The US presidential election was to take place in November and the British had their general election scheduled for October. Consequently neither the President nor the British Prime Minister, Sir Alec Douglas-Home, were prepared to do anything drastic. In addition, German parliamentary elections were planned for September 1965 and the Atlanticist Chancellor Ludwig Erhard wanted any agreement on the MLF to be concluded well beforehand, as success in this regard would represent a triumph for him. This left only November and December 1964 for signing a treaty.[14]

On 10 April 1964, the MLF supporters went to the White House to try to persuade the President to approve the new timetable.[15] By accident or by design, the proponents of the MLF dominated the meeting. In attendance were the President, Ball, Bundy, Finletter, Smith and several other officials, mostly from the State Department. Both Robert McNamara, Secretary of Defense, and Dean Rusk, Secretary of State, were unavailable. Generally speaking, these two men had a more pragmatic and flexible attitude towards the MLF. Thomas Finletter made his case at the meeting by stating that 'the educational phase' of the MLF had given way to 'the action phase'. The President needed only to give 'the go-ahead sign' and the project would be accepted by a number of countries. Even a reluctant Labour government under Harold Wilson would eventually agree to join the MLF if the US stated clearly that this organisation of European nuclear defence was 'the only alternative for them'. By contrast, Bundy maintained that although there was a consensus within the US government supporting the MLF, McNamara, the Joint Chiefs of Staff and William C. Foster (Director of the Arms Control and Disarmament Agency) all had 'serious reservations'. The MLF would not work if it was 'forced upon the Europeans', nor should it be handled 'in such a way as to complicate the [British election] campaign'. For his part, Foster highlighted Moscow's opposition to the MLF and indicated that pushing the project would complicate arms control.[16]

However, it was Ball, Finletter and their fellow supporters of the fleet who won the day. As the meeting closed, Johnson emphasised the need for further discussions with Congress; for the Europeans to be told that the MLF was the best way to proceed; and for movement towards an agreement on the MLF by the end of the year.[17] Ball and Finletter soon informed the European capitals that the United States now sought an agreement on the MLF by the close of 1964. Finletter visited Ludwig Erhard in Bonn just days later and restated Johnson's decisions. The German leader supported these points firmly.[18] The Joint Communiqué of a meeting between him and Johnson in Washington on 12 June 'reaffirmed the continuing importance of NATO to the defence and cohesion of the West', asserted that the MLF would augment NATO's military and political strength and indicated that efforts should be continued to ready an agreement for signature by the end of the year.[19] MLF advocates in the Johnson Administration now had the deadline they wanted, and work intensified in the Working Groups. Initially, the main purpose of the Working Groups was to investigate 'the principal questions involved' and not to draft an actual treaty.[20] This changed after 10 April 1964, when efforts turned towards preparing a treaty for signature by the end of the year, that is, within the time frame advocated by Johnson and Erhard.

It is worth saying a little more about the 10 April meeting, as it was an important occasion in the history of the MLF. It has been suggested that the MLF coalition, almost wilfully, misread the directives from President Johnson in order to further their own crusade for the establishment of a mixed-manned sea-borne force.[21] While it might be true that at the time Johnson did not realise the full implications of his decisions, it would be wrong to suppose that he was duped into something he would otherwise have found objectionable. Johnson's public statements after the meeting, as well as the ones given by Rusk, support the interpretation made by Finletter and his colleagues, that is, the need to push the MLF post-haste. Given that he had never expressed any particular enthusiasm for the scheme, why then did the President yield to pressure from his pro-MLF advisers? First, in the spring of 1964 he was preoccupied with legislative concerns and, second, the MLF supporters saw the meeting as an especially valuable opportunity to gain a presidential determination on the MLF and therefore pressed their case with zeal. More generally, there was the fact that the pragmatists never felt compelled to join forces and embark upon a joint crusade *against* the project, ensuring that the MLF advocates tended to hold the upper hand – at least in the short term.

It is worth underlining here that the main difference of opinion between the more pragmatic policy advisers and the so-called 'cabal' of MLF enthusiasts concerned not whether or not the MLF was worthwhile, but how vigorously it should be pushed. Advisers such as Bundy and Rusk were reasonably satisfied with the status quo and more afraid of causing a split among the European allies.[22] Rusk expected that in common with the Marshall Plan of 1947 the initiative should come from Europe instead of the United States. Since economic reconstruction and nuclear management were different matters, no concerted European initiative ever emerged – a state of affairs captured well by the Secretary's comment that there was 'no such thing as Europe' so far as the MLF was concerned.[23] Finletter, and to a lesser extent Ball, thought that strong American leadership on the issue was the only way to proceed and that the Europeans could never agree among themselves on such a sensitive matter.

British Reservations

Johnson and Erhard's June statement made it clear to the British that the United States sought to fit the MLF into a timetable suited to the German elections. Thus, British concerns were of only marginal importance and the new schedule meant that a decision on the MLF in the House of Commons would have had to be taken only a couple of months after the general election in October. This caused resentment in Whitehall. Conservative Prime Minister Alec Douglas-Home had taken over the post only in October 1963, after Harold Macmillan had resigned as a result of ill health, economic problems and political scandal. The fact that the Douglas-Home government was essentially a stop-gap until the election would play an important role in determining British attitudes toward the MLF. As Foreign Minister for Macmillan, Douglas-Home had attended the Nassau meeting in December 1962 and was an ardent defender of an independent British deterrent. So too were most of the ministers in his government, including Foreign Secretary Rab Butler and Minister of Defence Peter Thorneycroft.[24] The armed forces were not MLF enthusiasts either. The Navy regarded mixed-manning as unworkable, saw the MLF as a potential drain of resources from its existing activities and feared that the demand created by the MLF for skilled personnel might undermine the British Polaris programme. The RAF and the Army were worried that the MLF might drain funds from their activities.[25] Memorably, Chief of the Defence Staff Lord Mountbatten dismissed the MLF as 'the greatest piece of military nonsense he had come across in fifty years'.[26]

The reservations of the military left the arguments in favour of the MLF to be made solely on political grounds. The Foreign Office accepted that Britain could not remain outside this project if the US went ahead with the other NATO allies. The political costs of such isolation would be severe.[27] The British therefore put forward a modified version of the MLF known as the 'Thorneycroft proposals', partly with the intention of delaying the project until after the elections.[28] The main aim of these proposals was, from a British point of view, to lower costs. This could be done either by decreasing the size of the sea-borne force or by applying the MLF concept of mixed-manning and joint ownership to already-planned weapon systems. Either of these revisions would still achieve the political objective of giving the FRG, Italy and the smaller members of NATO 'a sense of participation'. The second of the Thorneycroft proposals called for a 'massive multilateralisation' of planned or already available aircraft and missiles belonging to the British, American and German defence forces. The British Polaris submarines were not to be included.[29] Financially, avoiding the need to purchase new military hardware promised to reduce costs significantly. Politically, the American MLF proposal would be dominated by the US and the FRG since they each had a 40 per cent share in the force. Since the British were only scheduled for a share of 10 per cent, Britain would exert only minimal political influence over this force. On the other hand, if Washington adopted Thorneycroft's proposals, Britain would play a leading role along with the Americans.

During the summer and autumn of 1964, the MLF supporters in Washington prepared for the post-election period when action would be taken on the MLF and a treaty prepared for signature. The British MLF proposals, injected into the negotiation process during the summer, did not cause as much delay as the Germans and the American MLF supporters had feared. This was because the FRG and the United States did much of the negotiating bilaterally, outside the Working Groups. This annoyed the British, and to a lesser extent the smaller NATO countries, but little could be done to resolve the situation.[30] By autumn 1964, the key question still to be resolved in the MLF negotiations was how political control and military command should be managed in the force. A settlement on this issue was unlikely to be made in the Working Group as a whole, leaving the possibility of signing an agreement on the MLF by the end of the year, with only the United States and the FRG as participants. On 30 September, Erhard wrote to Johnson suggesting the possibility of a bilateral German–American MLF.[31] However, Johnson's response stressed the importance of keeping to the agreed timetable and avoiding 'this great undertaking' looking like 'merely a German–American venture'. The issue could not in any case be decided before the British elections.[32] Thus the President had dampened the idea of a bilateral MLF, which the MLF supporters had sometimes suggested mainly as a means of putting pressure on the British. Now, Johnson awaited the British election in October and the US presidential election in November.

The British Labour Government and the MLF

Labour won the general election of 14 October by a narrow margin, while Johnson won the presidential election by a landslide the following month. On 6 December – the day before Prime Minister Harold Wilson was due to visit Washington – the President, Ball, McNamara, Rusk, Bundy and US Ambassador in London David Bruce held a meeting. The opportunity had arrived to take further steps to bring the MLF to fruition. However, Johnson's attitude was now very different from his passive stance at the 10 April meeting, and demonstrated that he could exert forceful command over his advisers. He stated that he had given the project much more thought than he had in the spring, noting among other things that there was little support for the MLF in the Senate, especially if Britain was in effect forced into joining. His advisers should be much more 'prudent' in what they pushed him to go for.[33] It was also the case that he had plenty to contend with in Vietnam, and he could not help but acknowledge that Moscow was vehemently hostile to the idea that Bonn should have its finger on the nuclear trigger – even with an American veto. While he did not want to give the Soviets the final say over any aspect of American foreign policy, he did want to 'build bridges' between East and West.

The British delegates to the summit proposed an 'Atlantic Nuclear Force' (ANF), comprising the British V-bomber force, the four British Polaris submarines then under construction, an equal number of American Polaris submarines and a mixed-manned element in which only the non-nuclear forces would participate.[34] Some historians have presented the ANF quite favourably, arguing that far from being a device to neutralise the concept of nuclear sharing, the proposal was more modest and realistic than the MLF and served several important purposes for the Labour government and the Atlantic community: it would have eased the concerns of Labour left-wingers who advocated unilateral disarmament; it would have gone some way in fulfilling the multilateral element of the Nassau agreement; and it would have resolved the impasse over the nuclear non-proliferation treaty that was blocked by the Soviets because of the MLF proposal.[35] These points have some validity, but more significant was the fact that there was no particular enthusiasm within the Labour government for any variant of the MLF – even the ANF. The Prime Minister, like his Conservative predecessor, had been obliged to navigate several unattractive options: an outright rejection of the MLF leading to political isolation; uninhibited participation, with the associated compromise of independent great power status; and a middle path of trying to mitigate the worst features of the fleet – hence the ANF. Dean Rusk, for one, understood fully what had been going on; he reflected a few months later that the British had been 'playing a game. They have been for abandoning their independent nuclear weapon in principle, but against it in practice. They have advanced the ANF as a substitute for the MLF; then backed away from their own proposal.'[36]

THE END OF THE MLF

Yet the British were not the only ones to back away. After hearing from Wilson and his colleagues at the summit meeting, Johnson decided that it was now up to the British, the Germans and the Italians 'to get together' to resolve matters, 'rather than that we should appear to be telling our European friends what they should be thinking'.[37] A National Security Action Memorandum on 17 December 1964 expressed this view by calling a halt to pressing for a hardware solution. The US would not endorse any nuclear arrangements for NATO unless they were acceptable to both the FRG and Britain; any such arrangements had to be discussed in advance with France; and the United States should allow the Europeans themselves to take the initiative on any further moves towards greater integration.[38] However, the German government, having won the election of September 1965, still wanted a 'hardware' solution to the NATO nuclear problem.[39] Ambassador McGhee noted 'a widespread feeling here in all circles – government, diplomatic and press – that the US has abandoned interest in the MLF – "that it is dead"'.[40]

At one point Rusk tried to placate the Germans by saying that the United States had not lost interest in the problems that the MLF was designed to address, that is 'to strengthen and rationalise, on an Atlantic basis, the organisation of the Alliance's nuclear effort' and allowing the 'principal non-nuclear powers to share . . . the responsibility for their own nuclear defence'.[41] However, Rusk's response clearly did not indicate any confidence that a hardware solution was on the cards. The MLF was running out of steam, and by early 1966 – as a contemporary observer put it – schemes for a NATO fleet 'could legally and logically be pronounced dead'.[42] All this made the ANF what the German politician Franz Joseph Strauss described as the only fleet in history which had not been created, yet torpedoed another fleet that never sailed.[43] Of course, Lyndon Johnson as well as Wilson never lamented the demise of a hardware solution to NATO's nuclear problems.

Fortunately, those problems would be ameliorated by the establishment of something more practicable than a NATO fleet: the NPG.[44] To address the unease in Western European capitals about the few opportunities for dialogue about nuclear strategy with American policymakers, a Special Committee in NATO was established in 1965 to explore the possibility of allied participation in planning for the use of nuclear weapons. The idea then made low-key progress. It was notable that the summit communiqué of the Johnson-Erhard meeting in September 1966 did not refer to the MLF but to the establishment of a permanent nuclear planning committee to enhance nuclear consultation and planning.[45] Robert McNamara, one of the chief sponsors of the NPG, stated its advantages late in 1966: it 'meets the need of our allies, especially Germany. It will more closely tie in Germany with the US and the UK in the nuclear field. It will end talk of the Multilateral Force.'[46] The NPG comprised four permanent members – the United States, Britain, the FRG and Italy – plus three members from Belgium, Canada, Denmark, Greece, the Netherlands and Turkey rotated at eighteen-month intervals. In order to retain its nuclear independence, France chose not to join.[47]

The forum first met in April 1967 and had one of its successes in January the following year, when NATO formally abandoned the strategy of 'massive retaliation', which had prevailed in the 1950s, in favour of 'flexible response'. This strategy was more nuanced and left greater scope for negotiation in the event of a crisis.[48] A further benefit of the end of the hardware project was the Treaty on Nuclear Non-Proliferation (NPT). This was signed in July 1968 by the United States, the Soviet Union, Britain, the FRG and fifty-three other countries. Nations without nuclear weapons agreed not to seek to develop them; and nations that possessed nuclear weapons agreed to work towards arms control and disarmament.[49] The Treaty came into force in 1970.

THE OFFSET QUESTION: ORIGINS

For some years there had been growing concern in Washington about the foreign exchange burden that resulted from the 225,000 or so American troops in the FRG converting their dollars to marks for local spending. By 1966 this added about $800 million per year to the US balance of payments deficit.[50] A memorandum of understanding had been signed five years earlier to the effect that the FRG would cover or 'offset' US foreign exchange expenditures in the Federal Republic by purchasing an appropriate amount of military equipment in the United States for two years. This agreement was extended for another two years in 1963 and 1965.[51] However, the Bonn government, now spending more on social issues and experiencing reduced economic growth, was soon less able, or indeed willing, to pay for the purchases. In July 1966, Ludwig Erhard contacted

Johnson to ask for more time to fulfil the offset agreement.[52] Erhard gave little indication of how and when the agreement might be met. One of his problems in setting financial priorities was the widespread perception in the FRG that, as President Johnson understood, the payments were for the mere presence of American troops rather than 'simply offsetting abnormal foreign exchange earnings, by buying goods and services from the United States'.[53] As National Security Adviser Walt Rostow noted, some Germans believed that the payments were, in effect, upholding the presence of mercenaries.[54]

A tough budgetary situation in Washington meant that the Johnson Administration, in common with the government in Bonn, had little room for manoeuvre. In December 1966, the President stated that the United States government was facing outgoings of $142 billion with revenue estimates of $120 billion. One reason for this was, as the President noted, that 'expenditures for the poor . . . have increased tremendously since the Kennedy Administration'. There were limits to borrowing, too: 'We are now very near a debt limit.'[55] Growing burdens in Vietnam as well as defence spending in Europe compounded American financial problems. Further offset complications arose in relation to the British, whose 51,000 troops incurred about $200 million per annum in foreign exchange costs at a time of chronic balance of payments shortfalls for Britain. London and Bonn had a partial offset agreement until 1967. However, the British indicated in a Defence White Paper in February 1966 that to maintain the BAOR at current levels then the full foreign exchange costs would have to be met.[56] Thus, London was, like Washington, ill-positioned to make concessions to the German budgetary situation. This was a cause for concern – Francis Bator of the National Security Council feared that 'sharp cuts' in British forces in the FRG might initiate 'an unravelling process in NATO' with increasing 'domestic pressure on us to follow suit'.[57]

As the latter point suggests, the administration had to contend with an adverse climate of Congressional opinion as well as with economic problems. Most American politicians understood that Cold War tensions in Europe had eased since the end of the Berlin crisis in 1961 and the resolution of the Cuban Missile Crisis the following year, and, according to some observers, France's withdrawal from the NATO command structure and the wholesale eviction of US troops from French territory in spring 1966 (see Chapter Four) was an example of European perversity and unworthiness. In late August 1966, Senate Majority Leader Mike Mansfield introduced a 'sense of Congress' resolution with the support of twelve other Senators, maintaining that a 'substantial reduction of US forces permanently stationed in Europe can be made without adversely affecting either our resolve or ability to meet our commitment under the North Atlantic Treaty'.[58] Of course, the White House did not greet Mansfield's initiative with much enthusiasm; quite the opposite. Johnson complained in colourful language to Senator Russell Long that the resolution

> really murdered us on NATO . . . A goddamned sense of Congress resolution ain't worth a shit unless this President has some respect for the sense of it. And all it can do is notify every enemy that we're just a bunch of un-unified folks running off . . . in every goddamned direction![59]

TOWARDS TRILATERAL TALKS

Secretary of Defense Robert McNamara was more involved with the offset issue than any of the other advisers, not least because he had helped to negotiate the offset agreements in the first place. He saw offset predominantly in statistical rather than political terms; an example perhaps of what George Ball suggested was a tendency to 'distort any kind of policy in order to achieve some temporary alleviation to the balance of payments'.[60] McNamara was not as politically inept as Ball suggested, but the Secretary's views on offset were certainly uncompromising. He felt that if the FRG did not cover the foreign exchange cost of US troops then a corresponding level of withdrawals should take place. He considered, probably with some justification, that on strict military terms a much smaller American presence in the FRG would suffice, and he was also worried that in the absence of adequate protection for the balance of payments, pressure from the Senate might lead to troop cuts so deep that they rendered the American presence in the FRG militarily useless.[61] Moreover, substantial troop withdrawals would be at odds with McNamara's desire to raise the nuclear threshold and to end reliance on the first use of nuclear weapons.

McNamara's patience was also eroded by the view that the German government was not spending what it ought on the German armed forces, leaving the United States to carry extra burdens – a recent report indicated that some $4 billion was needed for equipping, modernising and training, and for reserve stocks. Bonn's failure to keep its armed forces up to scratch gave the lie to various German statements that they did not need to buy the items stipulated by the terms of offset.[62] Finally, there was the background concern that the FRG was not doing enough to help in Vietnam, with McNamara once complaining to Johnson that the Germans were not providing 'a damn thing apart from the hospital ship. The [German] Ambassador came in the other day and asked if the hospital ship was satisfactory as the substitute for combat troops and I told him absolutely not.'[63] But the Bonn government felt that it had gone a long way in providing support for American policy in Vietnam short of sending troops, making German politicians and diplomats especially sensitive to how the Americans treated them.[64]

President Johnson's upbringing in an ethnically diverse community in Texas had given him a particular respect and affection for the German people. He often made effusive statements about German–American relations, once telling Erhard, for example, that the FRG was 'the most trustworthy of all allies'.[65] Johnson was more than willing to consider German needs and sensibilities – after all, the FRG was one of the three leading members of NATO – but obviously he had American interests to defend, too. He held a meeting with his chief advisers in Washington on 24 August 1966 to find the best way forward. McNamara, with the support of Secretary of the Treasury Henry Fowler, maintained that there were too many troops in the FRG; the payments drain was too much; the Germans should stick to the terms of the deal; and the United States should tell the British to hold the line, but they had to make their own deal with the Germans. George Ball reflected the State Department's more accommodating approach and he made various efforts to counter these arguments. However, he had only limited success, as Dean Rusk had allowed McNamara to take the lead on the offset question and thus provided Ball with little support. Moreover, Ball was on the verge of leaving the government, making his position all the weaker. While Johnson had sympathy with the McNamara line, he was politically more aware and knew that it made more sense to seek a new, mutually acceptable agreement, with some compromises if absolutely necessary, rather than to take drastic, unilateral action. Although immediately beneficial to the balance of payments, the latter would compound the problems of the transatlantic alliance, not ease them. The decision was taken to invite London and Bonn to participate in trilateral talks with representatives from Washington. The goals of the talks were to address the German need for financial respite; keep US forces in the FRG in adequate numbers to remain militarily effective, but make some troop cuts to placate Congress and to provide some balance of payments relief; and to provide financial respite to the British, to avoid substantial cuts from the British Army of the Rhine (BAOR).[66]

Harold Wilson consented to the idea of trilateral talks, but Ludwig Erhard, fearing that the Anglo-Americans might act in concert to squeeze concessions from him, was noncommittal, agreeing only to discuss the issue when he was next in Washington.[67] His reticence was a source of irritation in the White House, because of the urgent need to prevent the British from making cuts.[68] At the summit meeting, the Chancellor complained, only half-jokingly, that the 'US wanted money [from] the FRG and Britain wanted money [from] the FRG, and now they wanted to gang up together to put Germany in a 2:1 minority'.[69] However, some well-applied pressure from Johnson led him to consent, albeit begrudgingly, to trilateral discussions.[70] John McCloy was to be Johnson's envoy in the talks. His credentials for the role were impeccable. He had once served as High Commissioner in Germany and had garnered a great deal of respect among the German people, and his background in banking had given him a firm grasp of financial affairs. At the same time, he was a tough negotiator.[71] Manlio Brosio, NATO's Secretary General, also participated in the talks, which began in October 1966 and comprised a mixture of formal sessions, informal consultations and several Working Groups.[72]

THE RESOLUTION OF OFFSET

The offset issue generated continued friction in German–American relations and in German domestic politics. There were attacks against Robert McNamara in the German press for some statements interpreted as casting doubt upon the FRG's commitment to uphold its obligations, and against Defence Minister Kai-Uwe von Hassel and Chancellor Erhard for being too accommodating to the Americans.[73] Ambassador McGhee predicted that if too much pressure was placed on the Erhard government then it would fall or would be severely weakened, with the result that German–American relations would become more distant.[74] Indeed, on 27 October the Free Democratic Party members of Erhard's cabinet resigned. The Christian Democratic Union, the Christian Social Union and the Social Democratic Party agreed on a 'grand coalition' with Kurt-Georg Kiesinger as Chancellor. Erhard resigned on 30 November.[75] There were various issues behind Erhard's demise, including the awkward economic situation, but a key factor was his failure to return from Washington with concessions.[76] It was not until the end of January 1967 that Kiesinger, who was less Atlanticist in his foreign policy outlook than was his predecessor and with whom Johnson got on less well personally, was able to resume the offset talks. In the meantime, the United States had been obliged to ease London's budgetary situation by agreeing to additional military purchases from Britain amounting to $35 million.[77] This move required Johnson to fend off some additional Congressional pressure, but the concession was enough to get Wilson to keep British troops in the FRG until June 1967, by which date the offset negotiations should, it was hoped, have reached their conclusion.[78]

A further American contribution to the offset negotiations was a troop rotation technique called 'dual-basing'. Here two of the three brigades in a division would move back to the United States, while the third brigade stayed in the FRG. The German-based brigade would in due course return to the United States to be replaced by another brigade.[79] The same approach was proposed for American air wings.[80] The dual-basing concept drew on the lessons of 'Exercise Big Lift' of 1963, which demonstrated that an entire armoured division could be flown to Europe and be ready to participate in manoeuvres with little delay.[81] The attraction of dual-basing, according to Johnson, was that as well as easing the foreign exchange burden 'the entire division would remain ready for combat and committed to NATO'. There was some debate in the Administration about how many troops should participate in the dual-basing procedure,[82] but Johnson was able to issue his final instructions to McCloy on 1 March.

These provided that the FRG should decide what levels of procurement in the United States and Britain it wished to undertake in order to bring its military forces up to appropriate strength levels; and that the Allies should address the remaining balance of payments impact of allied troops stationed in Germany by cooperating in the management of monetary reserves or by other agreed means.[83] The last point, according to Johnson, was 'a departure from established policy'. It meant easing the pressure on the Germans to make military purchases in the United States and an openness to other ways of dealing with the problem.[84] By the end of April, the government in Bonn had agreed to offset US foreign exchange costs by purchasing $500 million worth of medium-term bonds. While McNamara considered anything other than straightforward military purchases to be 'hocus-pocus',[85] the agreement was satisfactory to both parties and helped to ease pressure from the Senate. The Germans promised to refrain from converting their dollar holdings into gold, thereby avoiding additional pressure on the dollar. This was probably the most important part of the 'offset' package, as it meant that the FRG, despite its huge and persistent payments surpluses, would not put any pressure on US reserves. There was no evidence of serious German unhappiness with this part of the package.[86] It was also agreed that 35,000 men (2 army brigades) and 96 warplanes (three tactical fighter wings) out of the 216 presently in the FRG would be deployed back to the United States under the aegis of 'dual-basing'. At the same time, there was a mutually acceptable British-German deal on offset, with some American assistance in the form of additional military purchases in Britain. The British would withdraw only a nominal number of troops.[87]

Undoubtedly, all this represented progress, but the trilateral negotiations did not fix forever the size of the American and British presence in the FRG. Nor did they settle the problem of offsetting the related foreign exchange burdens, as the purchase of medium-term US bonds was only a short-term answer.[88] Critics in the Senate complained that the FRG would be profiting from its investments instead of carrying a fairer burden on defence in Europe.[89] Critics also argued that the German purchase of the bonds only postponed the problem.[90] Early in 1968 Undersecretary of State Nicholas Katzenbach noted that 'the trilateral talks last year bought us some time, but it is important that we begin discussions with the FRG as soon as we can on [an] arrangement for the next two years'.[91] There were questions about the efficacy of dual-basing, as there was no escaping the fact that Warsaw Pact forces were close to the potential battle zone while a significant proportion of the American commitment to NATO would be thousands of miles away. There was the psychological dimension to consider, too. Sir Fitzroy Maclean, chairman of the North Atlantic Assembly, warned in 1967 that 'however mobile a force might be, the United States mobile strategic reserve does not have the same effect as uniforms on the street'.[92] Yet overall the trilateral talks made the best of a difficult situation by avoiding major troop cuts, and by affirming the principle that security concerns within NATO should take precedence over political ones. They also demonstrated that, in Johnson's words, 'military cooperation in NATO could not be separated from financial cooperation'.[93]

Both the MLF and offset questions emerged from centrifugal forces in the transatlantic alliance. So far as the MLF was concerned, Johnson, for one, came to appreciate that vigorous efforts to promote greater cohesion could be counterproductive – pushing reluctant allies into 'grand designs' would do little to strengthen the Alliance in the long term. The MLF was therefore allowed to slip away. It had come about in large part from the desire to control German aspirations for a national nuclear deterrent. George Ball has made the case that the strength of these aspirations has been exaggerated, and the main concern of Bonn as time went on was not with obtaining nuclear weapons but with pursuing *Ostpolitik* and the ultimate goal of unification.[94] Nevertheless, the prospect, however remote, of a German national deterrent was greeted with abhorrence in most quarters and would do severe damage to NATO as well as to East–West relations. Washington was successful in redirecting German goals away from the hardware project towards the consultative mechanism of the NPG, while the latter also permitted the progress of the NPT.

Notably, Ambassador at Large Averell Harriman advised Johnson and Rusk late in 1966 that if Washington 'abandoned the hardware option' in US proposals for a nuclear non-proliferation pact then Moscow might be induced to help negotiate a settlement in Vietnam.[95] Harriman's suggestion was well-timed given that the prospects for a nuclear hardware solution were by then very limited, and that Bonn had intimated that it would be happy if a NATO nuclear planning body was set up instead.[96] However, keen as the Administration was on the prospect of a non-proliferation treaty, it did not pursue any triangular connection between the MLF, the NPT and Vietnam – probably out of the recognition that Soviet influence over Hanoi had distinct limits.

Centrifugal forces also helped to generate the offset question. What Johnson described as the 'brutal blow' of France's withdrawal from the NATO command structure in March 1966 had made it all the more important to neutralise any further threats to the strength and coherence of the alliance.[97] But the improving climate of East–West relations had eroded the case for preserving a large contingent of American troops in the FRG. President Johnson considered that a substantial American military commitment in the FRG was vital to European and therefore US security, and wanted security considerations to take precedence over financial and political ones. He was 'more anxious than any man on that goddamn [Senate] committee on balance of payments to get troops out. But I sure as hell don't want to get them out with 22 divisions there and kick off World War III.'[98] The view that the Warsaw Pact was restrained from invading Western Europe only by Western arms may in retrospect seem exaggerated, but it was the symbolic impact of withdrawals made under financial pressure that concerned Johnson the most: where might such cuts end? The Administration was taking steps to develop the post-Cuba détente (see Chapter Six), but it would be some time before the Cold War came to an end. In his handling of the offset question, the President won the gratitude of the United States' NATO partners for his 'determination not to play into the hands of those in the US who want . . . to see substantial American troop cuts in Europe'.[99] Despite the undoubted demands of Vietnam, Johnson played an important role in resolving two serious challenges to NATO and to the German–American relationship.

Notes

1. This chapter is partly based on J. J. Widén and Jonathan Colman, 'Lyndon B. Johnson, Alec Douglas-Home, Europe and the NATO Multilateral Force, 1963–64', *Journal of Transatlantic Studies*, 5, 1 (2007), pp. 179–99.

2. See Chapter Four for more on the reform of NATO, as well as the challenge posed by French policies.

3. See Francis J. Gavin, *Gold, Dollars and Power: The Politics of International Monetary Relations, 1958–1971* (Chapel Hill, NC: University of North Carolina Press, 2004), pp. 135–6.

4. See Pascaline Winand, *Eisenhower, Kennedy and the United States of Europe* (Basingstoke: Macmillan, 1993), pp. 203–22.

5. On Skybolt and Polaris, see, for example, Jan Melissen, *The Struggle for Nuclear Partnership* (Groningen: Styx, 1993); Ian Clark, *Nuclear Diplomacy and the Special Relationship: Britain's Deterrent and America, 1957–1962* (Oxford: Clarendon Press, 1994); Donette Murray, *Kennedy, Macmillan and Nuclear Weapons* (Basingstoke: Palgrave, 2000); Nigel Ashton, *Kennedy, Macmillan and the Cold War* (Basingstoke: Palgrave, 2002); Ken Young, 'The Skybolt Crisis of 1962: Muddle or Mischief?', *Journal of Strategic Studies*, 27, 4 (December 2004), pp. 614–35.

6. 'The Nassau Agreement', 21 December 1962, reproduced in John Baylis (ed.), *Anglo-American Relations Since 1939* (Manchester: Manchester University Press, 1997), pp. 139–41.

7. Bundy to Johnson, 8 November 1964, *Foreign Relations of the United States* (hereafter FRUS) *1964–1968 XIII Western Europe Region* (Washington, DC: USGPO, 1995), p. 106.

8. Humphrey–McGhee conversation, 1 September 1965, *FRUS 1964–1968 XV Germany and Berlin* (1999), p. 324.

9. Johnson-Erhard meeting, 20 December 1965, *FRUS 1964–1968 XIII*, p. 289.

10. Bonn to State, 25 August 1966, *FRUS 1964–1968 XV*, p. 395.

11. George W. Ball, *The Past has Another Pattern: Memoirs* (New York: Norton, 1982), p. 271. In fact, the Treaty came to very little, with France not even consulting Germany on the decision to withdraw from the NATO command structure in 1966. Ibid., p. 273.

12. The positions of these men were: Undersecretary of State George Ball, Permanent Representative to NATO Thomas Finletter, Policy Planning Staff member Henry Owen, Deputy Special Assistant to the President for National Security Affairs Walt Rostow, Deputy Assistant Secretary of Defense for International Security Affairs Henry Rowan, Special Assistant to the Secretary of State for Multilateral Force negotiations Gerard Smith and Assistant Secretary of State for European Affairs William Tyler.

13. Bundy to the President, 15 June 1963, *FRUS 1961–1963 XIII Western Europe and Canada* (1994), pp. 592–5.

14. United States National Archives and Records Administration, College Park, Maryland, RG 59, Central Files, DEF (MLF) 3, Box 1759, SECUN 3, Bonn to Washington, 4 March 1964, no. 3133, Central Files, DEF (MLF) 4; and Geneva to Washington, 25 March 1964, and Bonn to Washington, 4 March 1964.

15. See Walt Rostow, *The Diffusion of Power: An Essay in Recent History* (New York: Macmillan, 1972), pp. 391–2; Philip Geyelin, *Lyndon B. Johnson and the World* (London: Pall Mall, 1966), pp. 159–61; and John D. Steinbruner, *The Cybernetic Theory of Decision: New Dimensions of Political Analysis* (Princeton, NJ: Princeton University Press, 1974), pp. 286–9. See also memorandum of conversation, 10 April 1964, *FRUS 1964–1968 XIII*, pp. 35–7.

16. Memorandum of conversation, 10 April 1964, *FRUS 1964–1968 XIII*, pp. 35–7.

17. Ibid.
18. Embassy Bonn to State, 16 April 1964, *FRUS 1964–1968 XIII*, pp. 37–9.
19. For the communiqué see *Documents on American Foreign Relations 1964* (Washington, DC: USGPO, 1965), pp. 93–5.
20. See TNA, PREM 11/4739, 'Concept Multilateral Nuclear Force given new impetus', US Information Service, 14 October 1963.
21. For a discussion of the different interpretations of the 10 April meeting see Geyelin, *Lyndon B. Johnson and the World*, pp. 160–1; Steinbruner, *Cybernetic*, p. 289 (particularly note 55).
22. Rusk's pragmatic view of the MLF can be studied in Dean Rusk Oral History Interview IV, 8 March 1970, by Paige E. Mulhollan, Internet Copy, Lyndon B. Johnson Presidential Library, Austin, TX (hereafter LBJL). A 'radical' view from an ardent MLF supporter, Finletter, is in Helga Haftendorn, *NATO and the Nuclear Revolution: A Crisis of Credibility, 1966–1967* (Oxford: Clarendon Press, 1996), pp. 182–3 (note 52).
23. Rusk to State, 17 April 1964, *FRUS 1964–1968 XIII*, p. 41.
24. See Alec Douglas-Home, *The Way the Wind Blows: An Autobiography by Lord Home* (London: Collins, 1976), pp. 176–204.
25. Andrew J. Pierre, *Nuclear Politics: The British Experience with an Independent Strategic Force, 1939–1970* (London: Oxford University Press, 1970), pp. 245–6.
26. Quoted in Stephen Twigge and Len Scott, *Planning Armageddon: Britain, the US and the Command of Nuclear Forces, 1945–1964* (Amsterdam: Harwood Academic Press, 2000), p. 188.
27. Pierre, *Nuclear Politics*, pp. 243–50.
28. TNA, PREM 11/4740, Shuckburgh to FO, 17 April 1964; and Shuckburgh to FO, 21 April 1964.
29. Pierre, *Nuclear Politics*, pp. 248–9.
30. TNA, PREM 11/4740, Shuckburgh to FO, 17 April 1964, and Shuckburgh to FO, 11 June 1964.
31. Erhard to Johnson, 30 September 1964, *FRUS 1964–1968 XIII*, pp. 78–9.
32. Johnson to Erhard, 7 October 1964, *FRUS 1964–1968 XIII*, pp. 82–3.
33. LBJL, NSF: Country File, Box 214, UK Wilson Visit I 12/7-8/64, 'Wilson Visit and the MLF', 6 December 1964.
34. State to Embassy in Bonn, 29 October 1964, *FRUS 1964–1968 XIII*, p. 94. For details of the Wilson–Johnson summit see Jonathan Colman, *A 'Special Relationship'? Harold Wilson, Lyndon B. Johnson and Anglo-American Relations 'at the Summit', 1964–68* (Manchester: Manchester University Press, 2004), Chapters 1 and 2; and Saki Dockrill, 'Forging the Anglo-American global defence partnership: Harold Wilson, Lyndon Johnson and the Washington summit, December 1964', *Journal of Strategic Studies*, 23, 4 (December 2000), pp. 107–29.
35. Andrew Priest, *Kennedy, Johnson and NATO: Britain, America and the Dynamics of Alliance, 1962–68* (London: Routledge, 2006), p. 94.
36. Rusk to Johnson, 11 April 1966, *FRUS 1964–1968 XIII*, p. 364.
37. Johnson–Erhard conversation, 9 February 1965, *FRUS 1964–1968 XV*, p. 223.
38. NSAM 322, 17 December 1964, *FRUS 1964–1968 XIII*, pp. 165–7.
39. Leddy to Rusk, 8 November 1965, *FRUS 1964–1968 XIII*, p. 261.
40. Embassy Bonn to State, 9 January 1965, *FRUS 1964–1968 XIII*, pp. 169–71.
41. Rusk to Schroeder, 13 January 1965, *FRUS 1964–1968 XIII*, p. 173.

42. Geyelin, *Lyndon B. Johnson and the World*, p. 180. See also Priest, *Kennedy, Johnson and NATO*, pp. 93–121.
43. Quoted in Denis Healey, *The Time of My Life* (London: Penguin, 1989), p. 305.
44. See Haftendorn, *NATO and the Nuclear Revolution*, pp. 161–3, on the background of the NPG.
45. Rostow, *The Diffusion of Power*, p. 394.
46. Notes of the 566th NSC meeting, 13 December 1966, *FRUS 1964–1968 XIII*, p. 512.
47. Haftendorn, *NATO and the Nuclear Revolution*, p. 167.
48. Secretary of State to FCO and Minister of Defence, 24 March 1969, FCO 41/413, TNA.
49. For recent coverage of the NPT, see Susanna Schrafstetter and Stephen Twigge, *Avoiding Armageddon: Europe, the United States and the Struggle for Nuclear Nonproliferation, 1945–1970* (Westport, CT and London: Praeger, 2004), pp. 163–201.
50. Lyndon B. Johnson, *The Vantage Point: Perspectives of the Presidency, 1963–1969* (New York: Holt, Rinehart, Winston, 1971), pp. 306–7.
51. Haftendorn, *NATO and the Nuclear Revolution*, pp. 240–1.
52. Francis Bator, 'Lyndon Johnson and Foreign Policy: The Case of Western Europe and the Soviet Union', in Aaron Lobel (ed.), *Presidential Judgment: Foreign Policy Decision Making in the White House* (Hollis, NH: Puritan Press, 2000), p. 44; Erhard to Johnson, 5 July 1965, *FRUS 1964–1968 XV*, pp. 375–6.
53. Johnson, *The Vantage Point*, p. 307.
54. Rostow, *The Diffusion of Power*, pp. 396–7.
55. 566th NSC meeting, 13 December 1966, *FRUS 1964–1968 XIII*, p. 513.
56. Haftendorn, *NATO and the Nuclear Revolution*, pp. 240–1. For the British side, see Geraint Hughes, *Harold Wilson's Cold War: The Labour Government and East-West Relations, 1964–1970* (London: Boydell, 2008), pp. 99–105; and John W. Young, *The Labour Governments 1964–1970, Volume Two: International Policy* (Manchester: Manchester University Press, 2003), pp. 124–7.
57. Bator to Johnson, 23 August 1966, *FRUS 1964–1968 XIII*, p. 453.
58. Johnson, *The Vantage Point*, p. 307.
59. Johnson–Long telephone conversation, 1 September 1966, *FRUS 1964–1968 XV*, p. 404.
60. George Ball Oral History Interview II, 9 July 1971, by Paige E. Mulhollan, Internet Copy, LBJL.
61. Bator, 'Lyndon Johnson and Foreign Policy', in Lobel (ed.), *Presidential Judgment*, p. 56.
62. McNamara to Johnson, 19 September 1966, *FRUS 1964–1968 XV*, p. 415.
63. Johnson–McNamara telephone conversation, 17 January 1966, *FRUS 1964–1968 IV Vietnam 1966* (1998), p. 415.
64. Embassy Bonn to State, 17 August 1966, *FRUS 1964–1968 XV*, p. 388.
65. LBJL, NSF: Country File, Boxes 185–6, Germany: Memos VIII 4/65–7/65, 'US-German Relations', 4 June 1965.
66. Bator, 'Lyndon Johnson and Foreign Policy', in Lobel (ed.), *Presidential Judgment*, p. 57. According to the editors of *FRUS 1964–1968 XIII*, no record of the meeting has emerged but the results are evident in Johnson's letter to Wilson, undated, ibid., pp. 457–8, as well as in Bator's testimony.
67. Erhard to Johnson, 7 September 1966, *FRUS 1964–1968 XIII*, pp. 464–5.
68. Ball to Embassy Bonn, 8 September 1966, *FRUS 1964–1968 XIII*, pp. 465–6.

69. Conversation between Rusk, Erhard et al., 25 September 1966, *FRUS 1964–1968* XV, p. 426.
70. Conversation between Johnson, Erhard et al., 26 September 1966, *FRUS 1964–1968* XIII, p. 473.
71. H. W. Brands, *The Wages of Globalism: Lyndon Johnson and the Limits of American Power* (Oxford and New York: Oxford University Press, 1995), p. 112. See also Thomas Alan Schwartz, *America's Germany: John J. McCloy and the Federal Republic of Germany* (Cambridge, MA and London: Harvard University Press, 1991).
72. 'Final Report on Trilateral Talks', undated, *FRUS* XIII, p. 562.
73. Embassy Bonn to State, 7 July 1966, *FRUS 1964–1968* XV, p. 377.
74. Embassy Bonn to State, 20 September 1966, *FRUS 1964–1968* XV, pp. 417–19.
75. Note 2, *FRUS 1964–1968* XV, p. 446.
76. Thomas Alan Schwartz, *Lyndon Johnson and Europe: In the Shadow of Vietnam* (Cambridge, MA: Harvard University Press, 2003), pp. 132–3, 145–6.
77. Johnson to Wilson, 15 November 1966, *FRUS 1964–1968* XIII, p. 491.
78. Embassy London to State, 22 November 1966, *FRUS 1964–1968* XIII, p. 499.
79. Brands, *The Wages of Globalism*, p. 113.
80. Johnson, *The Vantage Point*, p. 309.
81. Lawrence Kaplan, 'McNamara, Vietnam, and the defense of Europe', in Vojtech Mastny, Sven G. Holtsmark and Andreas Wenger (eds), *War Plans and Alliances in the Cold War: Threat Perceptions in the East and West* (Abingdon: Routledge, 2006), p. 288.
82. Johnson, *The Vantage Point*, p. 309. According to the editors of *FRUS 1964–1968* XIII, p. 536, note 3, no record of the 24 February meeting has been found.
83. Johnson to McCloy, 1 March 1966, *FRUS* XIII, p. 536.
84. Johnson, *The Vantage Point*, p. 310.
85. Editorial note, *FRUS 1964–1968* VIII *International Monetary and Trade Policy* (1998), p. 303.
86. Bergsten to Kissinger, 24 March 1969, *FRUS 1969–1972* III *Foreign Economic Policy, 1969–1972; International Monetary Policy, 1969–1972* (2001), pp. 32–3.
87. Johnson, *The Vantage Point*, p. 310. For the terms, see 'Final Report on Trilateral Talks', undated, *FRUS 1964–1968* XIII, pp. 562–70.
88. Johnson, *The Vantage Point*, p. 311.
89. Kaplan, 'McNamara, Vietnam, and the defense of Europe', in Mastny, Holtsmark and Wenger (eds), *War Plans and Alliances*, p. 296.
90. Bergsten to Kissinger, 24 March 1969, *FRUS 1969–1972* III, pp. 32–3.
91. Quoted in Kaplan, 'McNamara, Vietnam, and the defense of Europe', in Mastny, Holtsmark and Wenger (eds), *War Plans and Alliances*, p. 296.
92. Quoted in ibid., p. 289.
93. Johnson, *The Vantage Point*, p. 311.
94. Ball, *The Past has Another Pattern*, p. 274.
95. Harriman to Johnson and Rusk, 3 October 1966, *FRUS 1964–1968* IV, p. 691.
96. Bonn to State, 7 July 1966, *FRUS 1964–1968* XV, pp. 378–9.
97. Johnson to Wilson, undated, *FRUS 1964–1968* XIII, p. 460.
98. Johnson–Long telephone conversation, 1 September 1966, *FRUS 1964–1968* XV, p. 404.
99. European balance of payments trip, 7 January 1968, *FRUS 1964–1968* VIII, p. 499.

Chapter Six

Two Adversaries: The Soviet Union and the People's Republic of China

The Cold War rivalry between East and West had emerged in earnest by around 1947, with Washington's enunciation of the 'Truman Doctrine' pledging economic and military support for allies facing a communist-inspired uprising. By the time President Johnson entered office in 1963, a mixture of crises such as that over Berlin, and more relaxed periods, had come to characterise the Soviet–American relationship. In particular, the experience of the Cuban Missile Crisis of 1962 led both sides to reflect especially hard on the value of less adversarial policies. As was evident in relation to Vietnam, Johnson was very much a supporter of the Cold War consensus that the chief international aim of the United States was to inhibit the spread of communism, but he did recognise that in the nuclear age the superpowers bore a special responsibility to the world.[1] Despite the Vietnam War, the failure to initiate arms control talks and the fact that Johnson focused on the relationship with the Soviet Union only sporadically, his Presidency proved to be a constructive period for the Soviet–American relationship, as was shown by a range of accords.[2]

The relationship with the People's Republic of China (PRC) saw less tangible progress. China had become communist when Mao Zedong secured power in 1949 after years of civil war in which Washington had supported the Nationalists. The so-called 'loss' of China was seen as a profound setback for American Cold War interests. The US government refused to extend diplomatic recognition to the regime in Beijing, instead backing the Chinese Nationalist government based on the island of Taiwan (the Republic of China). The PRC's intervention in the Korean War in 1950, American resistance to the PRC's representation in the UN and periodic crises between the PRC and Taiwan over the islands of Quemoy and Matsu perpetuated the strain. For many observers, the 1962 border war with India confirmed the image of the PRC's belligerence, as did its efforts to develop a nuclear bomb. Although the PRC and the Soviet Union had been allies, an ideological 'split' between them had begun to emerge in the late 1950s, and in 1960 there was an open falling out at the World Communist Parties' meeting in Moscow.[3] The split could not be exploited by playing one power off against the other, as Richard Nixon and Henry Kissinger strove to do in the 1970s, because the Chinese were venomous in their rebuffs of the various tentative American initiatives in the Johnson years.[4] Nonetheless, in its efforts, however modest, to reach out to Beijing, the Administration had at least set a precedent. This, along with the progress in the Soviet–American relationship, helped to lay the foundations for the spectacular triangular diplomacy of détente in the 1970s.

Nascent Détente with Moscow

President Johnson strove to continue the improvement of relations with the Soviet Union that had begun under John F. Kennedy. In the United Nations in December 1963, Johnson announced the lofty goals of ending the Cold War; ending the dissemination of nuclear weapons; and making progress in arms control. There was in this early period the first of a number of reciprocal cuts in defence spending.[5] Johnson was sincere in his efforts to moderate the Cold War, but soon found himself pushed in that direction by Moscow. In January 1964, he bridled at a proposal from Khrushchev to end territorial disputes by peaceful means. For Johnson, the letter, which went to other governments too, was 'designed for propaganda purposes rather than serious diplomacy', evident in attempts to blame 'imperialists' and 'colonisers' for the world's troubles.[6] He complained to National Security Adviser McGeorge Bundy that he was 'tired' of Khrushchev 'being the man who wants peace in the world and [Johnson] the guy who wants war'. He ordered Bundy to

> get [Dean] Rusk and the five ablest men in the State Department and go up to Camp David and lock the gate this weekend and to try to find some imaginative proposal or some initiative that we can take besides just reacting to actions and just letting Khrushchev wire everybody twenty-five pages every two days and us just sit back and dodge.[7]

The result was Johnson's first substantive letter to Moscow, building upon his address to the United Nations. He told Khrushchev that he wanted to prevent the spread of nuclear weapons; end the production of fissionable material for weapons; transfer large amounts of fissionable material to peaceful purposes; ban nuclear weapons tests; limit nuclear weapons systems; reduce the risk of war by accident or design; and move towards general disarmament.[8]

Johnson's proposals met with some interest in the Kremlin, because the Soviets had their own motives for developing the post-Cuba détente. The CIA maintained that Moscow sought to moderate defence spending, time to concentrate on internal and bloc problems, and to gain financial credits from the West.[9] Although the Chinese were critical, feeling that Moscow was selling out, the Soviets engaged with the Johnson Administration in a generally constructive manner. They assented to a range of accords which were in large part a product of American initiatives in 1964. In the summer of that year the United States and the Soviet Union agreed to restrict the production of plutonium and enriched uranium for military purposes,[10] although neither side made any real sacrifice. The United States already had enough such material, and the Soviets made smaller cuts than did the Americans.[11] There were developments in the cultural realm. Since 1956 the United States and the Soviet Union had participated in a programme of cultural and technical exchanges. The agreement expired in 1963, but was renewed in 1964.[12] Later, there were controversies over some of these exchanges, such as a performance of the musical *Hello, Dolly!* in Moscow, which the Soviets postponed repeatedly. The Kremlin was expressing symbolic disapproval of the United States, over matters such as Vietnam. Since the opening of Soviet–American diplomatic relations under President Roosevelt in 1933 there had been intermittent efforts to reach an agreement on the opening of consular centres to extend diplomatic representation in each nation. After seven months of bargaining, the Consular Convention was signed in Moscow in mid-1964. However, concerns from some senators and from the FBI about Soviet spying meant that it was not until March 1967 that the Convention was ratified.[13]

There was progress on a civil aviation agreement to enable direct flights between New York and Moscow. The agreement had been negotiated in late summer 1961 but little had happened since because of tensions over Berlin and then Cuba.[14] Johnson's Assistant Secretary of State for Inter-American Affairs, Thomas Mann, was worried that the agreement would make it more difficult for the United States to keep Cuba in isolation and for Latin American and African countries to deny landing and overflight rights to Eastern bloc aircraft, and it took some time to overcome various technical difficulties. However, the first regular flights between New York and Moscow began in 1968.[15]

In May 1964, Johnson announced that the United States would work to 'build bridges' to Eastern Europe, by means of trade, visitors and humanitarian aid. Initially, Johnson was reluctant to try to expand trade links with the Soviet Union, largely because of domestic opposition and a growing preoccupation with the US election. Some members of Congress were worried that expanded trade with Eastern European states might strengthen the Soviet Union and its satellites, and there was also concern about Soviet support for Hanoi – it was felt that in the circumstances the United States should not be doing any favours for Moscow. The East–West trade bill did not get through Congress.[16] Nonetheless, there was still an increased number of American visitors behind the Iron Curtain in these years, and trade grew despite the failure of the bill. A further 'building bridges' initiative was to raise the status of American diplomatic missions in Hungary and Bulgaria from legations to embassies. Similarly, Johnson appointed John Gronouski, who was of Polish extraction, to the post of Ambassador in Warsaw in 1965. The appointment was a popular one among the Polish people.[17] Although there were obviously limits to what could be achieved, Johnson's first year or so in office was a constructive one for the Soviet–American relationship, and as such can be described as a period of nascent détente.

THE VIETNAM WAR

However, the growing commitment in Vietnam undermined the nascent détente. The Soviets had protested at the Gulf of Tonkin Resolution in August 1964, and, fatefully, Alexei Kosygin, who had had emerged as the key figure in Moscow after Khrushchev was ousted in October 1964, visited Hanoi for several days from 6 February 1965. The North Vietnamese failed to forewarn Kosygin of the attacks on the US base at Pleiku on 7 February, and in fact Hanoi may have launched the raids with an eye on entrapping the Soviet Union into extending greater military support: according to the CIA, once the United States had launched its retaliatory raids Moscow had to 'choose between giving North Vietnam military support or opening itself to Chinese charges of capitulation to the imperialists'. The Kremlin even suspected that the Chinese might have 'inspired the Viet Cong raid in order to embarrass Kosygin and disrupt Soviet-US relations'.[18]

If so, then the Chinese had some success, by causing the Soviets to step up aid to Hanoi. Soviet Ambassador Anatoli Dobrynin asked Vice-President Hubert Humphrey, 'Don't you understand as a socialist state we are morally and ideologically bound to come to the assistance of a sister Socialist State? We can't be a leader and stand by and ignore the bombing of the North Vietnamese.'[19] At the same time, the war in Vietnam was a complication that Moscow could do without, given that historically the Soviet Union had few direct interests in the region. A November 1965 US intelligence report summarised Soviet policy as 'supplying military aid, playing down their own involvement, and seeking opportunities to urge the US and North Vietnamese to negotiate'.[20]

There were demonstrations in Moscow against US policy in Vietnam. The demonstrations undoubtedly had the imprimatur of the Soviet authorities. In March, the US Embassy reported an attack by a 'mob in excess of 3,000 persons, mostly Asians, in what developed into most aggressive and nastiest demonstration here in living memory'.[21] Within a few weeks of Johnson's July announcement that he was raising the number of US troops in Vietnam to 125,000, the Soviets broke the exchange agreement by cancelling reciprocal trade exhibitions; made aggressive pronouncements in the press; refused to permit an American vessel to visit Yalta or Sevastopol despite the visit of a Soviet ship to Honolulu; imposed tougher travel restrictions for US diplomats in the Soviet Union; and gave the KGB an increasingly free hand in spying on the Embassy.[22]

Concerns about the possible expansion of the war in Vietnam encouraged Kosygin to participate in the unsuccessful 'Sunflower' peace initiative in London in February 1967 (see Chapter Three), but he complained to Ambassador Llewellyn Thompson in Moscow that a late-night message from the White House in which the Administration toughened its negotiating position was simply an 'ultimatum' that left Hanoi with little time to respond. Washington, Kosygin suggested, should have prolonged the bombing pause, and although the President and his colleagues had demanded that the North Vietnamese stop their infiltration of the South, nothing was said about American reinforcements. Finally, Washington was mistaken in ignoring the Chinese role, which, Kosygin said, sought to prolong the conflict.[23]

The CIA concluded in the wake of the failed peace initiative that Soviet policymakers now doubted the 'prospect of movement towards a political solution for several months at best'. The Soviets had 'concluded that for the time being they have no alternative but to help Hanoi carry on the war, hoping that a change of attitude in either Hanoi or Washington, or both, will make a political solution possible later'.[24] Yet Soviet–American cooperation after the escalation of the Vietnam War in 1965 was not lost entirely. As well as continued progress in bilateral agreements such as the Civil Air Agreement, Washington and Moscow kept one another informed via the 'hot-line'[25] – the first substantive messages through this medium since it was set up after the Cuban Missile Crisis – during the Six-Day War in the Middle East in June 1967 (see Chapter Seven). The Soviets had provided the Arabs with arms and diplomatic support, and Israel was a close American ally. On 10 June, Kosygin, perhaps feeling the sting of Chinese taunts, came on to the hot-line threatening military action if the Israelis did not withdraw. Moscow would 'adopt an independent decision' if military action was not ended within a few hours. 'These actions may bring us into a clash, which would lead to a grave catastrophe.' There was some debate within the Administration about the veracity of the threat, but the possibility of a clash led Johnson to order the withdrawal of the US Sixth Fleet.[26] More constructively, Johnson and Kosygin agreed on the importance of an early end to the war.[27]

THE GLASSBORO SUMMIT

Johnson sought to build upon the Nuclear Test Ban Treaty of 1963 and to initiate arms control talks with Moscow. Arms control would moderate budgetary pressures, which were greatly exacerbated by spending in Vietnam, and would also restrain the Soviets' rapid progress in expanding their nuclear arsenal since the Cuban Missile Crisis. The State Department pointed out in 1967 that the Soviet Union was likely to gain parity with the United States in ICBM launchers in the next year and would end up expanding its force beyond 1,000 missiles. In 1968 or 1969 the Soviet Union would surpass the United States in 'total intercontinental megatonnage', and in Polaris-type submarines within a few years after that.[28] The first step would be a conference between Johnson and Kosygin, but arranging the meeting was tricky. Johnson said that he told the Soviet leader that 'we're ready to meet with you but you come to Washington or go to Camp David'. However, Kosygin

> wouldn't go to Camp David because Khrushchev had been there. Wouldn't come to Washington because the Chinese and Arabs would give him hell, and wanted me to come and sit down in the United Nations, and I said I'm not going to do that.[29]

Neither party wanted to look like a supplicant. The White House suggested meeting at MacGuire Airforce Base in New Jersey, but Kosygin refused because it might look as if the United States was showing off its 'guns or rockets'.[30] Finally, Glassboro State College, in a small town in New Jersey halfway between New York and Washington, was chosen, in response to a suggestion from the New Jersey governor. The summit took place on 24–5 June 1967.

The main topics were the Middle East, Vietnam and the possibility of opening arms reduction talks. Kosygin's position on the Middle East, according to Johnson, was simple: 'there must be complete, absolute, immediate withdrawal' of Israeli troops from Arab lands. On Vietnam, the Soviet leader insisted that 'we've got to stop our bombing. We've got to pull out . . . That we're an aggressor there. We are an invader there.'[31] Johnson tolerated the rhetoric because his prime concern was 'to explore the questions of restraint in developing anti-ballistic missiles and intercontinental ballistic missiles with the government of the Soviet Union'. However, Kosygin would not engage with the issue.[32] Given that the Soviets were making rapid progress in expanding their nuclear arsenal, they had little inclination to engage in arms limitation. Kosygin's main goal at Glassboro, in Johnson's assessment, was propaganda:

> to give Israel hell, and to give us hell and try to get some of that polecat off him. He smelled bad in sending them [the Arabs] all that arms and just, by God, getting whipped in three days, and he wanted to divert the attention and get us on the defensive.

Similarly, the ideological contest with the Chinese, who suggested that Kosygin was in the United States to 'sell out someone', limited the scope of what might be achieved.[33]

At least in his own estimation President Johnson felt that he had presented himself at Glassboro as 'prudent . . . firm and determined and not being a fraidycat or a bully either'. For what it was worth, the atmosphere had been relatively cordial: 'pleasant, no vitriolic stuff, no antagonistic stuff, no bitter stuff'.[34] The very fact that a relatively harmonious meeting of the principals had taken place facilitated some of the developments in the Soviet–American relationship over the next year or so. These developments included the signing of the Nuclear Non-proliferation Treaty by the Soviet Union; a treaty on the return of astronauts; the inauguration, with Soviet–American cooperation, of a UN conference on the future of the sea-beds; cooperation in a UN Security Council resolution on the Middle East; the first flights under the Soviet–American Bilateral Air Agreement; bilateral Soviet–American talks on the Law of the Sea; progress in other matters such as the Cultural Exchange Agreement, and negotiations to improve Embassy sites. According to National Security Adviser Walt Rostow, the year after Glassboro was 'the most intensive and successful postwar year in US–Soviet relations' despite the lack of progress on the Middle East, Vietnam and arms control.[35]

ARMS CONTROL AND CZECHOSLOVAKIA

Soviet reluctance at Glassboro to begin arms limitation talks led Johnson to proceed unenthusiastically with the construction of a limited or 'thin' ABM system ('Nike-X') in the United States. Despite the immense cost and major technical difficulties involved, there had long been military and political pressure in favour of such defences, in part due to recent evidence that the Soviets had built a rudimentary ABM system around Moscow. Rusk had explained to Dobrynin the Administration's concerns about proceeding with a missile defence system: 'in a democratic society with two Senators from each state, it would be extremely difficult to have an ABM system limited to one city or one region'. American ABM development would accelerate the arms competition: Soviet marshals would soon be 'pressing the government in Moscow for many more offensive missiles to which, inevitably, there would be another US response'.[36] Similarly, Robert McNamara had argued that the construction of an ABM system would merely force the Soviet Union to increase its offensive nuclear force with the result that the risk of a Soviet nuclear attack on the United States would not be decreased, nor would the damage from any such attack.[37] Officially, the Nike-X system was designed to provide protection against the less potent Chinese nuclear missile threat, and the door was still open for Washington and Moscow to engage in the limitation of ABMs or ICBMs.[38] At the same time, if arms limitation talks failed, the United States could go ahead with a more comprehensive ABM system.[39] Johnson had kept his options open, but he much preferred the idea of arms talks.

After continued overtures from the Johnson Administration, the Soviets decided in June 1968 to discuss the control of strategic weapons.[40] According to the CIA, the change of course derived mainly from the Soviets' growing 'confidence in their possession of an assured destruction capability' and the desire to end American competition in this field, given the economic and technological burdens of a continued arms race.[41] In July, Kosygin proposed to Johnson that the strategic missile talks between technical experts begin within six weeks, in Geneva, a suggestion to which the President assented.[42] There was a further agreement that the two leaders would meet, to establish some basic principles for the arms control and to discuss issues such as the Middle East and Vietnam.[43]

However, within a few weeks a crisis erupted. A reformist regime under Alexander Dubcek had emerged in Czechoslovakia, and the liberalising 'Prague Spring' threatened Soviet sway over that country and beyond. Walt Rostow commented in July that armed Soviet intervention – comparable to that in Hungary in 1956 – could, among other things, raise the question of 'why the UN Charter protects Korea against aggression, but not Czechoslovakia'. Czechoslovakia's presence in 'the Soviet sphere of influence hardly justifies murder in broad daylight'. Rostow urged the sending of 'strong signals' of disapproval as a deterrent to Moscow.[44] Other officials, such as Ambassador Llewellyn Thompson in Moscow, suggested that the Soviets themselves would be the greatest losers if they intervened militarily: 'the free world will be deeply shocked, NATO strengthened, hope of reducing military expenditure by agreement with the US jeopardised, etc. Moreover, internal dissatisfaction with Soviet leadership will increase.'[45] The Administration did not have many means of influencing Soviet behaviour short of threatening war over the fate of a country which, as Rostow had noted, was in the Soviet 'sphere of influence', and it was also the case that the Dubcek government did not ask the United States for help. Dean Rusk told Dobrynin that the American government did not want to 'involve itself in this situation', although 'there should be no misapprehension as to the feelings and sympathies of the American people'.[46]

The Soviets gave statements such as this a hearing but did not change their behaviour. On 20 August, after staging military exercises in East Germany as a show of intimidation, Soviet troops launched what Johnson described as a 'callous, outrageous assault on Czechoslovakia'.[47] The administration was reduced to what Vice-President Hubert Humphrey described as 'snort and talk'.[48] The policy that emerged was a rhetorical one, to mobilise 'world opinion through the United Nations' as a means of 'influencing the Soviets towards moderation'.[49]

What was the impact then of the invasion of Czechoslovakia on the Soviet–American relationship? The CIA reflected that 'small accommodations, such as . . . Moscow–New York air services, do not appear jeopardised, but proposals for arms control and disarmament, already difficult of accomplishment, face formidable new obstacles'.[50] The idea of negotiating with the Soviets, always a difficult proposition among some elements in Cold War America, was now even more controversial. However, Johnson, having withdrawn from the presidential nomination in March and wanting to leave much more than Vietnam as his foreign policy legacy, was still keen to meet with the Soviet leadership and begin arms talks. He had some support within the Administration. Secretary for Defense Clark Clifford, for example, believed that it was important to begin arms discussions while the strategic balance was still favourable to the United States.[51] Walt Rostow feared that the opportunity for arms control might be lost for a long time unless a beginning was made immediately.[52]

There was also some reticence within the Administration towards arms talks. Dean Rusk and the State Department believed that talks would antagonise NATO members unless there was extensive consultation.[53] Presidential envoy John McCloy felt that priority should be given to consolidating the transatlantic alliance rather than making agreements with Moscow.[54] Johnson understood the need to work with NATO allies, but was determined to make whatever progress was possible.[55] Just days before Nixon's inauguration in January 1969, the Administration presented a draft of the principles and objectives for arms agreements to the North Atlantic Command to create an impetus for early talks. However, there was a justified suspicion in NATO capitals that they were not being consulted but merely informed of something that had already been agreed with Moscow.[56]

There was also the question of the proposed Johnson–Kosygin summit meeting. Ambassador Llewellyn Thompson in Moscow had reservations. He suggested in connection with the Middle East that the Administration would have little leverage over the Israelis given that Nixon was soon to take office, and that the Soviets would not be able to exert much pressure on North Vietnam because a summit would generate the usual 'noise about sell-out and collusion' from the Chinese.[57] What was more significant than any reservations among Johnson's advisers, though, were the doubts of the incoming Administration about beginning Soviet–American negotiations prior to the inauguration. President Nixon's National Security Adviser Henry Kissinger suggested with good reason that a summit with the Soviets just months after the invasion of Czechoslovakia would cause serious concern in Europe, and that any agreements reached by the outgoing Administration would have to be implemented by officials who had played no part in shaping them. After hearing of Nixon's views, Moscow professed that it was now 'difficult' to judge the likely success of a summit with the outgoing President.[58] So the Soviet invasion of Czechoslovakia and the incoming Administration cost Johnson his arms limitation talks – which began in autumn 1969 – and a lame-duck summit with Kosygin.

THE CHINESE NUCLEAR BOMB

Arms issues also featured in US policy towards the PRC; a key concern for the Administration in 1964 was the Chinese nuclear programme. In April, the State Department's Policy Planning Council suggested that the Chinese sought a nuclear capability largely for political reasons such as bolstering their claim to great power status, and that Beijing was unlikely ever to initiate the use of the bomb.[59] There were worries about nuclear proliferation,[60] and there was the psychological impact on American allies in Asia to consider. In the run-up to the bomb test, the Policy Planning Council considered the wisdom of launching a pre-emptive attack on Chinese nuclear facilities, concluding that 'the significance of such a capability is not such as to justify the undertaking of actions which would involve great political costs or high military risks'.[61] One of the problems, as Robert Johnson of the Council pointed out, was that any attack would bolster Beijing's argument that 'US hostility towards Communist China was the main source of tensions and the principal threat to peace in Asia'.[62]

The White House foreign policy advisers also concluded that a unilateral attack could not be justified on either security or political grounds. However, there was an option that might benefit the nascent détente with the Soviet Union. Washington could work with Moscow to warn the Chinese against tests, to seek a commitment to end underground testing and perhaps to cooperate in military action.[63] Bundy raised the idea of cooperation with Dobrynin, but the Ambassador played down the significance of a Chinese bomb: 'Chinese nuclear weapons had no importance against the Soviet Union or against the US, and . . . therefore they had only a psychological impact in Asia'.[64] Dobrynin's response ended the possibility of direct action.[65] His efforts to play down the significance of the Chinese bomb may have concealed a touch of embarrassment because his country had played a critical role in 1955–8 in furthering Beijing's nuclear capabilities.[66] The Soviets had withdrawn the last of their advisers in 1959, as the relationship between Moscow and Beijing deteriorated.

President Johnson had taken a backseat in the policy deliberations over a pre-emptive strike on Chinese nuclear facilities. While ruing the fact that, in his own words, 'a large country with a hostile government had mastered the technology of nuclear explosives', he recognised that there was a 'long and expensive road' between 'setting off a nuclear blast and developing powerful and accurate weapons across seas and continents'.[67] Undoubtedly, the option of attacking China and the possibility, however remote, of precipitating a Sino-American war was a nightmare to him. As his wary approach to escalating the American commitment in Vietnam signified, he recalled vividly the Chinese intervention in Korea.[68] Furthermore, after the punitive strikes on North Vietnam in August it would hardly be fitting for the 'peace candidate' in the election campaign to be launching more military attacks, especially unprovoked ones.[69]

The President told his advisers that 'our position should not be provocative but we should not give the impression of being unconcerned'. A White House statement after news of the Chinese detonation of an atomic weapon in October 1964 maintained that the Chinese bomb 'would have no effect upon the readiness of the United States to respond to requests from Asian nations for help in dealing with Communist Chinese aggression'.[70] The statement helped to placate the PRC's neighbours – apart from, as one might expect, Taiwan, long a focus of the PRC's enmity.

According to President Chiang Kai-shek, the 'primary ChiCom [Chinese communist] aim was to destroy him and [the] GRC [Government of the Republic of China] and when this happened all of Asia would be threatened'.[71] But the Administration had weighed the policy options and decided that by far the best course was simply that of coexistence, with the future possibility of engaging Beijing, should a more receptive regime ever emerge, in arms control agreements.

PRESSURES FOR CHANGE IN SINO-AMERICAN RELATIONS

In December 1963, Roger Hilsman, Assistant Secretary of State for Far Eastern Affairs, suggested in a public speech that the United States was 'determined to keep the door open to the possibility of change' in Sino-American relations and that 'we should like to be less ignorant of them and for them to be less ignorant of us'.[72] Johnson is said to have endorsed the speech without reading it.[73] The favourable response, or at least the absence of hostility, in the United States to Hilsman's tentative advocacy of improved relations with the PRC, along with the French recognition of Beijing in January 1964 (see Chapter Four) and the Chinese atomic bomb test later that year, encouraged advocates of a change of course in American policy towards the PRC. One of the most persistent advocates of change was James Thomson of the National Security Council (NSC). In October 1964 he presented arguments that would feature in many of his memoranda. He argued that seeking to isolate China was largely futile, because eventually China would be voted into the United Nations, participate in international negotiations on the control of nuclear weapons and enjoy growing travel and economic links with the non-communist world.[74] Robert Komer of the National Security Council argued, among other things, that the Sino-Soviet split was a good reason to deal with 'both Communist centres, not only one', and that the United States' strong stand in Vietnam made it easier to make concessions to the PRC without appearing weak. Efforts could be made to gain international recognition that there were two Chinas, just as there were two Germanys and two Koreas.[75] McGeorge Bundy favoured progressive measures towards the PRC,[76] and the CIA also supported a more flexible approach.[77] In part, these opinions reflected changes in the broader political climate in the United States. According to Alfred Jenkins of the NSC, the 'majority of American public opinion – public, academic, congressional and bureaucratic' felt that 'effort should be made to bring Communist China into the world community'.[78]

Exploratory Initiatives

Since 1954 Washington had engaged in consular talks with the Chinese in Geneva and then ambassadorial talks in Warsaw. These talks provided one of the few opportunities for dialogue, but little came of them. According to Henry Kissinger, the only real success of the 134 talks between 1954 and 1968 was an accord to repatriate soldiers taken prisoner in Korea.[79] The Chinese used the talks as a pulpit for ideological tirades. At a 1964 meeting, for example, the US Ambassador depicted his interlocutor as 'loud, tendentious, arrogant, virtually spitting out his accusations, often with finger wagging. We were subject to lengthy lectures delivered from an offensively professorial height.'[80] However, the meetings did provide a way for the Administration to warn the Chinese, at least in general terms, of intensified efforts in Vietnam, and stress that there was no intention to take the ground war in Vietnam into the North or into the PRC.[81] How far the authorities in Beijing were moved by what they heard in Warsaw is not clear, but what is more apparent, and paradoxical, is that the waging of war in Vietnam offered an incentive to reach out, in however small a way, to Beijing.[82] Neither party sought a clash.

American policymakers looked with interest towards the Cultural Revolution, which began late in 1965 and lasted, with periods of varying intensity, for three years. The lack of official representation in Beijing meant that the United States' understanding of what went on could have been better, but it was evident from other sources that the Revolution featured ideological purges, social upheaval and intensified xenophobia. Chinese people demonstrated in capitals across the world, ambassadors were withdrawn and in 1967 Red Guards even ransacked and burned the British Embassy in Beijing.[83] Walt Rostow maintained that during the Revolution 'mainland China almost ceased to have a foreign policy', although work on nuclear weapons and missiles continued.[84] (There was the launch of an IRBM in 1966 and the detonation of a hydrogen bomb in 1968.) For many Americans, the upheavals in China made reaching out less compelling than it would have been in different circumstances.[85] However, the Cultural Revolution did not end the search for a more flexible policy – not least because of hopes for the emergence of more sober-minded leaders in Beijing.

Dean Rusk believed that the PRC was an expansionist power that might, among other things, use nuclear weapons to construct a balance of power that would permit the use of 'potentially almost unlimited conventional forces'. However, in his view, this made it all the more necessary to pursue a policy that might be described as 'exploratory engagement' with Beijing.

In an address to the Senate in spring 1966, he suggested expanding the range of unofficial Sino-American contacts, and stated that if the Chinese so wished they could purchase grain from the United States. He indicated a readiness to permit Chinese journalists to enter the United States and for American universities to invite Chinese scientists to visit their institutions. Rusk emphasised the importance of maintaining diplomatic communication with the Chinese in Warsaw, and expressed willingness to discuss disarmament and non-proliferation of nuclear weapons with Beijing.[86]

In April 1966, the State Department disclosed steps towards easing travel restrictions for certain categories of American citizens. In July, President Johnson followed up Rusk's intimations by assuring Beijing in a televised address about Vietnam that the United States sought a 'peace of conciliation' rather than of conquest in Asia, and he reiterated the offer of concessions that Rusk had presented.[87] According to Thomson, Johnson's speech met with a high degree of approval at home and abroad and, similarly, generated little criticism even from Taiwan.[88] The following summer, President Johnson made an overture to China, when the Romanian Prime Minister, Ion Gheorghe Maurer, visited Washington prior to visiting Beijing. Johnson explained to the Romanian leader that he did not seek war with China nor to change its social system. He wanted to see the Chinese join the international community and to engage in nuclear non-proliferation talks.[89]

Nothing came of the American initiatives. The main reason for the minimal progress in Sino-American relations at this stage was that the Chinese did not take any steps to meet US proposals halfway or even quarter-way, with Beijing's rhetoric remaining as vitriolic as ever. A Chinese Foreign Ministry spokesman rejected the State Department's travel concessions in 1966 as 'a fraud'. It was 'obvious', he maintained, that the US government's goal was to 'deceive the American people and world opinion and exploit the American people's friendly sentiments for China'.[90] All references to China in Johnson's July 1966 speech were ignored; instead, the Chinese condemned his statements about Vietnam.[91] In May 1968 the Chinese unilaterally suspended the Warsaw talks, saying that there was 'nothing to talk about' with the Americans.[92] By then, Dean Rusk, for one, had long rued the making of 'empty gestures' to the Chinese.[93]

CHINESE REPRESENTATION IN THE UNITED NATIONS

Although in 1966 Rusk had outlined a number of proposals to improve the Sino-American relationship, they were not government-to-government proposals, nor could they be, in the absence of American diplomatic recognition for the regime in Beijing. The possibility of Chinese representation in the United Nations, which among other things would accord legitimacy to Beijing and might end up displacing Taipei, had been a matter of controversy for some time. However, there was a view in some quarters that participation in the UN might moderate Chinese support for communist movements in the developing world. Adlai Stevenson, the American representative to the UN, argued late in 1964 that it would be beneficial to 'get the ChiComs into the community of nations' in order to 'manage them better'. But it was Rusk who was more influential on President Johnson. The President's response was that he 'did not pay the foreigners at the UN to advise him on foreign policy, but that he did pay Rusk and that he was inclined to listen to him'.[94]

Rusk felt that UN membership would not exert much of a moderating effect on Chinese behaviour; if anything, it would encourage the hardliners because Beijing would only join if Taipei withdrew. A Security Council seat for communist China would paralyse the UN on disputes such as those between India and Pakistan, and Greece and Turkey. Beijing's membership would antagonise the Soviet Union at a time when the United States was trying to improve the relationship, and among most Asian nations there was hostility to the PRC's representation, according to Rusk.[95] It has to be said that the Chinese communists gave fair grounds for arguments of this nature. As well as demanding the expulsion of Taiwan, the PRC wanted the abrogation of the resolution during the Korean War that had branded them as aggressors, the adoption of a resolution branding the United States as an aggressor in Vietnam and the revision of the UN Charter to include the exclusion of all 'imperialist puppets'.[96]

While President Johnson sympathised with Rusk's views, he could not continue to ignore the advocates of Chinese membership of the UN. Arthur Goldberg, who succeeded Adlai Stevenson and was a personal friend of Johnson, suggested in April 1966 that Washington should 'move towards a policy which would recognize the right of both the Government of the Republic of China and Communist China to UN seats'.[97] This was not a radical policy because it did not entail the displacement of Taipei. Although Walt Rostow maintained that Washington had a 'solemn, secret commitment to Taiwan', hailing from the Kennedy years, that 'we would use our Security Council veto to keep the ChiComs out',[98] the President had come round to the possibility of representation for both Chinas in the UN. He asked his advisers to suggest 'imaginative ways of handling the China problem, which would get us off the defensive, and deal with the ChiRep issue in the next General Assembly'.[99]

A resolution from Albania – with whom Beijing had cultivated a strategic friendship – to expel Taipei and seat Beijing had been under discussion in the UN, as had a further, more moderate resolution inviting the communists to join while retaining Taipei as a member. The second alternative was better from the American point of view but would not find favour in Taipei, because any measure that legitimised the mainland regime undermined Taiwan's claim to leadership of all the Chinese people.[100] Although, as noted, Rusk had deep reservations about PRC representation in the UN, he did come to take the view, in Rostow's words, 'that we begin to shift off our present policy toward Communist China in the UN, starting with talks in Taipei'.[101] Later, Rusk arranged for newly-appointed Ambassador Walter P. McConaughy to raise with Taiwan the question of communist Chinese representation in the UN, as a 'softening up exercise' to be followed by further representations.[102]

A number of allies had helped to push Rusk into moderating his position. The Canadians, for example, believed that Chinese representation in the UN would help moderate China's international behaviour and might enhance the possibility of peace in Vietnam. Late in 1966, the Canadians collaborated with Belgium and Italy on the idea of a study committee that would put forward a report on the matter at the next UN General Assembly.[103] The Canadian representative to the UN stated that without an exploration of the question of representation for both Chinas, his country would abstain from rather than vote against the Albanian proposal.[104] What made this especially awkward for the United States was that Goldberg had to vote in favour of the study committee resolution, because doing so would help win the support of certain countries who might otherwise support the Albanian position.[105] The Canadian initiative forced Rusk to defend himself against an accusation from Taipei's Ambassador that there had 'never been any collusion between Canada and the US'.[106] However, as things turned out, the study committee initiative suited American and Taiwanese interests, because it offered an alternative to UN members who otherwise might have supported the Albanian resolution. The study committee and the Albanian resolutions failed, while a resolution declaring the question of PRC membership of the UN to be an 'important question' succeeded.[107] Generally, though, the issue of Chinese membership of the UN became less compelling as a result of the damage the Cultural Revolution wrought upon China's international standing.

In many ways the Soviet–American Cold War continued through the Johnson years much as it had ever done, with tension and suspicion stemming from a deeply rooted ideological and political rivalry. For example, after defecting to the United States in 1964, Yuri Nosenko of the KGB spent three years in solitary confinement and interrogation at the hands of the CIA, under suspicion of being part of a Moscow 'master plan' to spread disinformation. Johnson was probably correct to believe that Nosenko was a bona fide defector, although otherwise he evinced little concern for the Russian's plight.[108] In April 1964, there was the discovery, from information provided by Nosenko, of an extensive recording system in the Moscow Embassy.[109] In September that year Soviet officials forced their way into a hotel room occupied by US military attachés and searched their possessions. The Soviets maintained that the attachés were 'engaged in activities incompatible with their diplomatic status', that is, spying.[110]

Johnson recognised that the idea of ending the Cold War was good as political rhetoric but more aspiration than probability, short of the United States converting to communism or the Soviet Union to capitalist liberal-democracy. Policies such as 'building bridges' were less progressive than they appeared, given that the United States was behind its European allies in forging political and economic ties with Eastern European countries.[111] The pursuit of détente was as much to with waging the Cold War by other means as much as with reducing tensions for its own sake – one goal of building bridges, as noted by the State Department, was to foment a 'quiet revolution' of 'internal liberalisation . . . establishment of a certain degree of national independence from Soviet control' and 'progress in re-association with the West'.[112] This may have had the unintended consequence of the Soviet invasion of Czechoslovakia in 1968, after the Prague Spring.[113] Policymaking was flawed in some instances. Johnson first spoke of building bridges in May 1964, but without further elaboration or follow-through of the idea. Extraordinarily, the government bureaucracy was not formally instructed to 'develop areas of peaceful cooperation with Eastern Europe and the Soviet Union' until July 1966.[114] Johnson's personal attention to the Soviet–American relationship was somewhat intermittent, in large part because of the expanding commitment in Vietnam.[115]

Accords such as the Outer Space Treaty, which was signed by Washington, London and Moscow early in 1967 and was designed to avoid the militarisation of space, had publicity value but were of limited practical value – in this case, space-based weapons were unlikely to be a cost-effective alternative to earth-based missiles.[116] Johnson's quest for arms control negotiations was laudable, but as his Presidency drew to a close it was motivated increasingly by a wish (understandable in the light of Vietnam) to enhance his historical reputation. Yet the President did have an absolutely sincere and realistic view that, given the danger of nuclear war, the Soviet–American relationship could and should be a peaceable one. Johnson's time in office did not see any dangerous Soviet–American confrontations such as the crises over Berlin and over Cuba. Despite Vietnam and Czechoslovakia, the relationship between Washington and Moscow under his stewardship can be characterised overall as one of low-key progress. As he noted, there were 'more significant agreements with Moscow in the years 1963–1969 than in the thirty years after which we established diplomatic relations with the Soviet regime'.[117] All considered, American policy toward the Soviet Union in the Johnson years was a very creditable one.

Possibilities for the Sino-American relationship were compromised in part by the use of the spectre of Chinese-led communism as a justification for escalating the commitment in Vietnam. In his Johns Hopkins speech in April 1965, for example, the President argued that 'the rulers in Hanoi are urged on by Peiping' ('Peiping' was the Nationalist word for Beijing, and, as such, was offensive to the communists).[118] Johnson displayed less imagination and ambition for the Sino-American relationship than he did for the Soviet–American one. Perhaps quite fairly, he had little hope for substantive progress in the absence of a major change of attitude on the part of the Chinese and far-reaching concessions from the United States, such as the abandonment of Taiwan. Yet Washington and Beijing shared a desire to prevent the war in Vietnam from expanding and both were engaged in varying degrees of Cold War with Moscow. Johnson said privately in 1964 that the United States could not evade recognising China forever,[119] and two years later he noted that American public opinion had moderated.[120] His initial unwillingness to make concessions did not stop him making a number of tentative proposals later on. Beijing's lack of reciprocity was the main reason for the limited progress in Sino-American relations, but the very fact that Washington was at last reaching out to the PRC established a precedent. Sino-Soviet border clashes in 1969 finally offered an opportunity to exploit the split between Beijing and Moscow, for the purpose, among other things, of trying to end the war in Vietnam. One result of Beijing's unprecedented openness to American initiatives was the vaunted 'opening' to China in 1972, when President Nixon paid the first ever visit there by a US president.[121] In its contribution to both Soviet–American and Sino-American relations, the Johnson Administration played a largely unheralded role in paving the way for the triangular diplomacy of détente.

NOTES

1. Walt Rostow, *The Diffusion of Power: An Essay in Recent History* (New York: Macmillan, 1972), p. 390.

2. Other accounts of Soviet–American relations under Johnson include Hal Brands, 'Non-Proliferation and the Dynamics of the Middle Cold War: The Superpowers, the MLF, and the NPT', *Cold War History*, 7, 3 (August 2007), pp. 389–423; John Dumbrell, *President Lyndon Johnson and Soviet Communism* (Manchester: Manchester University Press, 2004); and John Prados, 'Prague Spring and SALT: Arms Limitation Setbacks in 1968', in H. W. Brands (ed.), *The Foreign Policies of Lyndon Johnson: Beyond Vietnam* (College Station, TX: Texas A&M University Press, 1999), pp. 19–36.

3. Paul M. Kennedy, *The Rise and Fall of the Great Powers: Economic Change and Military Conflict from 1500 to 2000* (New York, Random House, 1987), p. 398.

4. The most recent and comprehensive account of Sino-American relations in the Johnson years is Michael Lumbers, *Piercing the Bamboo Curtain: Tentative Bridge-Building to China during the Johnson Years* (Manchester: Manchester University Press, 2008).

5. Lyndon B. Johnson, *The Vantage Point: Perspectives of the Presidency, 1963–1969* (New York: Holt, Rinehart, Winston, 1971), p. 464; Raymond Garthoff, *A Journey Through the Cold War: A Memoir of Containment and Coexistence* (Washington, DC: Brookings, 2001), pp. 190–1.

6. Johnson, *The Vantage Point*, pp. 464–5; Dumbrell, *President Lyndon Johnson and Soviet Communism*, p. 34.

7. Michael Beschloss (ed.), *Taking Charge: The Johnson White House Tapes, 1963–64* (New York: Simon and Schuster, 1997), pp. 144–5; editorial note, *Foreign Relations of the United States* (hereafter *FRUS*) *1964–1968 XIV The Soviet Union* (Washington, DC: USGPO, 2001), p. 1.

8. Rostow to Johnson, enclosing Rostow to Rusk, 20 August 1968, *FRUS 1964–1968 XIV*, pp. 683–4.

9. National Intelligence Estimate, 19 February 1964, *FRUS 1964–1968 XIV*, pp. 20–1.

10. Khrushchev to Johnson, 5 June 1964, *FRUS 1964–1968 XIV*, p. 85.

11. Garthoff, *A Journey Through the Cold War*, p. 192.

12. Johnson, *The Vantage Point*, p. 467.

13. Note 2, *FRUS 1964–1968 XIV*, p. 466.

14. Davis to Rusk, 9 November 1964, *FRUS 1964–1968 XIV*, p. 170.

15. Note 4, *FRUS 1964–1968 XIV*, p. 40; Johnson, *The Vantage Point*, p. 464.

16. See Alan P. Dobson, *US Economic Statecraft for Survival, 1933–1991* (Abingdon: Routledge, 2002), pp. 177–8.

17. Johnson, *The Vantage Point*, pp. 471–3.

18. CIA memorandum, 9 April 1965, *FRUS 1964–1968 XIV*, p. 280.

19. Humphrey–Dobrynin conversation, 12 March 1965, *FRUS 1964–1968 XIV*, p. 257.

20. Intelligence memorandum, 12 November 1965, *FRUS 1964–1968 XIV*, pp. 338, 339.

21. Embassy in the Soviet Union to State, 4 March 1965, *FRUS 1964–1968 XIV*, p. 252.

22. Embassy in the Soviet Union to State, 20 August 1965, *FRUS 1964–1968 XIV*, pp. 317–18.

23. Embassy in the Soviet Union to State, 18 February 1967, *FRUS 1964–1968 V Vietnam 1967* (2002), p. 187.

24. Intelligence estimate, 4 May 1967, *FRUS 1964–1968 XIV*, p. 482.

25. Although the hot-line was only a teleprinter link to the Pentagon, it was of symbolic as well as of practical value.

26. Dumbrell, *President Lyndon Johnson and Soviet Communism*, pp. 160–1.

27. Editorial note, *FRUS 1964–1968 XIV*, p. 491.
28. State Department paper, 18 December 1967, *FRUS 1964–1968 XIV*, pp. 607–9.
29. Johnson–Eisenhower telephone conversation, 25 June 1967, *FRUS 1964–1968 XIV*, p. 563.
30. Rusk to State, 22 June 1967, *FRUS 1964–1968 XIV*, p. 511.
31. Johnson–Eisenhower telephone conversation, 25 June 1967, *FRUS 1964–1968 XIV*, p. 559.
32. Johnson–Kosygin conversation, 23 June 1967, *FRUS 1964–1968 XIV*, pp. 519–20.
33. Johnson–Kosygin conversation, 25 June 1967, *FRUS 1964–1968 XIV*, pp. 555, 562.
34. Johnson's account of his talks with Kosygin, 23 June 1967, *FRUS 1964–1968 XIV*, p. 528; Johnson–Eisenhower telephone conversation, 25 June 1967, *FRUS 1964–1968 XIV*, p. 558.
35. Rostow to Johnson, enclosing Rostow to Rusk, 20 August 1968, *FRUS 1964–1968 XIV*, pp. 684–5. On the Non-proliferation Treaty as an issue in the Soviet–American relationship, see Hal Brands, 'Non-Proliferation and the Dynamics of the Middle Cold War: The Superpowers, the MLF, and the NPT', *Cold War History*, 7, 3 (August 2007), pp. 389–423.
36. Rusk–Dobrynin conversation, 27 January 1967, *FRUS 1964–1968 XIV*, p. 455.
37. McNamara to Johnson, undated, *FRUS 1964–1968 XI Arms Control and Disarmament* (1997), p. 422.
38. Joseph M. Siracusa, *Nuclear Weapons: A Very Short Introduction* (Oxford and New York: Oxford University Press, 2008), p. 89.
39. Rostow, *The Diffusion of Power*, p. 388.
40. Kosygin to Johnson, 27 June 1968, *FRUS 1964–1968 XI*, p. 624.
41. Huizenga to Helms, 15 July 1968, *FRUS 1964–1968 XIV*, p. 664.
42. Note 2, *FRUS 1964–1968 XIV*, p. 666.
43. Rostow to Johnson, enclosing Rostow to Rusk, 20 August 1968, *FRUS 1964–1968 XIV*, pp. 685–6.
44. Rostow to Rusk, 20 August 1968, *FRUS 1964–1968 XVII Eastern Europe* (1996), p. 206.
45. Embassy in the Soviet Union to State, 22 July 1968, *FRUS 1964–1968 XVII*, p. 212.
46. Rusk–Dobrynin conversation, 22 July 1968, *FRUS 1964–1968 XVII*, p. 213.
47. Johnson, *The Vantage Point*, pp. 486–90.
48. Emergency NSC meeting, 20 August 1968, *FRUS 1964–1968 XVII*, p. 245.
49. Read to Rostow, 23 August 1968, *FRUS 1964–1968 XVII*, p. 252.
50. National Intelligence Estimate, 7 November 1968, *FRUS 1964–1968 XVII*, p. 111.
51. Foreign policy meeting, 26 November 1968, *FRUS 1964–1968 XIV*, p. 767.
52. Rostow to Johnson, 20 November 1968, *FRUS 1964–1968 XIV*, pp. 758–9; Rostow to Johnson, 11 December 1968, *FRUS 1964–1968 XIV*, pp. 780–1.
53. NSC meeting, 25 November 1968, *FRUS 1964–1968 XI*, p. 741.
54. Rostow to Johnson, 14 December 1968, *FRUS 1964–1968 XIV*, pp. 782–4.
55. Rostow to Johnson, 11 December 1968, *FRUS 1964–1968 XIV*, pp. 780–1.
56. Garthoff, *A Journey Through the Cold War*, p. 213.
57. Thompson to State, 29 November 1968, *FRUS 1964–1968 XIV*, p. 777.
58. Henry A Kissinger, *The White House Years* (London: Weidenfeld and Nicolson, 1979), pp. 49–50; Raymond Garthoff, *Détente and Confrontation: American-Soviet Relations from Nixon to Reagan* (Washington, DC: Brookings, 1994), p. 11.
59. Policy Planning Council Paper, undated, *FRUS 1964–1968 XXX China* (1998), pp. 57–8.

60. Meeting with Congressional leadership, 19 October 1964, *FRUS 1964–1968 XXX*, p. 114.

61. Policy Planning Council Paper, 14 April 1964, *FRUS 1964–1968 XXX*, p. 39. See also William Burr and Jeffrey T. Richelson, '"Whether to strangle the baby in the cradle": The United States and the Chinese Nuclear Program, 1960–64', *International Security*, 25, 3 (Winter 2000–1), pp. 54–99.

62. Quoted in Lumbers, *Piercing the Bamboo Curtain*, p. 70.

63. Memorandum for the record, 15 September 1964, *FRUS 1964–1968 XXX*, p. 94.

64. Bundy–Dobrynin conversation, 25 September 1964, *FRUS 1964–1968 XXX*, p. 105.

65. Lumbers, *Piercing the Bamboo Curtain*, p. 73; Jeffrey T. Richelson, *Spying on the Bomb: American Nuclear Intelligence from Nazi Germany to Iran and North Korea* (New York: Norton, 2007), p. 164.

66. NSC meeting, 17 October 1964, *FRUS 1964–1968 XXX*, p. 110.

67. Johnson, *The Vantage Point*, p. 469.

68. Lumbers, *Piercing the Bamboo Curtain*, p. 73.

69. Richelson, *Spying on the Bomb*, p. 164.

70. Lumbers, *Piercing the Bamboo Curtain*, p. 74.

71. Meeting between Cline and Chinese Nationalist officials, 23–4 October 1964, *FRUS 1964–1968 XXX*, p. 116.

72. Robert Garson, 'Lyndon B. Johnson and the China Enigma', *Journal of Contemporary History*, 32, 1 (1997), p. 66.

73. Arthur Waldron, 'From Nonexistent to Almost Normal: US-China Relations in the 1960s', in Diane B. Kunz (ed.), *The Diplomacy of the Crucial Decade: American Foreign Relations During the 1960s* (New York: Columbia University Press, 1994), p. 229.

74. Thomson to Bundy, 28 October 1964, *FRUS 1964–1968 XXX*, p. 118.

75. Komer to Bundy, 23 November 1964, *FRUS 1964–1968 XXX*, pp. 130–2.

76. Bundy to Rusk, 16 June 1965, *FRUS 1964–1968 XXX*, pp. 174–6.

77. Thomson to Bundy, 2 June 1965, *FRUS 1964–1968 XXX*, p. 172.

78. Jenkins to Rostow, 6 September 1966, *FRUS 1964–1968 XXX*, p. 380.

79. Kissinger, *The White House Years*, p. 165.

80. Embassy Poland to State, 24 September 1964, *FRUS 1964–1968 XXX*, pp. 102–3.

81. Nancy Bernkopf Tucker, 'Threats, Opportunities, and Frustrations in East Asia', in Warren I. Cohen and Nancy Bernkopf Tucker (eds), *Lyndon Johnson Confronts the World: American Foreign Policy, 1963–1968* (Cambridge: Cambridge University Press, 1994), p. 108.

82. Lumbers, *Piercing the Bamboo Curtain*, pp. 137–76.

83. Tucker, 'Threats, Opportunities, and Frustrations in East Asia', in Cohen and Tucker (eds), *Lyndon Johnson Confronts the World*, p. 108.

84. Rostow, *The Diffusion of Power*, p. 372.

85. Jenkins to Rostow, 6 September 1966, *FRUS 1964–1968 XXX*, p. 380.

86. Kwan Ha Yim (ed.), *China and the US, 1964–72: From Johnson and Vietnam to Nixon and Détente* (New York: Facts on File, 1972), pp. 116–18.

87. Yim (ed.), *China and the US, 1964–72*, pp. 129–30.

88. Thomson to Rostow, 4 August 1966, *FRUS 1964–1968 XXX*, p. 365.

89. Rostow, *The Diffusion of Power*, p. 434.

90. Yim (ed.), *China and the US, 1964–72*, p. 115.

91. Rosemary Foot, *The Practice of Power: US Relations with China since 1949* (Oxford: Oxford University Press, 1995), p. 102.

92. Waldron, 'From Nonexistent to Almost Normal', in Kunz (ed.), *The Diplomacy of the Crucial Decade*, p. 241. The talks were resumed in November.
93. Dean Rusk Oral History Interview III, 2 January 1970, by Paige E. Mulhollan, Internet Copy, LBJL.
94. Memorandum for the record, 18 November 1964, *FRUS 1964–1968 XXX*, p. 127.
95. Rusk to Pearson, 9 November 1966, *FRUS 1964–1968 XXX*, pp. 421–2.
96. State to certain posts, 16 September 1966, *FRUS 1964–1968 XXX*, pp. 390–1.
97. Goldberg to Johnson, 28 April 1966, *FRUS 1964–1968 XXX*, p. 293.
98. Rostow to Johnson, 30 April 1966, *FRUS 1964–1968 XXX*, p. 295.
99. Note 3, *FRUS 1964–1968 XXX*, p. 295.
100. Rusk to Johnson, 14 May 1966, *FRUS 1964–1968 XXX*, pp. 301–2.
101. Rostow to Johnson, 17 May 1966, *FRUS 1964–1968 XXX*, p. 333.
102. Editorial note, *FRUS 1964–1968 XXX*, p. 314.
103. State to Embassy Thailand, 28 October 1966, *FRUS 1964–1968 XXX*, pp. 407–8.
104. Rusk to Johnson, 5 November 1966, *FRUS 1964–1968 XXX*, p. 418.
105. Embassy Republic of China to State, 28 November 1966, *FRUS 1964–1968 XXX*, p. 463.
106. State to Embassy Republic of China, 9 November 1966, *FRUS 1964–1968 XXX*, p. 427.
107. Popper to Rusk, 29 November 1966, *FRUS 1964–1968 XXX*, pp. 469–70.
108. Johnson-McCone meeting, 20 February 1964, CIA Electronic Reading Room; http://www.foia.cia.gov/browse_docs.asp; Tim Weiner, *Legacy of Ashes: The History of the CIA* (London: Penguin, 2007), pp. 265–70; Richards J. Heuer, 'Five Paths to Judgment', in H. Bradford Westerfield (ed.), *Inside CIA's Private World: Declassified Articles from the Agency's Internal Journal, 1955–1992* (New Haven, CT and London: Yale University Press, 1995), pp. 379–414.
109. Embassy in the Soviet Union to State, 19 May 1964, *FRUS 1964–1968 XIV*, p. 74.
110. Klein to Bundy, 1 October 1964, *FRUS 1964–1968 XIV*, p. 109.
111. Record of discussion, 27 July 1964, *FRUS 1964–1968 XVII*, p. 25.
112. State Department paper, undated, *FRUS 1964–1968 XVII*, pp. 43–4; Dumbrell, *President Lyndon Johnson and Soviet Communism*, p. 165.
113. See Mitchell B. Lerner, '"Trying to Find the Guy Who Invited Them": Lyndon Johnson, Bridge Building and the End of the Prague Spring', *Diplomatic History*, 32, 1 (January 2008), pp. 77–103.
114. Garthoff, *A Journey Through the Cold War*, p. 226; NSAM 352, *FRUS 1964–1968 XVII*, pp. 54–5.
115. Dumbrell, *President Lyndon Johnson and Soviet Communism*, p. 180.
116. Garthoff, *A Journey Through the Cold War*, p. 197.
117. Johnson, *The Vantage Point*, p. 476.
118. Kissinger, *The White House Years*, pp. 167–8.
119. Editorial note, *FRUS 1964–1968 XXX*, p. 3.
120. Memorandum of conversation, 21 August 1966, *FRUS 1964–1968 XXX*, p. 373.
121. See Margaret Macmillan, *Seize the Hour: When Nixon Met Mao* (London: John Murray, 2006).

CHAPTER SEVEN

Two Crises in the Middle East: Cyprus, 1964 and the Six-Day War, 1967

After the Second World War, American involvement in the Middle East reached unprecedented levels, as British power in the region declined. The United States backed the creation of Israel in 1948, participated in the overthrow of the left-wing leader Mohammed Mossadeq in Iran in 1953 and frustrated British, French and Israeli efforts during the Suez Crisis of 1956. In 1958, there was the so-called 'Eisenhower Doctrine', proclaiming that the United States would support any friendly government in the Middle East facing a communist threat. US troops were sent into Lebanon in 1958 under the aegis of the Doctrine. The United States' chief goals in the Middle East in the 1960s were maintaining regional security and stability (in part to preserve the flow of oil to the West), minimising Soviet influence and maintaining friendly ties with as many states as possible in the region while supporting Israel.[1]

These goals were challenged in two regional crises in 1964 and 1967, although the 1964 crisis was especially significant for its NATO dimension. That year, there was the chance that Greece and Turkey, both NATO members, might end up fighting one another over the ethnically divided island of Cyprus. Washington, seeking to put a lid on the crisis, attempted to mediate, and at one point suggesting to Ankara that the United States would abandon its NATO commitments to defend a fellow member should Turkey end up in a war with the Soviet Union, which was providing tentative backing for Cyprus under its Greek Cypriot leader. Later, when the Greeks were proving the most difficult in the search for a settlement, President Johnson vetoed a suggestion of his advisers to give Ankara the green light to invade and partition the island.

Further south, the United States' relations with Egypt under President Nasser, who was strengthening his ties with Moscow, deteriorated while US bonds with Israel grew closer. Both developments stemmed from intensifying Egyptian hostility towards Israel and were also consistent with Johnson's pro-Israeli outlook. This development ran contrary to the more even-handed outlook espoused by the State Department. Johnson's caution was evident once more when despite his sympathies for Tel Aviv in the Arab–Israeli crisis of May–June 1967 he refused to sanction an Israeli attack on Egypt and its allies, although the Israelis went ahead anyway. Among other things, Washington's handling of these two crises in a region of critical strategic concern raised questions of how much support to give to allies and friends, as will be seen in this chapter.

ORIGINS OF THE CYPRUS CRISIS

Although the ethnic conflict in Cyprus had deep roots, the short-term cause of the crisis with which Johnson had to deal was the island gaining its independence from Britain in 1959 and problems over the constitution. This was a long and complicated document that came into effect the following year, after negotiations held in London and Zurich between representatives of Greece, Turkey and Britain as well as leading Cypriots. The constitution reflected the ethnic composition of Cyprus – 80 per cent of the island's population of 600,000 was Greek and 18 per cent Turkish – in that the president would be Greek and the vice-president Turkish, with the Turkish minority possessing a veto over legislation. The three guarantor powers had the right to intervene if the London-Zurich agreements broke down.[2] Late in 1963, President Archbishop Makarios declared that the Constitution was inoperable, and proposed various changes. Vice-President Fazil Kutchuk was willing to negotiate, but the Turkish government proved unyielding.[3] There were outbreaks of violence between the two Cypriot communities. In January 1964, Makarios threatened to cancel the treaties binding the island to the guarantor powers.[4] Ankara felt the lure of military intervention to protect the Turkish Cypriots.

Britain, which had two 'Sovereign Base Areas' on the island, made initial efforts to conciliate the disputes but with little effect. In the face of the growing disorder on Cyprus, the British appealed for American help, arguing that because of their historic ties to Greece it was difficult for them to be seen as neutral.[5] However, the Johnson Administration believed that London was evading its responsibilities. Adlai Stevenson, US Representative to the United Nations, explained that the British were 'determined [to] at least share, if not pull back from, [the] responsibility for [a] rapidly deteriorating security situation'.[6] Robert Komer of the National Security Council suggested that the 'Brits are . . . determined to pull us in'.[7] According to President Johnson, 'the British are getting to the point where they might as well not be British anymore if they can't handle

Cyprus'.[8] He was determined not to let 'these damned British run us in there'.[9] He remembered very well Britain abandoning its security commitments towards Greece and Turkey in 1947, leaving Washington to take up the burden.[10] The result was of course the famous Truman Doctrine.

Much as he would have preferred to, Johnson could not ignore the crisis in Cyprus. Komer noted that the island was of 'major strategic interest because of its highly strategic location, US and UK bases, and fact of our closest allies being so emotionally involved'.[11] One interest in Cyprus was the presence of a substantial American, as well as British, signals intelligence gathering capability.[12] More generally, the near-civil war in Cyprus might, according to George Ball, 'blow up with the result that two NATO allies would be fighting each other'.[13] Washington also kept a wary eye on Moscow. According to the CIA, the Soviets sought to exploit the Cyprus situation 'with the aim of disrupting the Southern flank of NATO, bringing about the withdrawal of foreign troops and bases on the island, and complicating efforts to achieve a settlement'.[14] Johnson also had to consider US voters of Greek extraction, who were more numerous than those with a Turkish background.[15]

So, the stakes were high, but there were few arguments in Washington in favour of sending American soldiers. Dean Rusk feared that US troops could end up fighting the Turks, placing the 17,000 American soldiers stationed in Turkey at risk.[16] The Chiefs of Staff feared that participating in a multinational peacekeeping effort could result in a long-term occupation-type force, as in Korea and Germany. Similarly, there would be a precedent to the effect that the United States would 'participate in future such contingencies throughout the world'.[17] Worries such as these meant that Johnson would, in his own words, have to be 'shove[d] very hard' to get him to send American troops to Cyprus; the British should be the ones to send troops'.[18] There was the option of the UN, but this organisation did not inspire great faith within the Administration. It was already stretched thin with operations in places such as the Congo and the Sinai Peninsula, and it had not had much success on the Arab–Israeli question. Furthermore, according to Komer, 'Communists and Afro-Asians' would 'all buy in' on Cyprus 'and force a settlement to our disadvantage and that of Greeks and Turks, too'.[19] What was needed, said Komer, was to steer a course between the 'Scylla of uncontrolled UN intervention and the Charybdis of sending US troops unless absolutely necessary'.[20]

GEORGE BALL AS MEDIATOR

Johnson decided to send an American envoy to the Mediterranean. According to the President, the envoy could begin by telling Ankara, with a touch of bluff, that 'Now we're going to make preparations and we're ready for a quick entry and we're not going to support you Turks if you pull anything like this . . . you just behave yourselves'. The Greeks should be told something similar.[21] However, George Ball preferred the United States not to engage in mediation on the Cyprus question, as doing so would end up alienating the Greeks in particular, as they wanted nothing less than the union of Cyprus with Greece (*enosis*). Ball devised a plan involving a Western European mediator, a three-month cease-fire and a 1,200-person US contribution to an international peacekeeping force (Ball, along with Robert McNamara, was one of the few within the Administration who accepted, albeit reluctantly, the idea of providing troops). Johnson permitted further exploration of the scheme.[22] Ball recorded in his memoirs that the British leaked details of the plan to the press and therefore neutralised it, apparently with the intention of committing the Americans more deeply to the Cyprus dispute. The British action is said to have roused President Johnson to fury.[23] Foreign Office records do show that London had reservations about the Undersecretary's plan. D. S. L. Dodson suggested that the 'appointment of a mediator might well weaken our ability to influence the formulation of a final solution and to that extent might operate against our interests' which included military bases on Cyprus. But Dodson also saw 'advantages from the international point of view in prime responsibility for the achievement of a solution being removed from our shoulders'.[24]

It is likely therefore that any British leak was due to sheer carelessness, and not with the intention of scuppering Ball's scheme. In any case, the demise of his plan for Western European mediation meant that it was Ball himself who ended up as the mediator, though the UN also strove to conciliate the parties. Each operated independently of the other, but, seemingly, managed to avoid treading on one another's toes. When Ball began his work early in February the Turkish Cypriots were demanding Cyprus's partition and self-governance, and the preservation of Turkey's right of intervention. Of course, Ankara supported the Turkish Cypriots, while emphasising Turkey's right to intervene by force. Ball soon concluded that the Turks were 'not bluffing' when they threatened to invade. Greece, which pressed for *enosis*, would 'have to move if the Turks did', although if the government in Athens held back, 'the Greek military would get a new government that would'. Although the Greek Cypriots wanted *enosis*, for tactical reasons they demanded a fully independent Cyprus run by the Greek majority.[25]

It was Archbishop Makarios rather than Athens or Ankara who held the key to peace. According to Adlai Stevenson, Makarios was the 'undisputed leader of four-fifths of [the] Cypriot population and, while he cannot prevent minor incidents, he can prevent major hostilities.'[26] Unfortunately, he could have done more to staunch the violence. He had been criticised as 'a traitor to the Greek Cypriot cause' because of his acceptance of the Turkish right of intervention in 1960. To avoid similar charges in the future, he followed rather than tried to lead public opinion.[27] The Cypriot leader told Ball on 13 February that he was seeking a UN resolution affirming the island's territorial integrity and political independence. This would prevent Turkey from intervening to defend the Turkish Cypriots. For Ball, using the UN in this manner was 'criminally foolhardy', because 'the murder rate is rising steadily and . . . the tempo of the fighting is increasing'. If the Turks invaded, 'neither the United States nor any other Western power would raise a finger to stop them'. Ball and the British High Commissioner, Cyril Pickard, berated Makarios and his 'extremist ministers in a manner unfamiliar to diplomatic discourse . . . we shook the Archbishop. Even his beard seemed pale.'[28] For the Undersecretary, Cyprus was 'infected by blood lust and that there is no government that seriously wants to maintain order. Its only desire is to liquidate Turks.'[29]

Ball made little progress in getting the parties to reason with one another, nor did the UN. From March, after the initial American efforts to secure peace had achieved little, the UN provided a peacekeeping presence. That presence may well have prevented some bloodshed but it probably did not play a significant role in dissuading the Turks from invading. Ball explained to Johnson later in 1964 that:

> the orders that the component elements have given to their own elements is that if an invasion should start, they would retire into the British bases and not stop it, because with 6,000 men they are not capable of stopping a Turkish invasion. And anyway there isn't a one of the United Nations forces that's . . . prepared to fight the Turks.[30]

THE DIPLOMATIC 'ATOM BOMB' AND THE WASHINGTON SUMMITS, 22–4 JUNE

On 4 June, Ambassador Raymond Hare in Ankara reported that the Turks were poised to sanction an invasion.[31] There may have been an element of bluff in the Turkish suggestion. Ankara may have wanted to bring about a still-deeper involvement of the United States in the search for a settlement, and, as Hare suggested, to get Prime Minister Inonu 'off the hook politically and shift the blame for Turkish inaction to ourselves'.[32] Moreover, one assumes that if Ankara was ready to intervene it would hardly have chosen to telegraph its thinking to other countries. One cannot know for sure how matters would have turned out in the absence of a firm response from Washington: Dean Rusk telephoned the Turkish Ambassador to express 'grave concern' about the possibility of an invasion, for such an event would have a 'very serious effect on the problem of our security commitment with our allies'.[33]

Rusk, Assistant Secretary of State for International Organization Affairs Harlan Cleveland and his deputy Joseph Sisco also prepared a powerful presidential message for Inonu. The message stated that NATO countries must not wage war upon one another. Germany and France had 'buried centuries of animosity and hostility in becoming NATO allies; nothing less can be expected from Greece and Turkey'. If the Soviet Union became involved then there was a strong likelihood that there would be no support from NATO. Turkey must not use US-provided military equipment. An invasion could bring the 'slaughter of tens of thousands of Turkish Cypriots'. Inonu had 'posed the gravest issues of war and peace'. Unless he gave an 'assurance that you will not take such action without further and fullest consultation I . . . must immediately ask for emergency meetings of the NATO Council and of the United Nations Security Council'.[34]

Besides ignoring the point that Turkish intervention in Turkey was permissible under the 1960 accords, the letter implied that Washington was not obliged to abide by the terms of the North Atlantic Treaty. The rationale of a multilateral alliance, as Henry Kissinger has noted, is that the protection of one or more members is in the interests of all members, and not something to be dispensed as a favour or withheld as a whim.[35] Washington's implication that the North Atlantic Treaty was not necessarily binding appears all the more extraordinary when one considers the problems that had arisen in recent years over doubts about the American security commitment to Europe. One wonders what statesmen in France and West Germany might have thought about the letter to Inonu.

Ball described the communication as 'the most brutal diplomatic note I have ever seen' – the 'diplomatic equivalent of an atom bomb'.[36] Although drafted by aides, the message reflected the authentic feelings of President Johnson, who had never had any inhibitions about using strong words to either the Turks or the Greeks – in February he had urged Ball to 'talk in the toughest language if necessary to all parties'.[37] In response to the 5 June message, Inonu told Ambassador Hare that while he 'disagreed with certain points', he agreed that the Turkish government should 'delay any action on [the] understanding [that] there would be full and frank discussion with [a] view [to] reaching [a] peaceful solution'. The Turkish leader asked the United States to take a more central role in seeking a solution.[38]

On 11 June, Ball explained to Johnson that the Greek government had grown 'scared at the reality of the danger of a Greek-Turkish war and at the progressive extension of Communist control', via the Cyprus Communist Party, on the island. The Greeks were 'fed up with Makarios' – not least because he had flirted with Moscow – and wanted strong American intervention in the search for a settlement. Meanwhile, Ankara was doing its utmost to 'manoeuvre us into taking responsibility for bringing about a settlement'. All this enhanced Washington's influence.[39] Johnson met with Prime Minister Inonu and the Greek Prime Minister Papandreou in Washington on 22–3 June and 24–5 June respectively, with the intention of gaining their acquiescence to American-led face-to-face discussions. Johnson greatly liked the Turkish leader, who favoured the idea of talking to the Greeks.[40] However, Papandreou, no doubt fearing an outcome other than *enosis*, proved evasive: Greece and Turkey should only 'undertake a reconnaissance to see whether future negotiations are possible . . . there is little point at undertaking actual negotiations'. Former Secretary of State Dean Acheson, drafted in to help the Administration with the Cyprus dispute, doubted that 'any pacification is possible until the views of Turkey and Greece are closer than they are now'. Papandreou did at least agree to accede to the wishes of the UN mediator on the question of talks.[41]

The UN endorsed the talks, subject to certain conditions, while Johnson placed further pressure on the Prime Minister to negotiate.[42] Papandreou, who struggled with the magnitude of the crisis and was still bruised from his visit to Washington, even suggested that the pressure for negotiations was comparable to that imposed upon Greece by the Nazis in 1940.[43] Finally, in a meeting with Ambassador Henry Labouisse he conceded the need for talks, while pointing 'proudly to [a] new picture of President Johnson on his bookcase', to demonstrate his sincerity.[44]

THE FIRST ACHESON PLAN

Given his prestige in both Greece and Turkey as one of the chief architects of the Truman Doctrine and the 'containment' policy in the 1940s, it was time for Dean Acheson to take a more central role. Acheson came up with two 'plans' for a settlement. According to a British analysis, he 'took care not to produce them in written form because his method was to work away slowly at the Greek and Turkish positions, leaving certain points deliberately unclear where necessary'. So the 'plans' emerged in a piecemeal fashion, although the key elements are apparent. The first of Acheson's plans involved the establishment of a Turkish base on the island, either under Turkish sovereignty or leased from the Greek government. The negotiations touched on the possible location of the base. The Turks wanted a sovereign base in the north-eastern part of the island (the Karpas peninsula), while the Greek government were not willing to consider more than a leased base in the south. As an alternative to a Turkish sovereign base there was also some talk of Turkish troops being accommodated in the British Sovereign Base Areas. In addition, Turkey was to be compensated by obtaining part of the Greek island of Castellorizon. The position of the Turkish Cypriots would be safeguarded by two Turkish Cypriot prefects rotating between regions with a Turkish population of at least 30 per cent. There would be a Bureau of Turkish Affairs in the Central Administration manned by Turkish Cypriots to watch over their own interests, together with an appropriate percentage of Turkish Cypriots in the local administration. A UN Commission would hear complaints about alleged violations of minority rights.[45]

Acheson made little headway, though, largely due to resistance from Athens. As Ball suggested, the Greeks felt that they could 'work out a plebiscite followed by *enosis* simply by sitting tight' for a UN endorsement of the principle of self-determination. Athens was 'blind to its long-range interest in conceding enough to Ankara to provide a basis for improved relations after a Cyprus settlement'.[46] The Greek government was also influenced by Makarios, who voiced his disapproval of concessions to Turkish interests. Athens understood the impossibility of trying to implement a solution to which Makarios objected.[47]

The Second Acheson Plan and the End of the 1964 Crisis

Meanwhile, George Ball initiated underground contacts with General George Grivas, the former leader of Cyprus's armed struggle for independence and now the Commander of the Cyprus National Guard. Grivas had a plan for *enosis* that afforded protection for the Turkish Cypriots remaining on the island and offered compensation for those wanting to leave. The fact that his plan also called for the ouster of Makarios made it all the more attractive to American diplomats.[48] However, in August the situation took a turn for the worse. Makarios ordered intensified attacks on Turkish Cypriots, and in retaliation the Turkish air force strafed a number of Greek villages on the island. The Archbishop may have heard about Grivas' plan and wanted to disrupt it,[49] while the US Embassy in Cyprus surmised that Makarios was trying to blackmail the United States into transmitting another ultimatum to Ankara.[50] This would put the Archbishop in a dominant position. Johnson wrote to Papandreou, Inonu and Makarios, urging restraint.[51]

In part due to Johnson's promptings, a UN-proposed cease-fire was accepted.[52] There was further hope when on 12 August the Soviet leader Nikita Khrushchev rejected a request for military intervention from Makarios, saying that while he 'sympathised with the Cyprus government, a cease-fire would be an important contribution'.[53] Yet the peace was fragile. A few days later, Acheson surmised that 'even with luck we may be only four or five days away from an explosion'. The Turks were 'full of cockiness . . . Their military plans are hair-raising since they would involve among other things taking out all the Greek airfields on the mainland.' The Greeks would 'not be able to stand down if the Turks move'. Makarios was trying to provoke the Turkish Cypriots into violence, to frustrate any American settlement, while the Turk-Cypriots were in a 'Gotterdammerung mood'.[54]

On 20 August, Acheson unveiled a second plan. It closely resembled the first, but this one envisaged a leased base for Turkey on the Karpas peninsula for forty-five to fifty years to include the whole of the area east of a line near Komi Kabir. Ankara felt that fifty years was too short, but Athens was more amenable, at least initially. However, Makarios expressed hostility to the proposal and the Greek Prime Minister was unwilling to break with him. Within days of presenting his second 'plan', Acheson realised there was little point in continuing the negotiations.[55] Washington's patience had its limits, as was also evident in the brutal 'solution' that Dean Acheson and George Ball suggested early in September. They tried to persuade Johnson that the only answer now would be 'a fait accompli in which the Turks would move to occupy the Karpas peninsula'. This would trigger 'an instant *enosis* under Greek leadership, with a consequent supercession of Makarios'. Johnson summarised the argument in a sympathetic way, saying that 'we must expect a resort to action in one way or another', and that 'the choice was whether it should be messy and destructive and in accordance with a plan'. However, he doubted that 'the plan as put forward could in fact be neat and tightly controlled, without risk of escalation'. He anticipated that the Greeks would be 'very likely to move with all their strength on the island against a Turkish lodgement', and he felt that, with the challenging situation in Vietnam and with the imminent presidential election in the United States, 'the next two months were not a good season for another war'.[56] Caution had got the better of President Johnson. He refused to give the green light, and an uneasy peace prevailed in Cyprus.

RELATIONS WITH ISRAEL

'Uneasy peace' also characterised Israel's relationship with its neighbours. Two years after the creation of Israel in 1948, Washington, London and Paris pledged in a 'Tripartite Declaration' to resist any attempt to alter the borders of the Middle East by force. Congress supported the pledge in the Middle East Resolution of 1957.[57] These statements were intended largely to preserve Israel's existence in the face of Arab hostility, and it was the case that Lyndon Johnson's sympathies in the Arab–Israeli rivalry lay mainly with the Israelis. In 1948 he had sought to facilitate the clandestine flow of arms to the Haganah, and as Senate Majority Leader from 1954, he established a friendship with Abba Eban, Israeli Ambassador in Washington and later Foreign Secretary.[58] Johnson made use of his influential position in the Senate to support Israeli interests. He reflected that 'When [the Israelis] were in real problems [during the Suez war of 1956] and they [the Eisenhower Administration] were getting ready to impose sanctions . . . I stopped it'.[59] Early in 1964, he told Israeli Prime Minister Levi Eshkol that the 'close and friendly relationship . . . between our two governments must continue'.[60] Johnson had a number of pro-Israeli advisers, including Vice-President Hubert Humphrey, US Representative to the UN Arthur Goldberg, National Security Adviser Walt Rostow and Undersecretary of State for Political Affairs Eugene Rostow. Informal advisers who were keen supporters of Israel included Supreme Court Justice Abe Fortas and Democratic fundraisers Abe Feinberg and Arthur Krim.[61] The upshot was that, as Harold Saunders of the NSC suggested in 1967, the President had 'a political need as well as a personal desire to maintain a warm relationship with Israel'.[62]

The arms relationship represented an increasingly important bond between Washington and Tel Aviv in the Johnson years.[63] Komer pointed out that from 1948 to 1961 the United States had avoided becoming Israel's main arms supplier by 'indirectly subsidising Israeli purchases in Europe'.[64] Kennedy had sold the Israelis Hawk missiles in 1962. Two years later, Israel asked the United States for tanks, but was refused on the grounds that, in McGeorge Bundy's words, 'it would be hard for us to maintain our present position in the Middle East'.[65] The Israelis ended up buying tanks from the United Kingdom and Germany, with American help and on very favourable terms.[66] In 1965, Washington sold tanks to Jordan to bolster King Hussein's stature and to deter him from accepting Soviet weapons. Washington offered tanks to Israel as well, as it would hardly do to be selling military equipment to Arab states while neglecting Israel. Similarly, the following year, the United States provided advanced

'Skyhawk' military aircraft to both Israel and Jordan to counter Soviet sales to Egypt. These arms sales played out reasonably well, at least in the short term. Komer reported that the United States had now become Israel's 'chief backer, without it costing us our influence in the Arab world'. Komer also took the view that a 'judicious US arms supply, aimed at maintaining a deterrent balance' in the Middle East might be a good 'inhibitor' upon Israeli nuclear aspirations.[67]

However, he was too sanguine in this regard. Israeli nuclear ambitions had begun in 1952 with the creation of the Israeli Atomic Energy Commission. Early in 1964, Johnson explained his disappointment to Prime Minister Eshkol that Israel would not provide reassurance to President Nasser about the 'peaceful character' of the reactor at Dimona in Israel.[68] Johnson maintained a heart-felt determination to obtain an assurance from the Israelis that they would not develop nuclear weapons.[69] However, in 1966 Israel conducted some kind of nuclear test (the details of which are not known), and by the time of the Arab–Israeli war possessed two or three crude nuclear weapons.[70] It seems that Washington had no knowledge of these weapons, although there were suspicions among American policymakers that, in the words of Undersecretary of State Nicholas Katzenbach, they 'did not know the full story' of the Israeli nuclear programme.[71]

The fact that many of the leading critics in the United States of American policy in Vietnam was another matter of concern to President Johnson. When a prominent New York rabbi criticised the Administration, Johnson told the Israeli Ambassador, Avraham Harman, to get the Jewish community under control.[72] The President recognised the inconsistency in 1967 when liberal Jewish Americans, who had been among the 'doves' in relation to Vietnam, were now 'hawks' in the Middle East and demanding the benefits of American military might.[73] Early in 1968 there were intimations that Prime Minister Eshkol was considering 'an open endorsement of our Vietnam effort and even some active help', but Walt Rostow pointed to a need since the Six-Day War to avoid bolstering 'the image of Israel as our stooge'.[74]

There were further difficulties over heavy-handed Israeli responses to terrorist raids from neighbouring territories. In 1966, a new, radical and Soviet-backed government in Damascus increased terrorist raids against Israel, sending Arab guerrillas across the borders of Syria, Lebanon and Jordan. The intention was to force Israeli reprisals against Jordan and Lebanon, both of which had moderate pro-Western governments.[75] The Syrians succeeded in this goal when after terrorist attacks a 400-strong Israeli force raided the Jordanian town of Es Samu, which was supposed to be providing succour to al-Fatah guerrillas, in November 1966. The Israelis ended up clashing with Jordanian regular troops, and the result was a lengthy battle in which fifteen Jordanian soldiers, ten Israelis and three villagers were killed. The Israeli raid dented the Jordanian government's confidence in Israel and in the American commitment to Jordan's territorial integrity, and encouraged King Hussein to improve his ties with Egypt. This culminated in the signing of a five-year mutual defence pact in the run-up to the Six-Day War.[76]

RELATIONS WITH EGYPT

Egypt had been trying to boost its status in the Middle East since President Gamel Abdul Nasser had assumed power in 1956 and rued the existence of the Jewish state. Although John F. Kennedy tried to persuade Nasser to put aside the Israeli question and began providing food aid, US efforts to arm Israel remained a source of antagonism, as did Egyptian intervention in the favour of rebel forces in Yemen. But the Johnson Administration strove to continue the limited cooperation, and Johnson was gratified when in 1964 Nasser assured him that his country would not develop nuclear weapons or procure them.[77] Egypt's nuclear weapons stance was therefore a pleasing contrast to that of Israel. However, the general trend of the relationship between the United States and Egypt in the Johnson years was downward. In November 1964, a mob protesting American policy in the Congo (where Egypt was aiding a rebel movement) attacked the US Embassy in Cairo,[78] and soon after that, Egyptian forces shot down the private aircraft of oil prospector John Mecom, a friend of Johnson, when it flew off course into Egypt. The Egyptians had thought Mecom's plane was an Israeli reconnaissance aircraft, but Nasser was unsympathetic to American concerns, telling Washington 'to drink from the sea'.[79]

Another concern was Nasser's deepening relationship with Moscow, which, as the CIA noted, had become 'more willing to work somewhat more closely with him than in the past in espousing his kind of Arab nationalism, socialism, and opposition to Western influence'. Other causes of antagonism between Washington and Cairo included Nasser's resentment at tightened US aid policies toward Egypt, and his continued suspicions of the American relationship with Israel.[80] Problems such as these led to the termination of American food supplies, and Nasser ended up as one of the most prominent non-communist leaders never to receive an invitation to visit Washington.[81]

The United States would have liked to have remained on friendly terms with both Israel and its Arab neighbours. However, Johnson's pro-Israeli inclinations gradually came to prevail over the more Arabist outlook of Dean Rusk and the State Department. This development occasioned some complaints. Not long before the outbreak of the Six-Day War, Ambassador to Syria Hugh Smythe argued that 'on the scales we have Israel, an unviable client state whose ties, value to US primarily emotional, balanced with [a] full range [of] vital strategic, political, commercial/economic interests represented by Arab states'.[82] Yet the divergence of views between the Johnson White House and the State Department did not represent a violent breach, as few if any American diplomats and policymakers were anti-Israeli, and all feared the Soviet Union making inroads into the Middle East.[83]

RISING TENSIONS

There were armed clashes between Syria and Israel early in April 1967, in which the Israelis shot down six Syrian MIGs.[84] On 16 May, after Damascus had fed Cairo unfounded reports of Israeli mobilisation, Nasser pressured Secretary General U Thant into withdrawing UN observers in the Sinai. Nasser was within his rights to ask the UNEF to depart, but the UN obeyed a little too quickly for American and Israeli tastes. Even Nasser was said to be surprised at the speed of the pull-out.[85] U Thant's failure to stall left less room for diplomacy to moderate the tensions, and Israel mobilised in response to the replacement of the UNEF by the Egyptian forces.

On 23 May, Nasser closed the Gulf of Aqaba to Israeli flagships, blocking access to the Israeli port of Eilat via the Strait of Tiran. The eminent CIA analyst Sherman Kent argued that for Israel to concede the permanent closing of the Strait would be economically disastrous and a long-term political setback. Unless the Straits were reopened soon, the Israelis would 'feel compelled to go to war'.[86] On 30 May there was an announcement of a defence pact between Egypt and Jordan. The following day, after a discussion with US envoy and former Secretary of the Treasury Robert Anderson, Nasser agreed to send his Vice-President, Zakaria Mohieddin, to Washington on 7 June.[87] He would then be encouraged to accept a peaceful settlement of the dispute.

Although the planned trip to Washington suggested that there was still an openness to discussion and negotiation, Egyptian policy had grown increasingly strident. The CIA reflected that Nasser had for various reasons 'chosen to abandon his longstanding reluctance to risk military confrontation with Israel'. The Soviets might have encouraged Nasser's brinkmanship: Moscow's interests would 'obviously be served by successes for Nasser at the expense of Israel and the US'. Furthermore, there was, it was speculated, 'an element of desperation in Nasser's attitude, arising from the parlous condition of the Egyptian economy, a belief that some sort of US-Israeli plot against him existed', and 'perhaps a fatalistic conclusion that a showdown with Israel must come sooner or later, and might best be provoked before Israel acquired nuclear weapons'.[88]

It hardly needs emphasising in the light of the American commitment in Vietnam (some 450,000 troops by now) and Johnson's general reluctance towards military action, that there was no disposition in Washington towards involvement in a Middle Eastern war. As Townsend Hoopes of the Defense Department stated, if the United States became a belligerent 'the chances for limiting and ending hostilities would be infinitely worsened, in part because the UN would be rendered impotent (as in the case of Vietnam) by a fundamental split between the two superpowers'.[89] This meant that any war could escalate to involve the Soviet Union and the United States and its fellow members of NATO.[90] On 23 May, the day of the closure of the Gulf of Aqaba, Johnson expressed concern on television and radio about 'warlike acts', the 'hurried withdrawal' of the UN from Gaza and Sinai, and the build-up of military forces in the region. The United States considered the Gulf to be 'an international waterway' and the blockade of Israeli shipping 'illegal and potentially disastrous to the cause of peace'.[91] There was also, according to Dean Rusk, 'a general agreement in Congress that the Arabs should not be permitted to drive the Israelis into the sea', but no desire for unilateral American action.[92]

Taking up two British ideas, the Administration decided to try to get a public declaration from as many countries as possible asserting the right of free passage through the Gulf of Aqaba and to construct an international fleet to challenge the Egyptian blockade and force Nasser to back down.[93] It would, however, take a while to bring these ideas to fruition, and by the time war erupted on 5 June only eight countries including the United States and Israel had offered support for the public declaration of maritime freedom, and just four countries had agreed to participate in the international fleet. On 23 May, Johnson secretly approved a military and economic aid package for Israel. This included the sale of 100 armoured personnel carriers, tank spare parts and credit for aircraft spares.[94] Although the deal had been in the pipeline for some months, endorsing it at this critical stage was an obvious token of Johnson's sympathies for the Israelis. The secret aid package was especially significant in that the Administration declared an embargo on 5 June, the day of the outbreak of the war, on the shipment of US arms to the Middle East.[95]

US pre-war diplomacy included discussions with Israeli Foreign Secretary Abba Eban in Washington on 25–6 May. Eban stressed that unless the Straits were reopened soon then Prime Minister Eshkol would give the go-ahead to the military. Johnson, who had prepared himself extensively for the summit, told him emphatically that Israel 'must not be responsible for initiating hostilities'. 'Israel will not be alone unless it decides to go it alone.' He tried to boost Israeli confidence by saying that if Egypt and its allies struck, 'our judgment is that the Israelis should lick them . . . you will whip hell out of them'.[96] Abe Fortas and Clark Clifford, who was by no means over-sympathetic to Israel, had argued that the Administration should make a concession to Eban, providing reassurance that the United States would use force if required to reopen the Straits. However, Johnson felt that the Administration was doing all that it reasonably could: Eban 'would not get all he wants. The big question was whether we will regret . . . not having given him more.'[97] Johnson's concern was that the Israelis would strike Egypt and precipitate war. He did not want a war under any circumstances.

No 'Green Light'

By the time the fighting broke out on 5 June, the Administration had striven in various ways to act as a moderating influence. There were numerous presidential messages to the heads of state in the area urging restraint; efforts were made to control the Israelis including the treatment accorded to Eban in Washington on 25–6 May; there were preparations to deal with the crisis, such as the establishment of a Middle East Control Group staffed by personnel from the CIA, the Pentagon and the State Department; liaison with Britain on the maritime declaration and the establishment of the multinational fleet; continuing recourse to the UN Security Council; consultations with Congress; and the sending of private emissaries to the region.[98]

While counselling restraint, Washington had nevertheless taken sides. According to Harold Saunders, for nearly twenty years Israel had wanted a 'special relationship' – even a 'private security guarantee' – from the United States, which was always refused on the grounds of preserving 'our other interests in the Middle East'. Now Washington found itself 'committed to side with Israel and, in opening the Straits of Tiran, even to wage war on the Arabs . . . we have chosen sides – not with the constructive Arabs *and* Israel, but with Israel alone against all the Arabs'.[99] As a State Department diplomat suggested, the Israelis had little faith in the plan for the 'Red Sea Regatta',[100] and there were even fears that the Administration would pull some kind of 'Munich' with the Arabs.[101] Meanwhile, as the CIA noted on 2 June, Nasser's forces were being 'built up and digging in. The Arab military forces are being unified and consolidated. The economic costs for Israel are rising. The political and psychological pressures for a solution are increasing.' The Israelis had taken American advice to wait 'as a cold, responsible, calculus', but 'now the military cost to them of a war with Egypt is rising every day'.[102] The pressure was simply too great. On 5 June, at about 0800 local time, Israel raided airfields in Cairo and other areas. The war, which also pulled in Jordan, Syria and, briefly, Iraq, would last until 10 June.

Had Washington relented and finally given a secret 'green light' to the Israelis to strike? There is evidence to this effect, but it is insubstantial. On 2 June, Rusk had repeated Johnson's message of restraint to Ambassador Harman, but when Harman discussed the crisis with Abe Fortas soon after, the message of restraint was much less in evidence. According to Fortas, Johnson believed that 'Rusk will fiddle while Israel burns.' Fortas added that 'If you're going to save yourself, do it yourself.'[103] Undoubtedly, there were some in the Administration who saw virtue in a pre-emptive Israeli strike, or at least in not holding the Israelis back from such a strike. Saunders, for example, suggested to Rostow that 'we don't have a right' to restrain Eshkol further 'while his enemy gets stronger unless we take on the Arabs ourselves . . . We ought to consider admitting that we have failed and allow fighting to ensue.'[104]

Yet, in view of Johnson's numerous pleadings to representatives of the Israeli government not to attack, it would have been a decisive turn-around for him to have endorsed a war. Even if he had believed what turned out to be a highly accurate forecast from Richard Helms, Director of the CIA, that Israel would secure a military victory in a matter of days,[105] there were still serious dangers. Could anyone be absolutely sure, for instance, that Moscow would merely sit by as its allies fell? What if after receiving the go-ahead from the United States Israel began to lose? How much American support might be needed? Where might it end? From Johnson's perspective, precipitating a war was not a risk worth taking.

The President's statement to an audience of Democrats, including some influential Jews, in New York at a fundraising dinner on 3 June that he was working day and night to prevent a war in the Middle East was accurate and not intended to mislead.[106] Moreover, after the Israelis had attacked and despite their rapid successes, he deeply regretted that war had started. On 7 June he told the NSC that it was 'important for everyone to know we are not for aggression. We are sorry this has taken place . . . We thought we had a commitment from those governments, but it went up in smoke very quickly . . . By the time we get through with all the festering problems we are going to wish the war had not happened.'[107] Johnson said later that 'I had a firm commitment from Eshkol [to wait] and he blew it',[108] while Rostow reflected that the President had 'never believed that this war was anything else than a mistake by the Israelis'.[109]

One might add that although Israel was always keen to develop its 'special relationship' with Washington, it was capable of making its own calculations and acting independently of the United States. As noted earlier, the military balance of power was moving away from Israel day by day, and there was the economic drain of continued mobilisation and the closure of the Gulf of Aqaba to consider, too. Rusk commented on 3 June that 'you should not assume that the United States can order Israel not to fight for what it considers to be its most vital interests'.[110] So, the Israelis wanted the support of their friends in the White House as far as possible but the time came when they felt that they could wait no longer before attacking. Instead of receiving a green light from Washington, Israel ignored a red one.

BIASED NON-BELLIGERENCE, 5–10 JUNE

The war confirmed American intelligence forecasts and went well for the Israelis, meaning that the United States would not face the difficult choice of whether or not to intervene. The initial attack on the Egyptian air force put five airfields out of action, and Israel took control of the Gaza Strip and the Sinai Desert. Rostow recorded that despite the war having been initiated against American advice, 'there was a certain relief that things were going well for the Israelis'.[111] No effort was made to implement any sanctions on Tel Aviv when the advice was rejected. Similarly, while Washington worked with the United Nations for a cease-fire, there was no pressure on the Israelis to give up the ground they had conquered. On 8 June, the Soviets pointed out that it had been two days since a Security Council Resolution calling for an end to the fighting, but despite the appeal, Israel 'seized considerable territory of the Arab States – the United Arab Republic and Jordan – ignoring the Security Council Resolution'. What was needed was not simply a cease-fire but 'a withdrawal of Israeli troops behind the armistice line'.[112] But just as the Administration had sought to restrain the Israelis from waging war, it was hardly in much of a position to hold them back after they had begun that war.

When framing their policies Johnson and his colleagues also had to consider the influential Jewish community in the United States which was, understandably, in a state of heightened sensitivity to signals from the White House. When on the first day of the war, Robert J. McCloskey of the State Department affirmed to the press that the American position was 'neutral in thought, word and deed', White House aide Joseph Califano told Rusk that the statement was 'killing us with the Jews'. The Secretary of State should 'swamp McCloskey with a statement of his own'. Later, Rusk told the press that the United States was 'not a belligerent in the current fighting but . . . this did not mean indifference'.[113] The policy was, in effect, one of biased non-belligerence.

President Johnson's sympathy for the Israelis was demonstrated, among other things, by his response to an Israeli attack on 8 June on the signal intelligence vessel the USS *Liberty*, which had been deployed to monitor Israeli activities along the Syrian frontier.[114] American mistakes contributed to this incident. The *Liberty*'s sailing order was that it should stay at least 12.5 miles off the coast of Egypt and 6.5 miles from Israel. Although the Joint Chiefs of Staff later increased this distance to 100 miles, a series of lapses in communication meant that the vessel was much closer to the Israeli coast on 8 June.[115] Israeli aircraft and torpedo boats attacked the *Liberty* that day, killing 34 and wounding 171 crew members. A further communication failure meant that Johnson did not learn of the attack until two hours later. He assumed that it was perpetrated by the Soviets, and prepared to send a message to Moscow via the 'hot-line' warning that American aircraft were investigating a serious incident in the area.[116] However, it soon emerged that the Israelis were the perpetrators. Dean Rusk sent a toughly worded diplomatic note to Tel Aviv, stating that 'at the time of the attack the *Liberty* was flying the American flag and its identification was clearly indicated in large white letters and numerals on its hull'. Two Israeli aircraft circled the vessel three times, to try to identify it. This meant the *Liberty* was identified an hour before it was first struck. The attack by Israeli aircraft was 'quite literally incomprehensible. As a minimum, the attack must be condemned as an act of military recklessness reflecting wanton disregard for human life.' The subsequent torpedo boat attack 'manifest[ed] the same reckless disregard for human life'. The United States wanted not only material compensation but for the Israeli government to discipline the personnel concerned.[117]

Some weeks later, the President's Foreign Intelligence Advisory Board under Clark Clifford concluded that there were 'gross and inexcusable failures in the command and control of subordinate Israeli naval and air elements' and that the 'unprovoked attack on the *Liberty* constitutes a flagrant act of gross negligence for which the Israeli government should be held completely responsible, and the Israeli military personnel involved should be punished'.[118] Yet although President Johnson had permitted

Rusk his tough diplomatic note to the Israelis, he did not want the matter to become a major issue in relations between the United States and Israel. He never voiced the reasons for his restraint but one can speculate that holding back would ease the pressure from the friends of Israel in the United States and give him greater leverage over Tel Aviv.[119]

THE SOVIET DIMENSION

Contacts between Washington and Moscow, which had done much to encourage Arab belligerency, began soon after the Israeli strike. After a 'hot-line' message from Rusk to Gromyko emphasising the need for superpower cooperation, Premier Kosygin called upon Washington to work with Moscow in securing a cease-fire. There were seven hot-line messages during the first two days of the war, while between 5 and 10 June twenty messages were exchanged.[120] There was a minor faux pas when Johnson's first message to Kosygin was addressed to 'Comrade Kosygin'. The American hot-line telegraph operators had asked the Moscow operators how to address Kosygin, hence the epithet. When the first message from Washington came through, however, the Soviets wondered, according to Ambassador Dobrynin, if the President was 'making a joke, or making fun of them some way'. However, Dobrynin suspected what had happened, and realised that the Americans were not engaging in mockery.[121] More seriously, on 10 June, Kosygin, perhaps feeling the sting of communist Chinese taunts at the poor performance of the Arab states, came on to the hot-line saying that Moscow would 'adopt an independent decision' if the war was not ended soon: 'These actions may bring us into a clash, which would lead to a grave catastrophe.'[122] According to CIA Director Richard Helms, who was in the White House cabinet room when Kosygin's message came through, the 'atmosphere was tense' and the 'conversation was conducted in the lowest voices possible'. The entire US intelligence community was placed on alert. Signals intercepts revealed that a number of Soviet airborne divisions and part of the Soviet nuclear forces had been placed on alert.[123] Justified concern about the possibility of a clash led Johnson to order the withdrawal of the Sixth Fleet to the eastern Mediterranean.[124] The Soviets, who were monitoring its movements by electronic means, noted the gesture and the tension was defused.

If the Soviets had ever expected their Arab clients to prevail in the war with Israel, then they were wrong. Syria lost most of its 85 fighter aircraft and about 100 of its 425 tanks. The Jordanian air force was completely destroyed; two-thirds of Jordan's 200 tanks were captured or destroyed.

Egypt, with the largest Arab armed force, lost about two-thirds of its 365 fighter aircraft, 55 of its 69 bombers, and about half of its 1,000 tanks. Egyptian pilot losses were small, but Egypt had only 200 pilots who were combat ready in jet fighters when the war began. There were heavy losses among armoured vehicle crews and ground forces. Fighting in the Sinai eliminated two of Egypt's four infantry divisions, one of its two armoured divisions, and fifteen of its twenty-three independent brigades. Morale was severely dented in all three Arab armies. Israel gained much greater military security relative to its Arab neighbours. Fewer than a hundred of the country's 1,100 tanks were destroyed. Of Israel's 256 aircraft, 48 were lost – including 14 of its 46 fighter bombers; 24 of its 450 jet pilots were killed. Even with these losses – and subsequent resupply of Soviet aircraft to the Arabs – the Israeli air force remained, as the CIA suggested, 'qualitatively much stronger than all the Arab forces combined'. While there were 7,000 Arabs killed, the Israelis lost just 700 military personnel. In addition, the Israeli army now occupied territory which would give it a great advantage if hostilities were to recur. Israel also managed to capture large quantities of ground force equipment, some of which was integrated into its units.[125]

In his memoirs, George Ball cited the praise of two journalists about American policy in the Cyprus crisis:

> . . . on most counts, the 1964 US venture into crisis diplomacy can be judged a success. It prevented the establishment of a Soviet satellite in the eastern Mediterranean. It staved off a Turkish invasion of Cyprus and, perhaps, a full-scale war between Greece and Turkey, two NATO allies. The US managed to preserve its firm, if somewhat cooler, relations with both Greece and Turkey, in spite of the harsh words and pressures exerted in trying to prevent conflict. It also succeeded in avoiding increased tension with the Soviet Union.
>
> And, more importantly, the entire enterprise was accomplished without commitment of American soldiers or equipment or the expenditure of American funds, except a pro-rata share of UN peacekeeping costs. In this respect alone, the Cyprus incident is unique in the history of US crisis diplomacy.[126]

These arguments have some merit but they are not completely persuasive. The Cyprus crisis of 1964 might not have reached such intensity had the United States intervened some months earlier, when Makarios first began pressing for changes to the Cypriot Constitution. Komer suggested in February that 'we let this crisis creep up on us', and that 'from a posture of let the UK do it', the State Department – as represented by George Ball – 'suddenly panicked in response to UK panic and reversed field by urging that we send troops'.[127] Moscow was certainly happy to see tension between NATO members, but Soviet policy was generally cautious and their influence never so pervasive that Cyprus was likely to fall into the Soviet orbit. But although Ball had always tended to regard Makarios as the most troublesome corner of the Cyprus triangle, it seems that for whatever reason he did little to modify the terms of the letter.[128] As noted earlier, the Kremlin turned down Makarios' request for military intervention during the intensified fighting in August.

It is fair to say, though, that despite worries about Soviet policy there was no increase in tensions between the two countries; the Cyprus conflict did not undermine the nascent détente of 1964–5 – unlike the issue of Vietnam (see Chapter Six). Notably, Washington saw Cyprus mainly through Cold War lenses; there was no particular interest in the nature of a settlement other than there should *be* a settlement to stabilise NATO's southern flank. Whether or not Johnson's tough letter to Inonu on 5 June 1964 was decisive in turning Turkey away from invasion is a matter for conjecture. The letter was accepted with reasonable grace, but there was now an assumption in Ankara that American policy was biased towards Greece. The following year the Turks asked Washington to stop using Turkish bases for intelligence flights over the Soviet Union. This began a gradual accommodation with Moscow that loosened Ankara's connections with NATO.[129] Yet the very fact that Johnson's advisors considered encouraging Turkey to invade Cyprus two months later indicates that there was no bias in American policy, only a desire to settle matters as expediently as possible. Johnson's decision to restrain his advisers and prevent them from giving the go-ahead for war may have prevented a more serious conflict. Overall, US performance in the 1964 crisis over Cyprus helped to keep a lid on the conflict, but at the price of alienating Ankara.

As with the Cyprus question, the Arab–Israeli war of 1967 raised questions about American commitments to friends and allies. The absence of a green light from the Administration was another token of the general caution and prudence with which Johnson tended to approach foreign policy issues. The White House was clearly disposed, as shown by aspects of its policies such as the military and economic aid package on 23 May, towards a successful outcome for Tel Aviv in the war of nerves and in the subsequent fighting. The bias did have an ethical justification, given that Israel's very existence was at stake rather than that of any of the Arab states. The defeat of the Arab states did not alter Moscow's conviction that, according to the CIA, 'Soviet interests in the area are best served by an alignment with radical Arab forces'.[130] Although Soviet prestige had suffered with the outcome of the war, Moscow helped to bolster the more intransigent aspects of its clients' policies. This was apparent with the Arab proclamation of the three 'no's' – 'no peace with Israel, no negotiation with Israel, no recognition of Israel' – at the Khartoum summit in August 1967. UN Security Council Resolution 242 a few months later spoke of 'a just and lasting peace', 'secure and recognised boundaries', Israeli withdrawal 'from territories occupied in the recent conflict' and the 'sovereignty, territorial integrity and political independence of all states'. The Resolution was acceptable to each party largely because of its ambiguity. For example, Israel took 'secure and recognised boundaries' to mean the newly captured territories, while Egypt and Jordan interpreted 'withdrawal from territories occupied in the recent conflict' to require withdrawal from the same territory.[131]

The intractability of some of the problems the Johnson Administration had to address in the Middle East was also shown by the fact that late in 1967 Washington had to dissuade the Turks once more from invading Cyprus, and in 1973 President Nixon had to deal with another Arab–Israeli war. In part due to intensified US support for Israel, the prospect of a superpower conflict was much higher than it had been in 1967, and the Administration took the decision to place US nuclear forces in a heightened state of alert. The following year the Cyprus issue blew up, when Turkey seized control of more than a third of the island.

NOTES

1. Arlene Lazarowitz, 'Different Approaches to a Regional Search for Balance: The Johnson Administration, the State Department and the Middle East, 1964–1967', *Diplomatic History*, 32, 1 (January 2008), p. 30.

2. See Hubert Faustmann, 'Independence postponed: Cyprus 1959–1960', and Joseph J. Joseph, 'The Political Context and Consequences of the London and Zurich Agreements', in Hubert Faustmann and Nicos Peristianis (eds), *Britain in Cyprus: Colonialism and Post-Colonialism* (Mannheim and Mohnesee: Bibliopolis, 2006), pp. 453–72 and pp. 413–30 respectively.

3. The National Archives, Kew, Surrey (hereafter TNA), FO 371/174750, 'Cyprus: Sir Arthur Clark's Valedictory Despatch', 12 May 1964.

4. George W. Ball, *The Past Has Another Pattern: Memoirs* (New York: Norton, 1982), p. 338; Press and radio briefing, 18 February 1964, *Foreign Relations of the United States* (hereafter *FRUS*) *1964–1968 XXXIII Organization and Management of Foreign Policy; United Nations* (Washington, DC: USGPO, 2004), pp. 987–8.

5. Meeting between Ball, Ormsby-Gore et al., 29 January 1964, *FRUS 1964–1968 XXXIII*, p. 954.

6. Mission to the UN to State, 25 January 1964, *FRUS 1964–1968 XXXIII*, p. 947.

7. Komer to Johnson, 5 February 1964, *FRUS 1964–1968 XXXIII*, p. 965.

8. Johnson–Ball telephone conversation, 25 January 1964, *FRUS 1964–1968 XVI Cyprus; Greece; Turkey* (2000), p. 3.

9. Michael R. Beschloss (ed.), *Taking Charge: The Johnson White House Tapes, 1963–1964* (New York: Simon and Schuster, 1997), p. 191.

10. Lyndon B. Johnson, *The Vantage Point: Perspectives of the Presidency 1963–1969* (New York: Holt, Rinehart, Winston, 1971), pp. 47, 422.

11. Komer memorandum, 28 January 1964, *FRUS 1964–1968 XXXIII*, p. 952.

12. Richard Aldrich, *The Hidden Hand: Britain, America and Cold War Secret Intelligence* (London: John Murray, 2001), p. 579.

13. Meeting with Johnson, 25 January 1964, *FRUS 1964–1968 XVI*, p. 7.

14. CIA report, 9 April 1965, *FRUS 1964–1968 XIV Soviet Union* (2001), pp. 282–3.

15. Meeting with Johnson, 25 January 1964, *FRUS 1964–1968 XVI*, p. 6.

16. TNA, FO 371/174746, Washington to FO, 24 January 1964.

17. Chiefs of Staff to McNamara, undated, *FRUS 1964–1968 XXXIII*, p. 964.

18. Meeting with Johnson, 25 January 1964, *FRUS 1964–1968 XVI*, pp. 6–7.

19. Komer memorandum, 28 January 1964, *FRUS 1964–1968 XXXIII*, p. 952.

20. Komer to Johnson, 5 February 1964, *FRUS 1964–1968 XXXIII*, p. 965.

21. Beschloss (ed.), *Taking Charge*, p. 191.

22. Editorial note, *FRUS 1964–1968 XVI*, p. 8.

23. Ball, *The Past Has Another Pattern*, p. 341.

24. TNA, FO 371/174746, Dodson memorandum, 29 January 1964.

25. Ball, *The Past Has Another Pattern*, p. 342; Memorandum for the record, 17 February 1964, *FRUS 1964–1968 XXXIII*, p. 985.

26. Mission to the UN to State, 25 January 1964, *FRUS 1964–1968 XXXIII*, p. 949.

27. Intelligence cable, 31 January 1964, *FRUS 1964–1968 XXXIII*, p. 962.

28. Embassy Cyprus to State, 1:45 a.m., 13 February 1964, *FRUS 1964–1968 XVI*, pp. 22–3.

29. Embassy Cyprus to State, 10:40 p.m., 13 February 1964, *FRUS 1964–1968 XXXIII*, p. 982.

30. Johnson–Ball telephone conversation, 9 August 1964, *FRUS 1964–1968 XVI*, p. 234.

31. Embassy Turkey to State, 4 June 1964, *FRUS 1964–1968 XVI*, pp. 103–4.

32. Embassy Cyprus to State, 6 June 1964, *FRUS 1964–1968 XVI*, p. 112.

33. Rusk–Menemencioglu telephone conversation, 4 June 1964, *FRUS 1964–1968 XVI*, p. 105.

34. Johnson to Inonu, 5 June 1964, *FRUS 1964–1968 XVI*, pp. 107–10.

35. Henry A. Kissinger, *Years of Renewal* (London: Weidenfeld and Nicolson, 1999), pp. 200–1.

36. Ball, *The Past Has Another Pattern*, p. 350.

37. Meeting between Johnson, Bundy et al., 17 February 1964, *FRUS 1964–1968 XXXIII*, p. 985.

38. Embassy Turkey to State, 5 June 1964, *FRUS 1964–1968 XVI*, p. 111.

39. Ball to Johnson, 11 June 1964, *FRUS 1964–1968 XVI*, pp. 132–4.

40. See memorandum of conversation, 22 June 1964, *FRUS 1964–1968 XVI*, pp. 146–51.

41. Meeting between Johnson, Papandreou et al., 24 June 1964, *FRUS 1964–1968 XVI*, p. 117.

42. State to Embassy Greece, 1 July 1964, *FRUS 1964–1968 XVI*, pp. 170–1.

43. Embassy Greece to State, 2 July 1964, *FRUS 1964–1968 XVI*, p. 172.

44. Embassy Greece to State, 19 July 1964, *FRUS 1964–1968 XVI*, p. 187.

45. TNA, FO 371/174775, Dodson memorandum, 8 January 1965.

46. NSC meeting, 7 July 1964, *FRUS 1964–1968 XVI*, p. 174.

47. H. W. Brands, *The Wages of Globalism: Lyndon Johnson and the Limits of American Power* (New York: Oxford University Press, 1995), p. 77.
48. Ball, *The Past Has Another Pattern*, p. 357.
49. Brands, *The Wages of Globalism*, p. 78.
50. Embassy Cyprus to State, 9 August 1964, *FRUS 1964–1968 XVI*, p. 238.
51. Note 2, *FRUS 1964–1968 XVI*, p. 241.
52. Meeting between Johnson et al., 10 August 1964, *FRUS 1964–1968 XVI*, p. 245.
53. Ball, *The Past Has Another Pattern*, pp. 358–9.
54. State to Mission in Geneva, 15 August 1964, *FRUS 1964–1968 XVI*, p. 255.
55. TNA, FO 371/174775, Dodson memorandum, 8 January 1965.
56. Memorandum for the record, 8 September 1964, *FRUS 1964–1968 XVI*, pp. 308–9; Brands, *The Wages of Globalism*, pp. 80–2.
57. Johnson, *The Vantage Point*, p. 287.
58. Douglas Little, 'Choosing Sides: Lyndon Johnson and the Middle East', in Robert A. Divine (ed.), *The Johnson Years: LBJ at Home and Abroad* (Lawrence, KS: University Press of Kansas, 1994), p. 152.
59. Beschloss (ed.), *Taking Charge*, p. 189.
60. Johnson to Eshkol, 2 January 1964, *FRUS 1964–1968 XVIII Arab-Israeli Dispute 1964–1967* (2000), p. 1.
61. Douglas Little, 'A Fool's Errand: America and the Middle East', in Diane B. Kunz (ed.), *The Diplomacy of the Crucial Decade: American Foreign Relations During the 1960s* (New York: Columbia University Press, 1994), p. 292.
62. Saunders to Rostow, 16 May 1967, *FRUS 1964–1968 XXI Near East Region; Arab Peninsula* (2000), p. 44.
63. See Abraham Ben-Zvi, 'Influence and Arms: John F. Kennedy, Lyndon B. Johnson and the Politics of Arms Sales to Israel, 1962–1966', *Israel Affairs*, 10, 1 & 2 (January 2004), pp. 29–59.
64. Komer to Johnson, 8 February 1966, *FRUS 1964–1968 XVIII*, p. 544.
65. Conversation between Bundy, Harman et al., 10 January 1964, *FRUS 1964–1968 XVIII*, p. 14.
66. NSC memo to Johnson, 19 October 1964, *FRUS 1964–1968 XVIII*, pp. 226–9.
67. Komer to Johnson, 8 February 1966, *FRUS 1964–1968 XVIII*, pp. 544, 545.
68. Johnson to Eshkol, 19 March 1964, *FRUS 1964–1968 XVIII*, p. 73.
69. Rostow to Johnson, 5 January 1968, *FRUS 1964–1968 XX Arab-Israeli Dispute, 1967–1968* (2001), p. 64.
70. Jeffrey T. Richelson, *Spying on the Bomb: American Nuclear Intelligence from Nazi Germany to Iran and North Korea* (New York: Norton, 2007), pp. 236–43.
71. Katzenbach to Johnson, 1 May 1967, *FRUS 1964–1968 XVIII*, p. 815.
72. Patrick Tyler, *A World of Trouble: America in the Middle East* (London: Portobello, 2009), p. 66.
73. Robert Dallek, *Flawed Giant: Lyndon Johnson and his Times, 1961–1973* (New York: Oxford University Press, 1998), p. 429.
74. Rostow to Johnson, 5 January 1968, *FRUS 1964–1968 XX*, p. 64.
75. Johnson, *The Vantage Point*, p. 289.
76. Clea Lutz Bunch, 'Strike at Samu: Jordan, Israel, the United States, and the Origins of the Six-Day War', *Diplomatic History*, 32, 1 (January 2008), pp. 55–6.
77. Johnson to Nasser, 13 August 1964, *FRUS 1964–1968 XVIII*, p. 206.
78. State to Embassy Cairo, 27 November 1964, *FRUS 1964–1968 XVIII*, pp. 242–3.

79. Association of Diplomatic Studies and Training, Arlington, Virginia (ADST), Foreign Affairs Oral History Project, Assistant Secretary Lucius D. Battle, interviewed by Paige E. Mulhollan, 14 November 1968.
80. CIA memorandum, 28 May 1966, *FRUS 1964–1968 XVIII*, pp. 590–1.
81. Lazarowitz, 'Different Approaches to a Regional Search for Balance', p. 44.
82. Embassy Damascus to State, 1 June 1967, *FRUS 1964–1968 XIX Arab-Israeli Crisis and War, 1967* (2004), p. 215.
83. Lazarowitz, 'Different Approaches to a Regional Search for Balance', p. 30. For Acheson's comment, see Rostow's recollections of 5 June 1967, 17 November 1967, *FRUS 1964–1968 XIX*, p. 291.
84. State to Certain Posts, 7 April 1967, *FRUS 1964–1968 XVIII*, pp. 789–90.
85. Embassy Portugal to State, 2 June 1967, *FRUS 1964–1968 XIX*, p. 233.
86. Kent to Helms, 26 May 1967, *FRUS 1964–1968 XIX*, pp. 149–50.
87. Walt W. Rostow, *The Diffusion of Power: An Essay in Recent History* (New York: Macmillan, 1972), p. 416.
88. Kent to Helms, 26 May 1967, *FRUS 1964–1968 XIX*, pp. 148–9.
89. Memorandum from Contingency Work Group on Military Planning to Middle East Control Group, 4 June 1967, *FRUS 1964–1968 XIX*, p. 282.
90. Johnson, *The Vantage Point*, p. 288.
91. Editorial note, *FRUS 1964–1968 XIX*, p. 80.
92. Johnson, *The Vantage Point*, p. 291.
93. Conversation between Rusk, Thomson et al., 24 May 1967, *FRUS 1964–1968 XIX*, pp. 85–7.
94. Note 4, *FRUS 1964–1968 XIX*, p. 73.
95. Michael B. Oren, *Six Days of War: June 1967 and the Making of the Modern Middle East* (New York: Oxford, 2002), p. 197.
96. Conversation between Johnson, Eban et al., 26 May 1966, *FRUS 1964–1968 XIX*, pp. 142–5.
97. Randall B. Woods, *LBJ: Architect of American Ambitions* (New York: Free Press, 1996), p. 775; meeting on the Arab–Israeli Crisis, 26 May 1967, *FRUS 1964–1968 XIX*, p. 136.
98. Meeting of the Middle East Control Group, 4 June 1967, *FRUS 1964–1968 XIX*, pp. 283–4.
99. Saunders to Rostow, 31 May 1967, *FRUS 1964–1968 XIX*, p. 210.
100. Interview with William Norris Dale in Dayton Mak and Charles Stuart Kennedy (eds), *American Ambassadors in a Troubled World: Interviews with Senior Diplomats* (Westport, CT and London: Greenwood, 1992), p. 112.
101. Conversation between Harman, Rusk et al., 2 June 1967, *FRUS 1964–1968 XIX*, p. 249; Little, 'A Fool's Errand', in Kunz (ed.), *The Diplomacy of the Crucial Decade*, pp. 302–3.
102. Rostow to Johnson, 2 June 1967, *FRUS 1964–1968 XIX*, pp. 244–5.
103. Little, 'A Fool's Errand', in Kunz (ed.), *The Diplomacy of the Crucial Decade*, p. 303.
104. Tyler, *A World of Trouble*, p. 93.
105. Stansfield Turner, *Burn Before Reading: Presidents, CIA Directors and Secret Intelligence* (New York: Hyperion, 2005), p. 119.
106. Tyler, *A World of Trouble*, p. 94.
107. NSC meeting, 7 June 1967, *FRUS 1964–1968 XIX*, pp. 347–8.
108. Tyler, *A World of Trouble*, p. 95.

109. Rostow's recollections of 5 June 1967, 17 November 1967, *FRUS 1964–1968* XIX, p. 288.

110. Quoted in Peter L. Hahn, 'An Ominous Moment: Lyndon Johnson and the Six-Day War', in Mitchell B. Lerner (ed.), *Looking Back at LBJ: White House Politics in a New Light* (Lawrence, KS: University Press of Kansas, 2005), p. 89; State to Arab capitals, *FRUS 1964–1968* XIX, p. 267.

111. Rostow's recollections of 5 June 1967, 17 November 1967, *FRUS 1964–1968* XIX, p. 288.

112. Kosygin to Johnson, 8 June 1967, *FRUS 1964–1968* XIX, p. 365.

113. Editorial note, *FRUS 1964–1968* XIX, pp. 311–12.

114. Little, 'A Fool's Errand', in Kunz (ed.), *The Diplomacy of the Crucial Decade*, pp. 303–4.

115. Thomas R. Johnson, *American Cryptology During the Cold War 1945–1989 Book II, Centralization Wins, 1960–1972* (National Security Agency, 1995), pp. 432–3. See also Matthew M. Aid, *The Secret Sentry: The Untold History of the National Security Agency* (New York: Bloomsbury, 2009), pp. 138–40.

116. Clark M. Clifford with Richard Holbrooke, *Counsel to the President: A Memoir* (New York: Random House, 1991), pp. 445–6.

117. Rusk to Harman, 10 June 1967, *FRUS 1964–1968* XIX, pp. 424–5.

118. PFIAB memorandum, 18 July 1967, *FRUS 1964–1968* XIX, p. 682.

119. Woods, *LBJ*, p. 781.

120. John Dumbrell, *President Lyndon Johnson and Soviet Communism* (Manchester: Manchester University Press, 2004), p. 159.

121. Conversation between Thompson and Davis, 4 November 1967, *FRUS 1964–1968* XIX, p. 411.

122. Dumbrell, *President Lyndon Johnson and Soviet Communism*, pp. 160–1.

123. Aid, *The Secret Sentry*, p. 139.

124. Dumbrell, *President Lyndon Johnson and Soviet Communism*, p. 161.

125. CIA analysis, 10 August 1967, *FRUS 1964–1968* XIX, pp. 771–2.

126. Ball, *The Past Has Another Pattern*, p. 359, citing Edward Weintal and Charles Bartlett, *Facing the Brink: An Intimate Study of Crisis Diplomacy* (New York: Scribners, 1967), p. 36.

127. Komer to Bundy, 15 February 1964, *FRUS 1964–1968* XXXIII, p. 983.

128. Monteagle Stearns, *Entangled Allies: US Policy Towards Greece, Turkey and Cyprus* (New York: Council on Foreign Relations, 1992), p. 36.

129. Ibid., p. 38; Nasuh Uslu, *The Cyprus Question as an Issue of Turkish Foreign Policy and Turkish-American Relations, 1959–2003* (New York: Nova, 2003), pp. 45–53.

130. CIA analysis, 13 July 1967, *FRUS 1964–1968* XIX, p. 651.

131. Henry A. Kissinger, *The White House Years* (London: Weidenfeld and Nicolson, 1979), pp. 344–5.

CHAPTER EIGHT

The Western Hemisphere: The Alliance for Progress, Cuba and the Dominican Republic

The United States had claimed a special relationship with Latin America since the early nineteenth century, when the Monroe Doctrine warned European powers from interference in the region. Since then Washington had asserted a protective relationship towards the Latin American nations, and by the time Lyndon Johnson came to power in 1964 a connective web of treaties and organisations known as the 'Inter-American System' had been woven. The web included the Organization of American States (OAS), the Rio Pact and the Alliance for Progress. Geography, ties of tradition and association, the widespread acceptance of the idea of community, and the formal international arrangements and commitments all meant that the United States was seen as heavily responsible for major developments in the Western Hemisphere.[1] There were, moreover, good reasons, from Washington's perspective, why it was in the interests of the United States to maintain close connections with Latin America. These included the region's major participation in US foreign trade; the need for diplomatic support; and Latin America's long-range development potential – the region possessed 11 per cent of the world's land area, major natural resources and a burgeoning population.[2] Furthermore, there was a particular concern in the wake of Fidel Castro's overthrow of the pro-American dictatorship in Cuba in 1959, his cementing of ties with the Soviet Union and his efforts to foster communism in the Western Hemisphere. The fear of communism was a pervasive influence on American policy in the region.

President Johnson, according to Lincoln Gordon, who ran the Alliance for Progress from 1966 to 1967, had 'a personal interest in Latin America which went way back to his early days in Texas as a young man. That experience gave him this very warm attitude, which was not purely vote-catching, directed toward the Chicanos.'[3] At the same time, Johnson was, at least in the first year or two in office, concerned not to make what he felt were unwarranted concessions in diplomacy and, whenever justified, he wanted to make Latin America a demonstration of his resolve and toughness in foreign policy: 'I know these Latin Americans . . . They'll come right into your yard and take it over if you let them.'[4] This chapter explores three issues. The first issue is Johnson's involvement in the Alliance for Progress, a US-sponsored body set up by John F. Kennedy in 1961 to foster political and economic modernisation in Latin America. Johnson had a less expansive vision of the Alliance than did the Kennedy Administration, preferring to prioritise economic modernisation over political reform, and while the organisation's achievements under him were by no means spectacular they were not insignificant either. Another topic to be examined is the Cuban challenge to the US naval base at Guantánamo early in 1964, at the very outset of Johnson's time in office. Although perceiving the challenge as a test of his mettle, the President dealt with the crisis with proportionality and restraint. The following year, fears of communist encroachment led the President to order military intervention in the Dominican Republic, whose government had fallen in a left-wing rebellion. Heightened sensitivities over Cuba meant that his fears of communism gaining a foothold were exaggerated, although not wholly far-fetched. Over the longer term the intervention played an important role in fostering constitutional government in the Republic.

THE ALLIANCE FOR PROGRESS

The Alliance for Progress was born to considerable fanfare and was an organisation in which liberals invested high hopes. Washington's thinking behind establishing the Alliance was to make Latin America less vulnerable to the sort of revolutionary upheaval that had struck Cuba. At the inter-American conference at Punta del Este in Uruguay in 1961, the United States pledged that over $20 billion of capital (mainly in the form of loans) from the United States and international organisations would be invested across Latin America over the next decade. During a reception in the White House for Latin American representatives a few days after he had become President, Johnson announced that relations with the Western Hemisphere would be 'among the highest concerns of my Government'. He was determined to 'improve and strengthen the role of the United States' to make the Alliance for Progress a 'living memorial' to the late President Kennedy.[5] According to Lincoln Gordon, Johnson had a particular sympathy with helping to provide electric lighting, clean water and schools in Latin America, because his modest Texan background made him 'much closer to the soil, so to speak, and to poverty than Kennedy'.[6] Johnson's priority therefore was to raise living standards by means of various New Deal-type measures, rather than pursuing political reform. He recognised that pressure for political reform sat uneasily with the need for close alliances in an important region.[7] The President's enthusiasm for the Alliance for Progress was generally limited. It was after all a Kennedy brainchild, and Johnson never felt much warmth for any international body: these 'international organisations ain't worth a damn, except window dressing'.[8] He also felt that the Alliance was badly administered, stating bluntly that it was 'being run by an alliance of misfits'.[9]

THOMAS MANN

To help improve the running of the Alliance, in January 1964 the President appointed Thomas Mann, a fellow Texan and former Ambassador to Mexico, to the post of Undersecretary of State for Inter-American Affairs and Coordinator of the Alliance for Progress. According to Gordon, Mann was sceptical about the Alliance, considering that it was just 'the enthusiasm of a bunch of political newcomers that don't really know Latin America the way we do'.[10] For Gordon, such a view was fair:

> If you'd worked mainly on Central America or Panama, or to a considerable extent Mexico, you had a lot of reason to be rather callous, to be hardened about corruption, the absence of any deep-rooted democratic cultural roots, and to be sceptical about the possibilities of rapid economic, political and social evolution of Latin American societies along the lines called for by the Alliance for Progress.[11]

There was some liberal controversy about Mann's appointment, with Johnson noting that 'We've got a little flak from [former Kennedy aide] Arthur M. Schlesinger and maybe [Ambassador at Large] Averell Harriman on Mann . . .' For the President, objections to Mann from liberal sources were to be expected, because the new appointee was unlikely to 'spend money quite as fast as they want him to'.[12] There was a minor storm when during a conference for American ambassadors and Agency for International Development (AID) administrators Mann seemed to suggest abandoning Kennedy's policy of trying to deter dictators.[13] Mann's comments did not cause President Johnson much grief, and generally he felt that the appointment would further American interests because 'everybody in Latin America is scared of this fellow Mann . . . because he's a tough guy'.[14] Mann was succeeded, though, in 1966 by Lincoln Gordon and then in 1967 by Corey Oliver, which meant that the Alliance for Progress would bear the influence of other leaders.

THE PUNTA DEL ESTE SUMMIT

In March 1964 Johnson began efforts to reaffirm the ideals of the Alliance for Progress,[15] but later felt he had not been given his due – in part because of how Vietnam came to overshadow foreign policies in other regions. In August 1965 he told Mann that he wanted 'a real good announcement' to the effect that he had taken and continued to take an active personal interest in the affairs of the Hemisphere.[16] Scepticism toward the Alliance for Progress aside, that interest was real. By early 1967, one official could write that Johnson had 'paid probably more personal attention to Latin America than probably any other President – the record of speeches, ceremonies, lunches, dinners, visits, boat rides, special delegations, personal letters, congratulatory messages, funeral planes, etc., is ample evidence'. Unfortunately, the political capital accruing from such efforts was limited, because Johnson had 'image problems . . . He does not project the sparkling intellectual image of Kennedy – young, scholarly, pretty wife, small children, Catholic, etc. – which so appeals to the Latins.' There was also the problem that President Johnson's image was tainted in some eyes by 'the distasteful – but necessary – job of sending troops into the [Dominican Republic in 1965] and of fighting the nasty war in Vietnam with all the "egghead" criticism that it has brought'.[17]

Prior to becoming Johnson's National Security Adviser in 1966, Walt Rostow was the US representative to the Inter-American Committee on the Alliance for Progress. Partly due to Rostow's promptings, the issue of regional economic integration became increasingly prominent and led to a summit meeting with Latin American leaders under the Organization of American States at Punta del Este in April 1967. As the summit approached, President Johnson sought an American contribution of up to $500 million to a fund that would ease some of the strains imposed by the development of a Latin American Common Market. He wanted $150 million to lodge with the Inter-American Bank for multinational projects that would foster growing physical and economic integration among the Latin American nations.[18] Johnson also requested a joint resolution prior to the conference. The House approved a modified version of Johnson's request for funds, but the Senate Foreign Relations Committee rejected the resolution, opting instead for its own resolution. The President, grappling with challenges that included the Vietnam War and Congressional pressure to pull troops out of Europe, did not push his relationship with Congress over the Alliance for Progress, and went to Punta del Este without a formal declaration of Congressional support.[19]

Johnson understood that aid to developing regions could accrue long-term political and economic benefits to the United States and was not averse to high-spending internationalist reform measures, but, as an incident at the summit revealed, ingratitude from aid recipients angered him. Experts from the Alliance had advised that Ecuador should raise taxes and raise more local currency before being granted loans to improve its transportation system. President Otto Arosemana struggled to get the tax increase, and decided to use the conference as a forum for criticising the United States, arguing that Washington was far too sparing.[20] Johnson told Arosemana to

> consider a hypothetical situation in which Ecuador would have to assist the poor people of the United States, and in which after taxing humble Ecuadorans heavily to obtain the assistance to send to the United States, the Americans would express their dissatisfaction and their President would say in a public meeting that assistance from Ecuador was insufficient, was slow because of red tape, and therefore was unacceptable.[21]

Minor irritations aside, the US President could consider the summit a success. The State Department noted that the summit communiqué, the 'Declaration of Presidents of America', was the 'product of a painstaking and long preparatory process in which every signatory government . . . was deeply involved' and went 'beyond what might reasonably have been expected a year ago'. The communiqué included a much stronger Latin American commitment to a Common Market than had seemed likely a year or so earlier; a greater focus on multinational projects to facilitate integration; more emphasis on important areas such as agriculture, education, science and technology; a statement on limiting military spending (although this was weaker than the Administration preferred); increased US assistance to Latin America; and a willingness on the part of the industrialised countries to consult on tariffs in favour of developing countries. It was also the case that 'personal relationships developed among Presidents were in almost all cases very satisfactory and should be helpful in future'.[22] Later, Congress voted appropriations to back a substantial portion of the programme that Johnson had outlined in March, just prior to the conference.[23] The summit was also beneficial for Johnson in that, according to Dean Rusk, it balanced how 'our own people have been hearing almost nothing else but Viet-Nam, President de Gaulle and China'.[24]

FAILURES AND SUCCESSES FOR THE ALLIANCE FOR PROGRESS

Yet there were limits to what the Alliance might have achieved in the Johnson years. Latin American difficulties such as high birth-rates, urban unemployment and the backwardness of rural society were deep rooted. The prospects of economic integration were overshadowed by inflation, nationalism and instability.[25] Reuben Sternfield, who worked for AID from 1961 and then joined the Inter-American Development Bank, noted in relation to the problem of instability that 'The countries changed governments, sometimes every six months, or every year. Very few governments lasted two years, [and there were] military takeovers, all of that on the one side.'[26] American economic aid proved less bountiful than the Kennedy Administration had envisaged. An analysis for President Nixon in 1969 noted that although the United States had 'formally met its Charter commitments . . . our net capital transfer to Latin America has been much less than the over $10 billion gross, and its impact on growth has been further reduced by US legal and policy constraints'.[27]

There were successes for the Alliance under Johnson nonetheless. The Economic and Social Act of Rio de Janeiro of November 1965 extended the life of the Alliance beyond its original ten-year span. The duration of the Alliance was very much a concern of Johnson, who considered the proposed duration of ten years to be insufficient – he told Milton Barall, Rostow's assistant on the Inter-American Committee on the Alliance, that there should be 'no calendar end to the program'.[28] Johnson succeeded in voicing the need for Latin America to do most of the work in meeting the challenges of the region, and, correspondingly, in facilitating the adoption by the United States of a more junior and less paternalistic role in Latin American affairs. This befitted the multilateral character of the Alliance for Progress, and was reflected in the principle of 'mutual aid' provided for in the Economic and Social Act of 1965. Mutual aid meant that the more advanced countries of the region (excluding the United States) undertook an obligation towards the less advanced ones.[29]

According to Deputy AID Administrator Rutherford M. Poats, the Alliance for Progress had 'a significant impact on reorienting political priorities . . . to development . . . at the end of about six years, it was fair to say that the Alliance had become truly an alliance for progress'.[30] Reuben Sternfield noted that the Alliance 'started some institutions which didn't exist before', such as 'water systems which were not just for the elite'. He noted how US aid helped to boost higher education in countries such as Ecuador, thereby 'producing trained people' necessary for national development.[31] Some of the statistics were creditable: official lending to Latin America, for example, rose from $981 million in 1963 to $1.7 billion in 1968. The average rate of growth of Latin American GDP rose from 2.5 per cent in 1965 to 3.7 per cent per annum in 1969 (although how far the United States contributed to this growth cannot be measured).[32]

But although aid to Latin America continued, the Nixon Administration chose not to refer to the Alliance for Progress, and efforts began in 1976 to bring the organisation to a formal end.[33]

CUBA

Since obtaining its independence after the Spanish–American war of 1898, Cuba had been a bastion of American influence. However, the seizure of power by Fidel Castro in 1959 saw the country building links with the Soviet Union. Washington, ruing the emergence of a communist beachhead so close to home, sought to isolate the new regime diplomatically and economically, as well as to implement a range of covert actions to undermine Castro. The most high-profile of these 'covert' actions was the Bay of Pigs invasion in April 1961, in which thousands of armed Cuban émigrés were rapidly defeated and captured, and whose sponsorship by the United States soon became clear. Apart from the sheer embarrassment for the Kennedy Administration, the event encouraged the Soviets to station nuclear missiles on the island to protect their ally. The stand-off with the United States in October 1962, the infamous Cuban Missile Crisis, is widely regarded as one of the most dangerous moments of the Cold War. In return for the missiles' withdrawal, Washington pledged in secret that there would be no future invasion of Cuba, and agreed to withdraw some US missiles from Turkey.[34] In contrast to his stance towards the Soviet Union, Johnson showed little dispensation to adopt a more conciliatory course towards Cuba, plumping instead for a strategy of isolating Cuba with the OAS, and strengthening the Free World embargo against Cuba. It was hoped that such an approach would destroy the regime, despite the danger in the short- to medium-term of strengthening Havana's reliance on Moscow. Thomas Mann concluded early in 1964, however, that Cuba was not a vital Soviet interest, and argued that Castro represented 'a successful defiance of the United States, a negation of our whole hemispheric policy of almost a century and a half'.[35]

American policymakers, including Johnson, were especially concerned about Cuba's efforts to export revolution and to establish allies across the region. In 1963, for example, some 4,600 Latin Americans visited the island to receive what the CIA described as 'formal indoctrination'. The CIA suggested that 'several hundred of these probably received training in the techniques of guerrilla warfare and urban terrorism'.[36] The following year it was noted that over a hundred members of the terrorist organisation known as the Armed Forces for National Liberation (FALN) in Venezuela had received paramilitary training in Cuba and elsewhere in the communist bloc. Cuban broadcasts to Venezuela endorsing the FALN's cause had boosted the insurgents' morale.[37] Johnson raised the issue of Cuban subversion at the June 1967 Glassboro summit with the Soviet leader Alexei Kosygin (see Chapter Six), stating that, in his own words, the Cubans were 'giving us hell in the Dominican Republic, and Haiti, and Bolivia, and half a dozen places'.[38] Moscow's influence was limited, however. Thomas Hughes of the State Department's Intelligence and Research Department suggested that Moscow was 'engaged in an effort to show its interest in Latin America and the revolutionary struggle there, without actually committing itself to give material assistance to Latin American guerillas'. The CIA reported that when Kosygin visited Havana after the Glassboro summit, he did tell Castro to back away from regional revolution. Castro accused him of leading a country that had 'turned its back upon its own revolutionary tradition'.[39] The following year, Havana was appalled at the Soviet invasion of Czechoslovakia.[40]

The issue of Cuban subversion gradually subsided, not least as a result of the death of the Cuban revolutionary Ernesto 'Che' Guevara in Bolivia late in 1967 at the hands of Bolivian troops. Bolivian counterinsurgency efforts had in fact drawn on covert US support.[41] According to Walt Rostow, Guevara had been Castro's 'leading guerrilla fighter and guerrilla theoretician'. According to the CIA, the Bolivian guerrilla movement was 'a Cuban show designed to spark a movement of continental magnitude', creating 'a Vietnam out of South America'.[42] Hughes suggested that Guevara's death was a major setback to Castro's hopes of exporting revolution across Latin America.[43] Supporters of covert action could point to the Bolivian example to show how it could benefit American interests at small cost.

THE GUANTÁNAMO CRISIS

It was some time earlier though that Cuba had reached its greatest prominence in the mind of President Johnson. On Sunday, 2 February 1964, a US Coast Guard vessel spotted four Cuban fishing boats just off the American coast in the Florida Keys. Thirty-six Cuban fishermen were turned over to the authorities in Florida for possible prosecution under State law, while two others appealed for, and gained, political asylum. Although the President's initial response to the event was that 'it doesn't amount to much one way or the other',[44] he soon concluded that 'the incursion of the Cuban boats was a deliberate provocation'. The captains of the vessels had been told that they were on a 'historic venture'.[45] Johnson shared the view of Thomas Mann that the Soviet Union was using Castro to test the mettle of the new President, noting on 7 February that he had told his advisers to 'get ahold of Khrushchev and tell him that [Castro]'s playing a mighty dangerous game with his marbles'.[46] There is little evidence that Khrushchev had much to do with it, though; as was seen earlier, Castro's ties with Moscow had their limits, and Soviet influence in the Western Hemisphere was if anything a conservative one.

The absence of direct diplomatic links between the United States and Cuba made communications between the two countries circuitous. On 4 February, the Czech Embassy in Washington protested about the capture of the fishermen, while the Swiss Embassy in Havana delivered an American protest about the violation of US territorial waters by Cuban vessels. The next day, the Cuban government told the Swiss Ambassador in Washington that it was cutting off the water supply to the American naval base in Guantánamo, Cuba, in retaliation.[47] The United States had leased the base since 1903, at the end of a five-year period of military occupation of the island. The question was how best to respond, beyond merely supplying the base with water from tankers.

On 7 February Johnson met twice with his advisers, stating at the end of the inconclusive first meeting that he wanted 'every man in the room to spend the rest of this day in hard study of every possible action that is available to us, short of war'.[48] Johnson emphatically did not want to take military action against Cuba, but he felt that a resolute stance was required. He was dismayed by what he regarded as the 'innocuous' counsel he had received: only Secretary of Defense Robert McNamara and Thomas Mann had 'guts'.[49] These two men felt that, in Mann's words, it was 'not wise to merely respond by using our own water. We want to do much more than that.'[50] The second meeting also featured some of the more 'innocuous' counsel that Johnson derided. In connection with one of the policy options, Attorney General Robert Kennedy made

> a very strong objection to the dismissal of Base employees on the grounds that it was (a) it was an overreaction to Castro's move and (b) it hurt the wrong Cubans who by and large had been loyal Base employees, some for more than a generation.[51]

DCI John McCone concurred with these points, and added that 'other countries might fear a similar action in the event of our disagreement with them'.[52]

However, Johnson chose to implement the stronger response not only of providing the base with a self-sufficient fresh water supply, but of dismissing all the 3,000 or so Cubans who worked on the base. The dismissal of these employees entailed a foreign revenue loss for the Cuban economy of up to $8,000,000 per year,[53] and was consistent with the policy of trying to isolate Cuba economically. The mass dismissal also seemed to have the added effect of undermining Castro's standing among his people. The President stated that 'when we fired 500 the first damned day, every one of them went bellyaching' to the Cuban leader about losing their jobs, blaming him for what had happened. Security concerns were another reason to fire the Cuban employees; he told Senator Richard Russell that the Guantánamo base had had 'over 300 known subversives'.[54] While the figure might be open to dispute, the notion that a significant proportion of the employees at the American base were reporting to the Cuban security services was a plausible one.

Moreover, there were public relations reasons behind Johnson's resolute stand, including his concern with perceptions across Latin America: 'if we get soft with them [the Cubans] . . . and everybody else will start kicking us in the pants 'cause they think they can'.[55] At this early stage in his Presidency, Johnson was anxious to prove to both international and domestic observers his ability to stand up for American interests. Richard Russell explained to Johnson in vivid terms that within Congress

> they're just tired of Castro urinating on us and getting away with it. They don't like the smell of it any longer and they just want to sort of show that we are taking such steps as are within our power without involving the shedding of a lot of blood . . .[56]

Fortunately, the crisis over Guantánamo was short-lived, in part because, to his credit, Fidel Castro's stance was generally restrained. According to McCone, his radio and television 'broadcasts are mild . . . not so nearly hysterical as was anticipated'.[57] As Johnson surmised, Castro 'wants Guantánamo, but he wants it peacefully'.[58] The Cuban leader's unwillingness to up the ante may even have stemmed from his desire to see Johnson rather than the Republican candidate succeed in the presidential election planned for later in the year.[59] On 13 February, Castro stated that he would resume the supply of water to the Guantánamo base as soon as the Cuban fishermen were released. A week later, the Florida court that had been hearing the case of the Cuban fishermen dropped all the charges against the crews but levied fines on the captains. All were released and sailed home. Castro ordered the return of the water supply, but by now it was superfluous because water was being shipped in.[60]

One close observer commended Johnson's handling of the February 1964 crisis with Cuba. John Hugh Crimmins, who was the Coordinator of Cuban Affairs in the State Department, noted that the President was 'not at all interested in posturing or taking a dramatic stand on this issue.

I was very impressed by his restraint . . . He didn't act like a president whose mettle was being tested and felt that he had to be very macho about this.'[61] By contrast, evidence cited earlier indicated that Johnson did consider that he was being tested and feared appearing soft. Yet his response to the Cuban action was still a reasonable one. He recognised that the employment of the Cubans was a holdover from the days when Cuba had a friendly government and as such was anomalous. Exploiting Cuban vulnerability in this manner was proportionate with how the Cubans had exploited American vulnerability over the water supply to Guantánamo. Furthermore, the construction of a desalination plant by December 1964 meant that Castro was no longer in a position to turn off the water. This meant that within less than a year of the crisis, the Guantánamo base was operating without dependence on Cuba for either water or manpower.[62] In October 1967, the CIA warned that Castro was considering an invasion of the base, partly in order to divert attention from the parlous state of the Cuban economy. It was suggested that the Cuban leader wanted to push Moscow to 'take a stronger position vis-à-vis the United States' and to 'inspire revolutionary emulation' throughout Latin America. It was maintained that the Soviets might even encourage such an attack to undermine the American commitment in Vietnam. However, the CIA saw such a course of events as improbable, given Moscow's conservative stance in relation to the Western Hemisphere.[63] Castro clearly thought better of it, too.

Covert Action and Intelligence Gathering

Another area of Cuban policy with which Johnson concerned himself was covert action. CIA activities in this realm had begun under President Eisenhower and, along with the Bay of Pigs paramilitary operation, included elements such as propaganda operations, efforts to foment a coup, assassination attempts and sabotage operations to destroy life and property. Records indicate that the period from June 1963 to April 1964 saw more than eighty acts of internal sabotage and sixty armed clashes between Cuban security forces and insurgents.[64] Though obviously having no sympathy for the Castro regime, Johnson loathed the use of covert action in Cuba, feeling that the sabotage efforts, for example, were 'both ineffectual and hypocritical'. There was the sheer 'hypocrisy of our seeking peace and talking peace and conducting this sort of activity on the side'.[65] It was inconceivable that in any circumstances Johnson would ever condone a large-scale covert paramilitary operation, having seen one blow up in the face of John F. Kennedy.[66] Johnson also detested the idea of trying to kill Castro, a goal pursued in a number of ill-conceived schemes during the Eisenhower and Kennedy years. Apart from the fact that these efforts threatened deep domestic and international controversy, the President speculated, as noted in Chapter One, that they may have played a part in Kennedy's murder.[67] In March 1967, after the journalist Drew Pearson alleged that the United States government was still trying to assassinate the Cuban leader, Johnson directed DCI Richard Helms to conduct an investigation. It emerged that the CIA was working with Major Rolando Cubela of the Cuban military to do away with Castro, but there was no evidence of any direct US involvement in the period since Johnson had become President.[68]

It is not clear how far other types of covert action in Cuba might have been scaled down under Johnson, but it is clear that he had no desire to moderate the continued gathering of intelligence, even though this had its risks. During the tensions over Guantánamo, he agreed that if the Cubans shot down a US surveillance aircraft then several surface-to-air missile sites on the island should be 'taken out'.[69] Johnson realised that the over-flights antagonised Havana but felt there was no alternative if the United States was to remain properly informed: 'We can't circle the island. We got to go over it.'[70] Johnson knew that photographic intelligence had enabled the detection of Soviet missile bases on Cuba in 1962. After the 1964 crisis over Guantánamo, there were no major flare-ups in the relationship with Cuba – although, as will be seen, Johnson would see Castro's hand in the uprising in the Dominican Republic in 1965.

THE REBELLION IN THE DOMINICAN REPUBLIC, 1965

The Dominican Republic gained its independence from Spain in 1821, and was subject thereafter to frequent meddling or intervention from regional and European powers. The United States began to exert particular influence over the island from the mid-nineteenth century onwards, culminating in military intervention under President Woodrow Wilson in 1912 to restore political and financial stability. Putting aside the impact of the twelve-year US presence on the development of the Dominican Republican, there is little doubt that the dictatorship (1931–61) of Rafael Trujillo was a brutal and corrupt one. According to the CIA in 1964, his leadership 'warped' the Dominican Republic's 'political and economic framework'. Many Dominicans had come to doubt that they could 'accomplish anything by themselves; there were few who have the experience, honesty and backbone to play effective roles as government leaders'.[71] By the 1960s, as one US diplomat described it, 'The country was deathly poor, overpopulated, undereducated, and a major source of legal and illegal immigration to the US . . . [economic] growth was slow to non-existent. And the elite were rich and intent to hold on to their positions.'[72] The United States backed Joaquin Balaguer as Trujillo's successor. Although Balaguer was closely associated with Trujillo and had a history of demagoguery, he had the virtues of being 'anti-communist and enjoy[ing] the support of some of the country's best people'.[73] The US government therefore felt that he was the best man for the job. However, an election in December 1961 brought a decisive victory for Juan Bosch, a writer and intellectual who had been in exile for twenty-four years. According to Thomas Mann, Bosch was 'a kind of literary man . . . he is the most impractical fellow in the world – sort of an idealist floating around on Cloud 9 type – he is a handsome man and a good orator . . . That is the way he got elected, by being a good orator.'[74]

The CIA confirmed that although Bosch had never been a member of the Communist Party, he was 'frequently . . . influenced and manipulated by those of his close associates who are Communists'.[75] After Cuba, the 'loss' of the Dominican Republic to communism would be another blow to the standing of a United States long accustomed to treating Latin America as its backyard. In September 1963, a military coup, with the backing of the conservative Union Civica Nacional (UCN), deposed Bosch, who retreated into exile in Puerto Rico.[76] Later, the Johnson Administration recognised the regime in Santo Domingo and supported Donald Reid Cabral, the head of the ruling triumvirate. On 24 April 1965 a countercoup erupted when elements of the Dominican armed forces rose to re-establish Bosch as the president. The anti-government movement was under the leadership of a mix of dissatisfied military, students and political agitators, including at least two prominent members of Bosch's Dominican Revolutionary Party.[77]

The Party soon seized control and appointed Rafael Molina Urena as President, pending Bosch's return from exile. On 26 April, loyalist forces bombed the rebel-held areas in Santo Domingo. Although the bombing lasted only a day, the situation deteriorated rapidly. What Robert McNamara described as 'extremist groups' soon moved to the assistance of the rebels, who distributed 'arms and ammunition' to 'thousands of irresponsible civilians'.[78] On 28 April, a new governing junta emerged, headed by Colonel Pedro Benoit of the Dominican air force. By now, the police and the loyalist armed forces had managed to gain control of most of the country, with the exception of part of Santo Domingo.[79]

The American military build-up proceeded simultaneously. On 24 April the Caribbean Ready Amphibious Squadron, with over 1,800 Marines, was moved to just off the Dominican coast. Two days later, two Army battalions of the 82nd Airborne Division were alerted. The next day, the amphibious squadron began the evacuation of American nationals.[80] On 28 April, Ambassador Tapley Bennett in Santo Domingo asked for the landing of Marines to protect the operation to evacuate American citizens and to help protect the Embassy.[81] It seems that Johnson had already anticipated the use of American forces, and after formal consultations with the Secretary of State, the Secretary of Defense and the Joint Chiefs of Staff he endorsed the request.[82] Some 400 Marines went ashore. The next day, the Ambassador requested that the rest of the Marine units and the two Army battalions be moved to the Dominican Republic 'to protect American lives'.[83] American troops moved between both camps and helped to bring about a cease-fire by 30 April.[84] There were further contingents of American troops, though, and by 14 May numbers had reached 21,000.[85] The burgeoning US presence reflected the breakdown of order on the island – 1,300 Dominicans were killed between 24 and 29 April, and some 6,500 men from 46 countries had to be evacuated.[86] There was also a large-scale feeding and relief programme to run.[87]

JOHNSON'S INVOLVEMENT

Undersecretary of State George Ball suggested that upon hearing the news of the rebellion President Johnson experienced an 'increasing absorption in the Dominican problem, to the point where he assumed the direction of day-to-day policy and became, in effect, the Dominican desk officer'.[88] Johnson felt, according to Ball, that 'his own position was very much at stake on this issue of whether we had another Cuba on our hands or not'.[89] The Johnson White House also had to consider the Dominican Republic not only in terms of American Cold War security interests but in the context of a powerful anti-communist constituency in the United States that had coalesced around the Republican candidate in the 1964 presidential election, Barry Goldwater.[90] So, as with the other crises in Latin America, both domestic and international politics shaped Johnson's outlook; for him, the 'worst political disaster' both at home and abroad 'would be for Castro to take over' the Dominican Republic.[91] This meant that, in effect, the Administration pursued what amounted to a policy of 'double containment' – restraining communism abroad and anti-communism at home.[92]

The fear of communism gaining ground in the Dominican Republic became nothing less than an obsession with the President. On 30 April he stated, with exaggeration, that 'our CIA says this is a completely led, operated, dominated . . . Castro operation. That it started out as a Bosch operation, but he's been moved completely out of the picture . . . and their people took over.' There is also the Vietnam dimension to explain the intensity of Johnson's worries. He felt that events on the island 'may be a part of a whole Communistic pattern tied in with Vietnam . . . The intelligence reports show that the Communist countries have felt that we were pulling out of Vietnam' and as such were seeking to take advantage of the United States' seeming lack of resolution.[93] Johnson asked, 'How can we send troops 10,000 miles away and let Castro take over right under our nose?'[94] Concerns about the spread of communism both in the Caribbean and in Southeast Asia meant that by the middle of May there were 100,000 American soldiers engaged in two 'wars' far apart from one another.[95]

The public justifications for sending troops to the Dominican Republic were those of restoring law and order, protecting American lives and preventing a possible communist takeover.[96] Somewhat incoherently, Johnson used both anti-communism and the need to protect American nationals as justifications: he told the former President of Venezuela, for example, that 'within hours of the landing of the Marines the US had names, addresses, and other information concerning Communists and Castroites who were in the rebel ranks', but the main reason for sending troops was 'to protect the lives of Americans and other foreign nationals who were in danger'.[97] Thomas Mann suggested that evacuating American citizens was but a 'fig-leaf' for the 'anti-communist argument'.[98] He feared that 'if we don't get a decent government in there . . . and we get another Bosch, it is just going to be another sinkhole'.[99] Similarly, it is fair to suggest that the views of the Embassy in Santo Domingo derived as much from the likelihood of rebel success than from the level of danger faced by American and foreign nationals.[100]

SECRET INTELLIGENCE

The crisis in the Dominican Republic was a rare occasion when Johnson went out of his way to use secret intelligence information, if only to bolster his preconceptions and to justify a course of action that had already been implemented. He was keen from the outset to 'get the CIA to give us name, address, chapter and verse . . . to show that we got proof . . . that this is a case of Cuba doing this job'.[101] The hasty procurement of intelligence material gave rise to some friction. On 29 April, McGeorge Bundy complained that some of the 'technical people were protecting their Goddamn code words, and it took one of their important messages five hours to get here'.[102] It was soon arranged that 'all really good intelligence' would be passed on via a faster 'ticker' which would be delivered to the President by his secretary. Additionally, Johnson would get a more general intelligence assessment twice daily.[103]

The new DCI Admiral William Raborn was happy to oblige his sponsor with what he wanted to hear: 'In my opinion, this is a real struggle mounted by Mr Castro.' The CIA had 'identified eight hard-core, Castro-trained guerrillas' who 'came in' and 'pushed aside the Bosch people and took command of the forces'. These 'Castroites . . . took over the situation rapidly. They raided the police station, took their arms, took their uniforms, and are sort of in command of the city in spots.'[104] FBI chief Edgar Hoover was also more than willing to feed Johnson's fervour by providing reports of known communists said to have been seen in the Dominican Republic.[105]

While none of the advisers challenged the need to intervene, there were some members of the Johnson entourage who questioned the hyperbole, at least in private. Bundy feared that it would be easy to go too far in identifying the rebels with communism, telling Johnson that a planned public statement might commit the United States to 'a civil war against Communists who aren't in charge'. Although the CIA had identified a number of communist-trained rebels, 'nobody has yet said that any one of these Communists is actually in command of a column'.[106] McNamara had similar concerns. He explained that it was 'a pretty tough job' to prove that external powers were in control and that Castro had done much more than provide training for the rebels. The claim that Castro was masterminding events placed Johnson's 'own status and prestige too much on the line'. The CIA had 'yet to provide any evidence that the communists were trying to gain control . . . to say you as President [have] personal knowledge that powers outside the hemisphere' was too much.[107] Bundy and McNamara, as well as Abe Fortas, rued the possibility of another Cuba, but they were equally interested in democracy and social reform and felt it necessary to appraise the possibility of a communist takeover in realistic terms.[108]

Johnson was willing, at least to a point, to cool his public rhetoric in response to comments from aides, but it has to be said that his fear of communism gaining control in the Dominican Republic was not solely a product of an over-heated imagination. On 7 May, a sober-minded CIA assessment reported that 'a modest number of hard-core Communist leaders in Santo Domingo' had 'managed by superior training and tactics to win themselves a position of influence in the revolt within the first few days'. Their influence expanded 'day-by-day', and soon 'there appeared to be no organization within the rebel camp capable of denying them full control of the rebellion within a very few days'. Now 'a movement increasingly under the influence of Castroites was threatening to gain ascendancy in the Dominican Republic'.[109]

The Prospects of a Communist Regime

John J. Crowley, Deputy Chief of Mission in Santo Domingo 1970–4, had thought in 1965 that the US invasion was 'an overreaction . . . Based on the evidence . . . it didn't look like we were about to have another Cuba.' Crowley added, though, that Colonel Camano Deno,

> who had been the leader of the '65 revolt, came back into the Dominican Republic clandestinely with about . . . 30 or 40 people, armed by the Cubans and apparently in a boat that they bought for him, came in and declared that the savior had returned and the people should all rise up.

The people did not 'rise up' but Crowley concluded that 'maybe LBJ was right' to send troops, in view of the fact that Deno had been 'living in Cuba all this time and he visited the Soviet Union. He's here with their arms and their money.' So the Dominican Republic 'could have gone the way of Cuba if we had not intervened'.[110] For Johnson, the very possibility that events in the Dominican Republic would lead to another Cuba was enough to justify large-scale intervention.[111] At the same time, Johnson seems never to have entertained the prospect that the emphasis on Cuban involvement might have encouraged Havana to intervene.[112]

The President was worried that the invasion had damaged his standing with liberals in the United States at a time when the Great Society legislative programme was at its height; he had to consider both anti-communist views on one hand and liberal sentiment on the other. To satisfy the former constituency, Johnson and his colleagues were anxious to link the rebels with Castro, even scrambling to procure 'some still pictures of rebels wearing Fidel Castro caps'. With liberals in mind, Johnson reassured himself that he was charting a moderate course between communism and right-wing authoritarianism. For him, the United States was 'being about as democratic as you can be . . . we're giving [the Dominican people] protection and we're giving them food and feeding them and giving them supervised elections'.[113] There were also concerns about how other countries perceived the intervention. Thomas Mann feared that Latin American states were going to give the United States 'a lot of trouble'. He suggested that although there was an acceptance of the principle of collective defence, it could not be forgotten that Washington and Latin American governments had all supported the principle of non-intervention. Latin American 'theology' did not admit the view that 'aggression does not have to be an armed military attack; it can also come in the form of subversion'. Now there was a view that the United States was engaged in 'gunboat diplomacy'.[114]

Johnson and his colleagues had in fact striven to legitimise the intervention by appealing to the OAS to authorise a joint military operation to restore peace, but the head of the Organization responded that it would take time even to get the delegates together, never mind to obtain a policy consensus.[115] The President concluded that the OAS was 'a phantom – they are taking a siesta while this is on fire'.[116] Fortunately, many countries in Latin America turned out to be at least tolerant of American policy. Averell Harriman, acting as the President's personal envoy, reported on 8 May that after visiting Colombia, Ecuador, Peru, Chile, Argentina, Uruguay, Brazil and Panama, the latter two were 'very friendly' and Argentina and Colombia 'would probably contribute troops'. The other countries would not provide soldiers, but would lend assistance in other ways.[117] Within a couple of years of the intervention President Johnson was working with eleven regional presidents at Punta del Este, Uruguay, to discuss the Alliance for Progress.[118]

Further Developments in the Dominican Republic

By September 1965 the American-backed provisional government of Hector Garcia Godoy was in place in Santo Domingo. Elections for a new constitutional president took place in June the following year. Joaquin Balaguer was elected with 57 per cent of the vote and a substantial majority in both houses of Congress (Bosch came second). The fact that elections could take place stemmed in part from the efforts of American officials such as John Bartlow Martin, Abe Fortas, McGeorge Bundy, Thomas Mann, Cyrus Vance and Jack H. Vaughn to bring the contending factions together so that they would participate in elections.[119] Ellsworth Bunker, US Ambassador to the OAS, played an especially important role in this development.[120]

The very public American intervention in the affairs of the Dominican Republic in 1965 gave way to secret involvement in the country's affairs. Early in 1966 it was decided, with Johnson's imprimatur, to provide covert support for Balaguer, the candidate who was 'most likely to be able to establish and maintain stable government in the Dominican Republic which is friendly to the US and which is capable of carrying out essential domestic reforms'.[121] Thus the United States played a clandestine role in the outcome of what the President described as 'one of the most closely watched elections ever held in the Western hemisphere'. Had OAS observers known of the US involvement, they might have been less inclined to depict the elections as 'an outstanding act of democratic purity'.[122] A small covert contribution in 1968 to the Revolutionary Social Christian Party towards the cost of participating effectively in the municipal elections[123] contributed to high voter turnout and made the victory of the Reformist Party 'more generally acceptable and had the net effect of strengthening both President Balaguer's image and the democratic process in the Dominican Republic'.[124]

Although by 1968, as one analysis noted, there was on the island 'a considerable degree of political stability . . . its continuation is far from certain'. Substantial US economic assistance since 1965 had contributed to the stability, but there was still 'massive unemployment and . . . only minimal economic growth and financial equilibrium'.[125] Johnson reflected after the intervention that he did not want to be seen as 'an intervener'. He told Abe Fortas that 'Sometimes I take other people's judgments, and I get misled. Like sending troops in there to Santo Domingo. But the man that misled me was Lyndon Johnson . . . I can't blame a damn human.'[126] The reality was that Johnson was as much an enthusiast for intervention as any of his colleagues, but the measure proved, on balance, to be a positive course of action. One official suggested fairly that 'the timely action of the United States' in 1965 'permitted rather than frustrated democratic expression of the will of the Dominican people'.[127] However imperfectly, the United States helped to advance the cause of constitutional government and political stability in the Dominican Republic.

Although he had an authentic sympathy for the people of Latin America, the examples explored in this chapter suggest that Lyndon Johnson did not bring much flair, ambition or imagination to US policy in the Americas. Instead, he charted a deeply conservative course, as was shown by his redirection of the Alliance for Progress to economic modernisation rather than political reform as well. The emphasis on the former rather than the latter meant that Washington could find itself backing dictators, an all too common situation that did little good for the standing of the United States in the Hemisphere. Johnson's policy of attempting to further Cuba's isolation and embargo showed continuity with the Kennedy Administration, although he demonstrated good judgment and restraint in dealing with the Guantánamo crisis. By the end of Johnson's time in office, the efforts to isolate Cuba had exerted at least modest effects in weakening Castro's regime. According to a 1968 report, Cuba's 'present economic straits and the signs of growing discontent would indicate that the pinch of isolation is having a real effect'.[128] Another effect of the policy of isolation and embargo was to create added material dependency and push Havana together with Moscow. Given the Soviets' conservatism, this would be an effective way to moderate Havana's policies in the absence of any means of destroying the regime, although whether it was an intended outcome is a moot point.[129] There was a touch of political immaturity evident in Johnson's shrill and exaggerated response in 1965 to the prospect of communism taking hold on the Dominican Republic. Yet the American military intervention and the promotion of a democratic and constitutional political system (albeit one manipulated covertly by the United States on occasion) did prove beneficial to the Republic's development. It seems that in at least one instance Washington did know what was best for one of its southern neighbours.

NOTES

1. Document 4, Study of US policy toward Latin America, 5 July 1969, *Foreign Relations of the United States (hereafter FRUS) 1969–1976 E–10 Documents on American Republics, 1969–1972* (http://history.state.gov/historicaldocuments/frus1969-76ve10). On the literature of US policy toward Latin America, see Darlene Rivas, 'United States-Latin American Relations, 1942–1960', and Stephen G. Rabe, 'US Relations with Latin-America, 1961 to the Present: A Historiographic Review', in Robert D. Schulzinger (ed.), *A Companion to American Foreign Relations* (Oxford: Blackwell, 2006), pp. 230–54 and pp. 387–403 respectively. See also Max Paul Friedman, 'Retiring the Puppets, Bringing Latin America Back In: Recent Scholarship on United States-Latin American Relations', *Diplomatic History*, 27, 5 (November 2003), pp. 621–36.
2. Document 5, 'Analytical Summary Prepared by the NSC Interdepartmental Group for Latin America', undated, *FRUS 1969–1976 E–10*.
3. Association for Diplomatic Studies and Training (ADST), Foreign Affairs Oral History Project, Ambassador A. Lincoln Gordon, interviewed by Charles Stuart Kennedy, initial interview date 30 September 1987.
4. Quoted in Robert Dallek, *Flawed Giant: Lyndon Johnson and His Times, 1961–1971* (Oxford and New York: Oxford University Press, 1998), p. 91.
5. Editorial note, *FRUS 1964–1968 XXXI Central and South America; Mexico* (2004), p. 1.
6. ADST, Ambassador A. Lincoln Gordon, interviewed by Charles Stuart Kennedy, 30 September 1987.
7. Dallek, *Flawed Giant*, p. 96.
8. Michael Beschloss (ed.), *Reaching for Glory: Lyndon Johnson's Secret White House Tapes, 1964–1965* (New York: Simon and Schuster, 2001), p. 300.

9. Michael Beschloss (ed.), *Taking Charge: The Johnson White House Tapes, 1963–64* (New York: Simon and Schuster, 1997), pp. 74, 87.

10. ADST, Ambassador A. Lincoln Gordon, interviewed by Charles Stuart Kennedy, 30 September 1987.

11. Ibid.

12. Beschloss (ed.), *Taking Charge*, p. 101.

13. Editorial note, *FRUS 1964–1968 XXXI*, pp. 28–9; Dallek, *Flawed Giant*, p. 96.

14. Beschloss (ed.), *Taking Charge*, p. 157.

15. Editorial note, *FRUS 1964–1968 XXXI*, pp. 27–8.

16. Johnson–Mann telephone conversation, 27 August 1965, *FRUS 1964–1968 XXXI*, pp. 81–3.

17. Bowdler to Rostow, 17 January 1967, *FRUS 1964–1968 XXXI*, pp. 107–8.

18. Walt Rostow, *The Diffusion of Power: An Essay in Recent History* (New York: Macmillan, 1972), pp. 425, 430.

19. Note 2, *FRUS 1964–1968 XXXI*, p. 120.

20. Lyndon B. Johnson, *The Vantage Point: Perspectives of the Presidency, 1963–1969* (New York: Holt, Rinehart, Winston, 1971), p. 351.

21. Memorandum of conversation, 13 April 1967, *FRUS 1964–1968 XXXI*, pp. 129, 130.

22. State to all American republics, 17 April 1967, *FRUS 1964–1968 XXXI*, p. 132.

23. Johnson, *The Vantage Point*, p. 351.

24. Embassy Argentina to State, 19 February 1967, *FRUS 1964–1968 XXXI*, p. 114.

25. Rostow, *The Diffusion of Power*, p. 425.

26. ADST, United States Foreign Assistance Oral History Program, Foreign Affairs Oral History Collection, Reuben 'Ray' Sternfeld, interviewed by W. Haven North, initial interview date 2 February 1999.

27. Document 4, Study of US policy toward Latin America, 5 July 1969, *FRUS, 1969–1976 E–10*.

28. ADST, Foreign Affairs Oral History Project, Milton Barall, interviewed by Charles Stuart Kennedy, initial interview date 10 April 1990.

29. Rostow, *The Diffusion of Power*, pp. 424, 425.

30. ADST, United States Foreign Assistance Oral History Program, Foreign Assistance Oral History Collection, Rutherford M. Poats, interviewed by W. Haven North, initial interview date 13 January 1999.

31. ADST, United States Foreign Assistance Oral History Program, Foreign Affairs Oral History Collection, Reuben 'Ray' Sternfeld, interviewed by W. Haven North, initial interview date 2 February 1999.

32. Rostow, *The Diffusion of Power*, p. 424.

33. ADST, Foreign Affairs Oral History Project, Foreign Assistance Series, Herman Kleine, interviewed by W. Haven North, initial interview date 14 February 1996.

34. Literature on the Cuban Missile Crisis includes Graham T. Allison, *Essence of Decision: Explaining the Cuban Missile Crisis* (London: Longman, 1999); Alexander Fursenko and Timothy Naftali, *'One Hell of a Gamble': Khrushchev, Castro, Kennedy and the Cuban Missile Crisis* (New York: Norton, 1997); Len Scott, *The Cuban Missile Crisis and the Threat of Nuclear War* (London: Continuum, 2008).

35. On the policy debate within the Administration, see John Dumbrell, *President Lyndon Johnson and Soviet Communism* (Manchester: Manchester University Press, 2004), pp. 139–42. Quotation, p. 142.

36. National Intelligence Estimate, 19 August 1964, *FRUS 1964–1968 XXXI*, p. 69.

37. National Intelligence Estimate, 19 February 1964, *FRUS 1964–1968 XXXI*, p. 1085.
38. Editorial note, *FRUS 1964–1968 XXXI*, p. 146.
39. Quoted in Dumbrell, *President Lyndon Johnson and Soviet Communism*, p. 145.
40. Ibid., p. 148.
41. 'Memorandum Prepared by the 303 Committee', 22 November 1967, *FRUS 1964–1968 XXXI*, p. 387.
42. Rostow to Johnson, 14 October 1967, *FRUS 1964–1968 XXXI*, p. 385.
43. Dumbrell, *President Lyndon Johnson and Soviet Communism*, p. 147.
44. Editorial note, *FRUS 1964–1968 XXXII Dominican Crisis; Cuba; Haiti; Guyana* (2005), p. 566.
45. Johnson, *The Vantage Point*, p. 185; editorial note, *FRUS 1964–1968 XXXII*, p. 566.
46. Beschloss (ed.), *Taking Charge*, p. 228.
47. Johnson, *The Vantage Point*, p. 185.
48. Notes of meeting, 7 February 1964, *FRUS 1964–1968 XXXII*, p. 571.
49. Johnson–Russell telephone conversation, 7 February 1964, *FRUS 1964–1968 XXXII*, p. 572.
50. Notes of meeting, 7 February 1964, *FRUS 1964–1968 XXXII*, p. 569.
51. Memorandum for the record, 7 February 1964, *FRUS 1964–1968 XXXII*, p. 584.
52. Memorandum for the record, 7 February 1964, *FRUS 1964–1968 XXXII*, pp. 584–5.
53. Beschloss (ed.), *Taking Charge*, p. 228.
54. Editorial note, *FRUS 1964–1968 XXXII*, p. 603.
55. Note 3, *FRUS 1964–1968 XXXII*, p. 584.
56. Johnson–Russell telephone conversation, 7 February 1964, *FRUS 1964–1968 XXXII*, p. 581.
57. Notes of meeting, 7 February 1964, *FRUS 1964–1968 XXXII*, p. 568.
58. Editorial note, *FRUS 1964–1968 XXXII*, p. 603.
59. Verbal message from Castro to Johnson, 12 February 1964, *FRUS 1964–1968 XXXII*, pp. 592–3.
60. Johnson, *The Vantage Point*, pp. 186–7.
61. ADST, Ambassador Hugh Crimmins, interviewed by Ashley C. Hewitt, Jr, 10 May 1989.
62. Johnson, *The Vantage Point*, pp. 186–7.
63. Dumbrell, *President Lyndon Johnson and Soviet Communism*, p. 144.
64. 'Review of Current Program of Covert Action in Cuba', undated, *FRUS 1964–1968 XXXII*, pp. 555–6.
65. Memorandum for the record, 18 January 1964, *FRUS 1964–1968 XXXII*, p. 548.
66. Beschloss (ed.), *Taking Charge*, p. 87.
67. Tim Weiner, *Legacy of Ashes: The History of the CIA* (London: Penguin, 2007), p. 271.
68. Editorial note, *FRUS 1964–1968 XXXII*, p. 741. See also Weiner, *Legacy of Ashes*, pp. 313–14, for a more conspiratorial angle.
69. Johnson–McCone meeting, 29 April 1964, *FRUS 1964–1968 XXXII*, p. 634.
70. Johnson–Mann telephone conversation, 11 June 1964, *FRUS 1964–1968 XXXI*, p. 46.
71. 'Special National Intelligence Estimate', 17 January 1964, *FRUS XXXII*, pp. 1–2.
72. ADST, Foreign Affairs Oral History Project, John T. Bennett, interviewed by self, September 1996.
73. White House Situation Room to Johnson at Camp David, 25 April 1964, *FRUS 1964–1968 XXXII*, p. 60.

74. Johnson–Mann telephone conversation, 27 April 1965, *FRUS 1964–1968 XXXII*, p. 65.

75. Intelligence memorandum, 26 May 1964, *FRUS 1964–1968 XXXII*, p. 245.

76. 'Special National Intelligence Estimate', 17 January 1964, *FRUS 1964–1968 XXXII*, pp. 2–3. There is some evidence of American involvement in the coup. See Weiner, *Legacy of Ashes*, pp. 197–9.

77. White House Situation Room to Johnson at Camp David, 25 April 1964, *FRUS 1964–1968 XXXII*, p. 59.

78. McNamara to Johnson, 26 May 1965, *FRUS 1964–1968 XXXII*, pp. 247–8.

79. Johnson, *The Vantage Point*, p. 194.

80. McNamara to Johnson, 26 May 1965, *FRUS 1964–1968 XXXII*, pp. 247–8.

81. Embassy Dominican Republic to Director of NSA, 28 April 1965, *FRUS 1964–1968 XXXII*, pp. 76–7.

82. Johnson, *The Vantage Point*, p. 192; 'Meeting with Congressional Leadership on Dominican Republic', 28 April 1965, *FRUS 1964–1968 XXXII*, p. 82.

83. McNamara to Johnson, 26 May 1965, *FRUS 1964–1968 XXXII*, pp. 247–8.

84. Johnson, *The Vantage Point*, p. 202.

85. McNamara to Johnson, 26 May 1965, *FRUS 1964–1968 XXXII*, pp. 247–8.

86. Johnson, *The Vantage Point*, p. 193; Solomon to Johnson, 17 June 1966, *FRUS 1964–1968 XXXII*, p. 419.

87. Solomon to Johnson, 17 June 1966, *FRUS 1964–1968 XXXII*, p. 420.

88. Ball, *The Past Has Another Pattern*, p. 329.

89. Lyndon Baines Johnson Library, George Ball Oral History interview conducted by Paige E. Mulhollan, 8 July 1971.

90. Randall B. Woods, 'Conflicted Hegemon: LBJ and the Dominican Republic', *Diplomatic History*, 32, 5 (November 2008), pp. 751–2, 753.

91. Beschloss (ed.), *Reaching for Glory*, p. 301.

92. Woods, 'Conflicted Hegemon', p. 755.

93. Beschloss (ed.), *Reaching for Glory*, pp. 297, 299.

94. Editorial note, *FRUS 1964–1968 XXXII*, p. 100.

95. Philip Geyelin, *Lyndon B. Johnson and the World* (London: Pall Mall, 1966), p. 238.

96. State to Embassy Dominican Republic, 27 April 1964, *FRUS 1964–1968 XXXII*, p. 66.

97. Conversation between Johnson and Betancourt et al., 3 May 1965, *FRUS 1964–1968 XXXII*, p. 128.

98. Memorandum for the record, 3 May 1965, *FRUS 1964–1968 XXXII*, p. 124.

99. Johnson–Mann telephone conversation, 26 April 1964, *FRUS 1964–1968 XXXII*, p. 62.

100. Geyelin, *Lyndon B. Johnson and the World*, pp. 245–6.

101. Telephone conversation between Johnson and Fortas, 30 April 1965, *FRUS 1964–1968 XXXII*, p. 105.

102. Beschloss (ed.), *Reaching for Glory*, p. 291.

103. Editorial note, *FRUS 1964–1968 XXXII*, pp. 152–3.

104. Johnson–Raborn telephone conversation, 29 April 1964, *FRUS 1964–1968 XXXII*, p. 89.

105. George W. Ball, *The Past Has Another Pattern* (New York: Norton, 1982), p. 329.

106. Editorial note, *FRUS 1964–1968 XXXII*, p. 111.

107. Beschloss (ed.), *Reaching for Glory*, pp. 302–3; editorial note, *FRUS 1964–1968 XXXII*, p. 109.

108. Woods, 'Conflicted Hegemon', p. 757.
109. CIA memorandum, 7 May 1965, FRUS 1964–1968 XXXII, p. 139.
110. ADST, Ambassador John J. Crowley, Jr, interviewed by Charles Stuart Kennedy, 27 June 1989.
111. Geyelin, *Lyndon B. Johnson and the World*, p. 254.
112. Woods, 'Conflicted Hegemon', pp. 759–60.
113. Telephone conversation between Johnson and his advisers, 18 May 1965, FRUS 1964–1968 XXXII, p. 193.
114. Memorandum for the record, 3 May 1965, FRUS 1964–1968 XXXII, pp. 124–5.
115. Woods, 'Conflicted Hegemon', p. 758.
116. Editorial note, FRUS 1964–1968 XXXII, pp. 100, 101.
117. Note 4, FRUS 1964–1968 XXXII, p. 141.
118. Johnson, *The Vantage Point*, pp. 348–51.
119. Ibid., p. 202.
120. Ball, *The Past Has Another Pattern*, pp. 329–30.
121. Memorandum for the 303 Committee, 30 December 1965 and memorandum for the 303 Committee, 11 January 1966, FRUS 1964–1968 XXXII, pp. 359, 368.
122. Johnson, *The Vantage Point*, p. 203.
123. Memorandum for the 303 Committee, 29 January 1968, FRUS 1964–1968 XXXII, p. 512.
124. Memorandum for the 303 Committee, 28 June 1968, FRUS 1964–1968 XXXII, p. 521.
125. Country analysis, 'The Dominican Republic', undated, FRUS 1964–1968 XXXII, p. 518.
126. Beschloss (ed.), *Taking Charge*, pp. 338–9.
127. Solomon to Johnson, 17 June 1966, FRUS 1964–1968 XXXII, p. 420.
128. Editorial note, FRUS 1964–1968 XXXII, pp. 753–4.
129. Dumbrell, *President Lyndon Johnson and Soviet Communism*, p. 150.

CHAPTER NINE

Dollars and Gold: Monetary and Trade Policy

American foreign policy in the Cold War was concerned primarily with national security conceived in military and political terms, but economic and financial issues had an intimate role. This was evident in the delicate question in 1966–7 of how far Bonn would 'offset' the cost of American troops in the Federal Republic of Germany (FRG). The failure to resolve this issue would intensify pressure in the United States to withdraw troops, but such withdrawals might lead to the FRG adopting destabilising bilateral or unilateral foreign policies (see Chapter Five). This chapter outlines the international monetary regime of the 1960s and then explores the chronic US balance of payments deficit, due in large part to defence spending in Europe and Asia. There is an assessment of the economic crisis of 1967–8, which arose initially from the devaluation of sterling and left the dollar exposed to speculative attack. The Johnson Administration exploited continued American influence and succeeded in the establishment of a two-tier gold market and the creation of a new international currency known as Special Drawing Rights (SDR).[1] Finally, there is coverage of the Administration's successful effort to liberalise trade among the developed countries through the Kennedy Round of tariff negotiations under the General Agreement on Tariffs and Trade (GATT). As with international monetary reform, the Kennedy Round involved intensive collaboration and negotiation with allies. The results achieved in these areas appear all the more creditable against a background that included, for example, strains in the NATO alliance, war in the Middle East, continued crisis in Vietnam, the British abrogation of a global defence role and social upheaval in the United States.[2]

187

THE BRETTON WOODS REGIME

The Free World monetary regime established at Bretton Woods in 1944 out-lawed discriminatory practices and exchange restrictions, and was based on fixed exchange rates. These were intended to facilitate international trade by stabilising the price of goods. The dollar was pegged to gold – which the Americans possessed in abundance at the end of the Second World War – at the rate of $35 per ounce, while the other members of the newly created International Monetary Fund (IMF) pegged their currencies to the dollar.[3] The United States undertook to sell gold for dollars upon the demand of foreign governments. The major currencies were to be mutually convertible, although gold and US dollars and, to a lesser extent, British sterling, were the main media of exchange. IMF members agreed to keep their currencies from deviating from their existing dollar parities. The IMF operated an inter-national fund to provide short-term credit for financing balance of payment deficits, on the basis that fundamental (that is, large and chronic) deficits might need an adjustment in par value.[4] When the United States' relative wealth began to wane due to the postwar recovery in Western Europe and Japan (itself facilitated by American economic support), problems arose. There was clear evidence in 1960, for example, that the American com-mitment to sell gold for dollars was becoming increasingly onerous. The US presidential contest fostered speculation that raised the price of gold on the London market from the official $35 to $40 per ounce. In the absence of sufficient sales by the gold-producing countries, the burden fell upon the United States to provide enough gold to satisfy demand in order to keep the price down. Only when John F. Kennedy pledged to defend the gold-dollar exchange should he be elected, did the markets cool.[5]

THE US BALANCE OF PAYMENTS DEFICIT

One factor behind the gold crisis of 1960 was the chronic US balance of payments deficit. The United States was in surplus in the years 1946–9 as most of the other industrial powers were still drained from the War, but a long-term deficit appeared. Initially, the deficit was relatively small and helped to fulfil the international need for dollars to pay for reconstruction. It was, according to a Johnson aide, 'a blessing to the world'.[6] However, the shortfall between earning and spending abroad persisted beyond the period of reconstruction. In 1961, Kennedy explained that

> The surplus of our exports over our imports, while substantial, has not been large enough to cover our expenditures for United States military establishments

abroad, for capital invested abroad by private American businesses and for government economic assistance and loan programs.[7]

Lyndon Johnson built on Kennedy's initiatives to ease the balance of payments deficit by introducing measures such as voluntary programmes to limit direct investment overseas and to reduce bank lending to foreign countries.[8]

Johnson complained in March 1965 that 'the biggest problem I've got outside Vietnam is balance of payments'.[9] The two were intimately connected. The Americanisation of the war in Vietnam in 1965 compounded the balance of payments problem because it meant spending additional billions of dollars outside the United States, while Great Society spending at home fed a domestic boom which caused inflation and increased imports. Johnson had cut taxes in 1964, and although by 1966 it was evident that a tax increase was needed he did not succeed in getting Congress to raise taxes substantially until 1968.[10] By 1967, the overall balance of payments deficit had reached nearly $3.4 billion.[11] Given that American foreign policy commitments contributed substantially to the deficit, the Administration believed that the shortfall was not solely an American responsibility. According to the President in 1967, the United States'

> role of world leadership . . . is the only reason for our current embarrassment in an economic sense on the one hand and, on the other, the correction of the economic embarrassment under present monetary systems will result in an untenable position economically for our allies'.[12]

However, ending the payments deficit would mean a retreat to isolation for the United States and would unhinge the international trading system.[13] As such, the deficit could be moderated but not eliminated.

INTERNATIONAL MONETARY REFORM

Devaluing the dollar could help to reduce the balance of payments problem, but might precipitate a wave of competing devaluations. Furthermore, Washington did not see the dollar as greatly overvalued, and there was a general sense that devaluation would represent a political humiliation, a sign of weakness.[14] Allowing the dollar to 'float' and to reach its own level was not considered desirable either, because that too might cause international economic instability. The preferred option was to reduce American vulnerability to foreign demands for gold. The French were especially challenging in this regard. In February 1965, President Charles de Gaulle called for a gradual return of the world monetary system to a gold standard rather than a gold exchange standard. Thinking of the glut of American dollars in Europe, he wanted countries to meet their balance of payments debts solely in gold. Gold, according to him, was 'the only 'unquestionable monetary basis which did not bear the mark of any individual country' and therefore the fairest way in which to conduct international financial transactions.[15]

French monetary policy generated acrimony in Washington. Secretary of the Treasury Henry Fowler noted in July 1966 how France strove to 'convert all dollar accruals into gold', thereby depleting American holdings of the precious metal. Monthly conversions during the first half of 1966 had averaged $54 million and were increasing.[16] Without French purchases of gold, 'we would actually have a net accumulation of gold so far this year'.[17] Assistant Secretaries of State Anthony E. Solomon and Walter J. Stoessel even suggested refusing to sell gold to France, a policy of 'selective non-convertibility'.[18] Little came of this idea, presumably because singling out France as a miscreant would exacerbate the already considerable strains in the Franco-American relationship over Vietnam and NATO, and of course Paris was perfectly within its rights to buy gold with dollars.

Johnson, as noted in Chapter Four, tried to deal with Franco-American differences stoically, and, according to Francis Bator, he also displayed 'calm good sense' on monetary affairs. He did not regard the tenets of Bretton Woods as sacrosanct, and doubted, in Bator's words, that another 'run on the US gold stock which led to a cessation of gold-dollar convertibility would be a first order national disaster to be avoided at all costs'. The President is said to have told William McChesney Martin, Chairman of the Federal Reserve Board, that 'I will not deflate the American economy, screw up my foreign policy by gutting aid or pulling troops out, or go protectionist just so we can pay out gold to the French at $35 an ounce.' He had heard Treasury Secretary Douglas Dillon and Undersecretary Robert Roosa using the threat of a run on gold to persuade President Kennedy to delay a tax cut, and was unwilling to experience similar pressure himself.[19]

In March 1965, the annual report of the Joint Economic Committee of the US called for a speedy reduction of the American balance of payments deficit and for reforms to the international monetary system. The Committee urged the 'serious consideration of the possibility of creating a new reserve unit'.[20] In June 1965, Johnson asked Henry Fowler to establish a Study Group to investigate the prospect of 'systematically producing the additional liquidity which has been supplied by the payments deficits of the United States'. This would ease the pressure on the dollar and gold as well as meet the growing demand for international liquidity.[21] Fowler announced that the President had authorised him to the effect that 'the United States now stands prepared to attend and participate in an international monetary conference that would consider what steps we might jointly take to secure substantial improvements in international monetary arrangements'.[22]

Washington decided to pursue the creation of SDR, a new international reserve currency, to supplement dollars and gold. The new asset would be created in a specific annual amount for a five-year period, say $1 to $2 billion per year. The asset would be gold-value guaranteed and backed by members' obligations to accept the asset and to pay convertible currencies in return. It would be an international legal tender that would ease the pressure on gold and dollars. Although creating the new currency would not address the balance of payments deficit, it would allow US reserve assets to increase and would support the continued growth of international trade. Negotiations to create the new reserves began in September 1965 in the Group of Ten and Executive Board of the IMF. In July 1966, agreements were reached on a number of points. At American prompting, it was agreed at the IMF annual meeting in September to broaden the negotiations to include representatives of all IMF members. This decision led to the Group of Ten Deputies and the IMF Executive Directors holding a series of joint meetings to reach agreement on the plan. At the fourth and last meeting in June 1967, the basic elements of a plan were laid down but many issues remained unresolved. By August the Group of Ten Ministers had made further progress but no agreement had been reached.[23]

THE DEVALUATION OF STERLING

International monetary affairs were complicated by an economic storm stemming initially from British problems in 1967–8. Britain had suffered long-term balance of payments shortfalls as a result of poorly performing industries and defence spending abroad. American policymakers did not want the British to cut back substantially on their foreign policy commitments and supported sterling as the first line of defence against the dollar by means of a number of 'bailouts'. Undersecretary of State George Ball, for example, argued in summer 1965 that a substantial devaluation of sterling could produce 'chaos' in the international monetary system that would 'mangle' US 'foreign and political policies'. The United States, 'as the leading Western power, could not engage in financial and economic warfare with other major trading nations of the world and still maintain functioning military alliances – or, in fact, effective cooperation of any kind'.[24]

The plight of the pound concerned President Johnson, who felt that the social spending of the British government was too high. He asked Eugene Black, President of the World Bank, in August 1965:

> What can we do about the British pound thing? We've told them how far they ought to go and they won't do it . . . then we're going to have to bail them out. We tell them we won't do it except multilaterally but I think we're going to have to. They know that we can't make good on our threats . . . we can't walk away from it and I just don't know what to do . . . They got us by the yin-yang. I want some smart fellow like you to figure how to tell them to go to hell.[25]

Johnson told William Martin of the Federal Reserve that the British were like 'a reckless boy that goes off and gets drunk and writes cheques on his father'. The father honours 'two or three or four' of the cheques before 'call[ing] him in and just tell[ing] him now we've got to work this out or you live off what you're making . . . if you don't, I can't come to your rescue any more'. But the boy just 'goes home' and writes another cheque.[26]

Britain's decision to seek membership of the European Economic Community (EEC) early in 1967 along with the Labour government's decision to try to boost the economy after various deflationary measures led to sterling being sold short on the markets.[27] The closure of the Suez Canal during the Six-Day War in June along with a dock strike in Britain compounded the problem. London wanted another bailout in order to avoid devaluation. However, by late 1967 there was a view that it might be manageable simply to let sterling go if there was only a small change in parity. A 10 to 15 per cent devaluation, according to Fowler, would be manageable and would relieve 'sterling's long agony' and help to 'get the UK economy on a more solid basis'. He anticipated, though, that even with a small devaluation the 'dollar would come under attack; the gold market would come under very great pressure – and might explode; the world might not believe a "modest" devaluation would be adequate and pressure on sterling would continue'.[28]

In keeping with Fowler's prediction, the devaluation of sterling by 14 per cent (from $2.80 to $2.40) on 18 November 1967 precipitated a wave of speculation in the gold market which left the dollar exposed. The demand for gold was already strong because of the Six-Day War, increased industrial use and because in 1966 and 1967 Moscow had refused to sell gold on the world market. Speculators gambled that the United States would have to abandon its commitment to buying and selling gold at the official rate of $35 per ounce. The gold pool – which consisted of the main central banks and which bought and sold gold in order to maintain the official price – incurred losses of $641 million (of which the American share was 59 per cent) in the week of 20–7 November.[29]

The French stance was problematic. France chose to announce its withdrawal from the gold pool, in the hope that doing so would force an increase in the official price of gold. In practice, the French had pulled out some months earlier, but the announcement complicated an already difficult situation. This, for Johnson, was 'one of several times when I was tempted to abandon my policy of polite restraint towards de Gaulle, but I forced myself to be patient once again'.[30] The CIA assessed that the attitudes of the French government 'and the actions of some French officials, were important factors contributing to the massive speculation against the dollar and gold'.[31]

On 18 November, the President affirmed the American commitment to maintain the $35 per ounce gold price, in order to placate the market. Measures were taken to ensure that the other major countries held their exchange rates along with the United States, and there were efforts to build confidence in the dollar. These involved, as Fowler put it, 'demonstrating fiscal responsibility and other constructive measures to improve the balance of payments situation'. In a meeting with Johnson and other officials, Fowler stressed that the 'enactment of the President's tax increase program at this session of Congress was the single most important and indispensable step the nation could take now to protect the dollar' and 'safeguard the international monetary system'. Increasing taxes would slow domestic demand and thereby improve the balance of payments.[32]

In the week from 11 to 15 December, gold losses reached $548 million, with National Security Adviser Walt Rostow telling the President that 'the gold market has come to a boil again'.[33] A beleaguered Johnson complained to Senator Mike Mansfield about the desire of the French and Soviets and 'all of our enemies' to 'get US gold and bring the dollar down', and that the failure of the American government to raise taxes was convincing 'all the bankers and all the money people' that US policy was irresponsible. Wilbur Mills, Chairman of the House Ways and Means Committee and an opponent of a tax increase without budget cuts, had been 'wrecking the damn world'. Now, with the US gold reserves depleted, the dollar might soon be 'busted like the pound was busted'.[34]

In the last week of December 1967, senior officials in the Administration devised various proposals concerning the balance of payments, to form the subject of a presidential announcement. While the Administration had been working on the balance of payments question for some time, the matter was especially critical in the midst of the economic crisis. Even so, there was no dispensation to scale back American commitments abroad. On 1 January 1968, the President announced a programme to cut the balance of payments deficit by $3 billion that year. The plan consisted of tighter regulation of US investment abroad, restrictions on foreign lending, cutbacks in military and economic assistance to other countries, a request that Americans reduce travel and spending outside the Western Hemisphere and an effort to expand US commercial sales in foreign markets.[35] The initial response was favourable – Undersecretary of State Nicholas Katzenbach and Undersecretary of the Treasury Frederick L. Deming reported a few days later, after visiting European capitals, that central bankers 'approved in general the program and its parts', although 'the government people', while generally approving, had 'reservations', such as the possibility of a shortage of American investment, 'about some of the balance of payments aspects'.[36]

Renewed Crisis

There was further trouble ahead, due to a combination of still poor US balance of payments figures, increasing inflation and continued doubts about whether the British could hold the new parity of sterling. Furthermore, the Tet Offensive raised the possibility that even more troops would be despatched to Vietnam, with a further burden on the balance of payments.[37] In Washington, there was continued frustration over the stalled income tax increase. Fowler complained that the 'attitude on the Hill' was 'one of almost anarchistic willingness to pull down the temple around their ears on the grounds that our budgetary expenditures are out of control'.[38] A public call in late February from Senator Jacob Javits for suspending the gold pool and the convertibility of the dollar contributed to another run on gold.[39]

Rostow recognised the need for new measures. On Thursday, 14 March, he made his own private suggestion to Johnson of closing the London gold market the next day, prior to weekend emergency talks with the central bankers. The closure would avoid the loss of up to $1 billion 'in gold tomorrow (we lost $372 million today)'. More losses on this scale would 'further shake the confidence of central banks and trigger their coming to us for gold'. Closing the market would make it easier to 'arrange an emergency meeting of the gold pool countries this weekend', and would provide 'evidence of US decisiveness'.[40] Johnson agreed to the suggestion. The day after, Secretary Fowler and Chairman Martin announced the US government's commitment to buying and selling gold in official transactions at the $35 rate and affirmed that they had 'invited the central bank governors to consult with us on coordinated measures to ensure orderly conditions in the exchange markets and to support the present pattern of exchange rates'.[41] Over the weekend of 16–17 March, Fowler and other economists agreed with European finance ministers and bankers that monetary gold would be exchanged among official authorities at the official price with the free market determining the price for other uses.[42] In other words, the American undertaking at Bretton Woods to sell gold at $35 per ounce applied only to foreign governments and central banks.

Just as important as the establishment of a two-tier gold market were the Administration's efforts to accelerate the SDR plan. Again, this would help to take the pressure off US gold. The result was that at the end of the weekend emergency meetings in Washington the central bankers announced that 'As the existing stock of monetary gold is sufficient in view of the prospective establishment of Special Drawing Rights, they [the central banks] no longer feel it necessary to buy gold from the market.' This, according to Johnson, was 'a historic turning point. The world's leading bankers were telling the speculators that henceforth the banks would be looking to the new international currency, not to gold, to enlarge monetary reserves.'[43]

The Stockholm Monetary Conference of the Group of 10, on 29–30 March 1968, completed, according to Rostow, 'another phase in the IMF Special Drawing Rights plan. It brings us close to creation of "paper gold"'. The 'Four' – Germany, Italy, Belgium and the Netherlands – had been willing to 'stand up against the French', who by now were beginning to struggle with their own balance of payment difficulties. In joining with the United States, the Four showed 'confidence that we would bring our financial house in order'.[44] Finally, in October 1969 the IMF decided to create $9.5 billion worth of SDR in 1970–2.[45] However, the Nixon Administration's decision in 1971 to dispense completely with the commitment to sell gold at $35 per ounce and to float the dollar made the emergence of SDR less salient. It also terminated the long-ailing Bretton Woods system, which the Johnson Administration had striven to patch up.

The bifurcation of the gold market in March 1968 was beneficial to the dollar, but there was continued trouble for sterling and trouble also for the French franc. The latter problem arose due to France's deteriorating balance of payments situation and from riots in May 1968 that were followed by strikes and wage rises. By September, the French Treasury had lost $3 billion.[46] In November, Rostow noted that the pound and the franc were under pressure, and that 'money is flowing to Germany in a big way'. He felt that the respective parities of the franc and pound should stay where they were and that the German mark should be revalued upward, as the FRG was an export powerhouse and heavily in surplus.[47] The upward valuation of the mark would benefit the pound, the franc and the dollar.

At a monetary conference in November, the United States, along with the French and the British, pressured the Germans to revalue. Finance Minister Franz-Joseph Strauss responded, however, that although the FRG would reduce its tax on imports, French and not German issues were responsible for the current difficulties. According to him, 'No other country has offered anything to solve the problem' and 'Other countries cannot decide what Germany will do.' Strauss noted that offsetting the cost of American troops was a major burden for the FRG.[48] While the United States had prevailed over the creation of the two-tier gold market and SDR, American power and allied unity had their limits. Fortunately, there was no devaluation of the franc or the pound in 1968, and the dollar remained relatively healthy.

THE KENNEDY ROUND

The Kennedy Round negotiations proved more constructive than the monetary discussions of November 1968. As John F. Kennedy's Vice-President, Lyndon Johnson had facilitated the passage of the Trade Expansion Act of 1962. This enabled the White House to cut tariffs under the aegis of GATT by up to half if other countries reciprocated. It was hoped that the Act would enhance American prosperity and improve the balance of payments by facilitating a net increase in exports, and it also reflected the long-standing view that trade barriers impeded economic growth and fostered political divisions.[49] Former Secretary of State Christian A. Herter represented the United States in the subsequent tariff reduction talks, which began in Geneva in 1964 and were dubbed the 'Kennedy Round'. Also participating were the countries of the EEC, along with the United Kingdom, Austria, Denmark, Finland, Norway, Sweden, Switzerland and Japan. Australia, South Africa, Canada, New Zealand and South Africa took part in a special category.[50]

Progress in the talks, however, proved erratic. Trade in agriculture was the most contentious issue. Possessing a modern and efficient agricultural sector, the United States sought a major liberalisation of trade in farm produce. For this to happen, France and Germany would have to agree to revise the EEC's Common Agricultural Policy, but both countries were resistant. With its small farms and old-fashioned farming practices, France was the most hostile to trade liberalisation, but Bonn was also resistant because it had no wish to antagonise Paris.[51] Problems such as these meant that during 1965 and 1966, the negotiations were 'in the doldrums', as Herter put it.[52] Delays were of great concern in Washington because the presidential discretion authorised under the Trade Expansion Act lasted only until July 1967.[53] In the run-up to the deadline, there was a growing sense of urgency to bring matters to a head. Ambassador William Roth, Herter's successor, moved to Geneva to participate directly in the negotiations, with the assistance of a special coordinating team in Washington and a number of technical specialists.[54] In April, Johnson ordered Bator to 'set up a small and secret command group operating from the White House to manage last minute Kennedy Round strategy', thereby 'backstopping' the team in Geneva. The 'secret command group' bypassed what Bator described as a 'large and leaky' Cabinet committee on trade. All communications on the talks were to be 'distributed on a strictly need-to-know basis' and classified, appropriately given the agricultural dimension of the Geneva negotiations, 'Limdis - Potatoes'.[55]

The US delegation engaged in some hard bargaining. On 1 May, Walt Rostow reported that the American representatives had 'conducted an effective campaign to convince the EEC that we are near the end of our rope. They *may* be beginning to believe us.' While progress had been made, there was still deadlock in two major areas. On agricultural tariffs, the EEC had, according to Bator, conceded only 'bits and pieces'. Chemicals were a sticking point in the industrial negotiations due to the tariff system in the United States known as the American Selling Price,[56] but by 11 May, the outline of compromise agreement had emerged. A major trade liberalisation in industrial products had been agreed, although the United States had gained a much smaller number of concessions for the export of American agricultural produce. The Administration had to consider whether to accept what was on offer, or abandon the effort entirely.[57]

AGREEMENT

To facilitate progress, the White House was willing to exploit the British commitment to a 'special relationship', and, in particular, Prime Minister Harold Wilson's personal respect for President Johnson. On 13 May, Bator complained to the President that the British were 'stonewalling on a number of critical issues with the risk that the entire house of cards will crumble'. Bator telephoned Michael Palliser, Prime Minister Harold Wilson's Foreign Office Secretary, laying it 'hard on the line that this is political business of the highest sort, and should receive immediate attention from his boss'. He added that President Johnson had been 'personally involved in managing our Kennedy Round over the past few days, and considers the successful outcome of the negotiations a matter of greatest concern'.[58] Palliser considered Bator's message to be exaggerated, but the British made a number of concessions, and a new agreement soon emerged.[59] On 15 May, Bator noted that so far there was an average industrial tariff cut of 30 per cent: 'We will be giving our industrial plant, the largest and most efficient in the world, access to markets several times the size of our own.' The agricultural package had its merits, too. It included a 'revolutionary Grains Agreement, and substantial tariff concessions on a wide variety of farm products. The Grains Agreement will guarantee a high international trading price for our wheat exports.'[60] All told, the Kennedy Round would

> go far to guarantee the kind of economic world most profitable to us. We export nearly $30 billion in goods and services every year – more by several billion than we import. We have an enormous stake in maintaining orderly rules of world trade. Each of the last eight Administrations tried to strengthen and liberalize those rules. We can do more now for this cause than they have done in 35 years of effort.[61]

Vice-President Hubert Humphrey, Secretary of State Dean Rusk and a number of other officials briefed Congress on 16 May about the results of the talks. Some of the Senators and Representatives 'expressed concern with respect to certain categories of products and certain domestic industries', with Senator John Pastore even asking bluntly whether 'we had lost our shirt in our anxiety to bring the Kennedy Round to a successful conclusion'. However, the attendees were broadly satisfied that the agreement was 'a balanced one and in the interests of the United States'.[62] After some last-minute changes, the United States agreed to tariff cuts on about $8 billion worth of industrial imports and benefited from tariff cuts on about the same amount of exports. The industrial cuts averaged 33–5 per cent. The average agricultural cut was smaller but the United States had 'obtained important concessions covering a substantial volume of trade'.[63] For Bator, the Kennedy Round had 'in one move . . . done more to promote the free and efficient exchange of goods in the Free World than any Administration, or any Congress has ever been able to do'.[64]

Moreover, the United States' partners in NATO were satisfied with the outcome of the Kennedy Round. Although they had their own economic problems to contend with, the British found the agreement 'highly satisfactory' and the Germans considered it to be the best result available. The French, who as noted had been the most resistant on agricultural issues, had at least given way. There were still reservations in Congress to contend with, and some economists have suggested that the Kennedy

Round contributed to the disappearance of the American trade surplus over the next few years. However, the United States did not have untold leverage in the talks, and the Administration played its hand well.[65]

Relative American decline is evident in the chronic balance of payments deficit and the haemorrhage of gold that peaked in 1967–8. The economist Milton Friedman noted of the 1968 balance of payments measures: 'How low we have fallen! The United States, the land of the free, prohibits its businessmen from investing abroad and requests its citizens not to show their faces or open their pocketbooks in foreign ports.'[66] By the 1960s economic and financial power were far more widely dispersed than they had been in the distinctly abnormal circumstances prevailing at the end of the Second World War, and, although problematic for American policymakers, the flight of gold from Fort Knox in the 1960s was an inevitable readjustment in the global economic balance. The fact that other countries went along with the American ideas for reform – especially the establishment of the two-tier gold market and refraining from buying gold – derived less from the inherent merits of the US case than from the fact that there were few alternatives other than painful unilateral American measures.[67] The American monetary initiatives of spring 1968 were more reactive, ad hoc improvisations than visionary blueprints for viable, long-term reform, but they provided some breathing space for the United States to address the balance of payments issue.[68] To its benefit, Washington had succeeded in encouraging the British to keep the devaluation of sterling a modest one, and helped to ensure that the major industrialised nations did not respond with competing currency realignments.[69] The preferences of American policymakers were fulfilled during the 1967–8 international financial crisis in that the dollar was neither devalued nor floated, and US military commitments abroad were maintained. All these developments demonstrated continuing American power and influence in the international monetary arena.

The Kennedy Round of negotiations was another area of achievement for the Administration, helping to overcome isolationist pressures in all the countries concerned. As with the international monetary issues, the Kennedy Round was a technical matter involving intensive collaboration with allies and saw the intimate involvement and leadership of President Johnson. His oversight of the talks brought a thorough sense of what was and what was not negotiable, and contributed to the favourable outcome.[70] That outcome played a role in promoting Western unity. The international monetary initiatives and the tariff negotiations brought at least qualified success for the United States in what was an especially challenging period at home and abroad.

Notes

1. See Raj Roy, 'The Battle for Bretton Woods: America, Britain and the International Financial Crisis of October 1967–March 1968', *Cold War History*, 2, 2 (2002), pp. 33–60, for the view that Washington's handling of the crisis demonstrated continuing American power.

2. On the latter, see Jeremi Suri, 'Lyndon Johnson and the Global Disruption of 1968', in Mitchell B. Lerner (ed.), *Looking Back at LBJ: White House Politics in a New Light* (Lawrence, KS: University Press of Kansas, 2005), pp. 53–77.

3. In 1945, US gold reserves stood at $20 billion, representing almost two-thirds of the global total of $33 billion. Paul M. Kennedy, *The Rise and Fall of the Great Powers: Economic change and Military Conflict from 1500 to 2000* (New York: Random House, 1987), p. 358.

4. Robert M. Collins, 'The Economic Crisis of 1968 and the Waning of the American Century', *The American Historical Review*, 101, 2 (April 1996), p. 399; Hubert Zimmerman, *Money and Security: Troops, Monetary Policy West Germany's Relations with the United States and Britain, 1950–1971* (Cambridge: Cambridge University Press, 2002), pp. 99–100.

5. Zimmerman, *Money and Security*, pp. 111–12.

6. Collins, 'The Economic Crisis of 1968', p. 399; Califano to Johnson, 22 December 1967, *Foreign Relations of the United States (FRUS 1964–1968) VIII International Monetary and Trade Policy* (1998), p. 466.

7. Quoted in Collins, 'The Economic Crisis of 1968', p. 400.

8. Ibid., p. 401.

9. Quoted in Francis J. Gavin, *Gold, Dollars and Power: The Politics of International Monetary Relations, 1958–1971* (Chapel Hill, NC: University of North Carolina Press, 2004), p. 117.

10. Walt W. Rostow, *The Diffusion of Power: An Essay in Recent History* (London: Macmillan, 1972), p. 528.

11. Robert Solomon, *The International Monetary System, 1945–1976* (New York: Harper and Row, 1977), p. 104.

12. Johnson to Califano, 23 December 1967, *FRUS 1964–1968 VIII*, pp. 473–4. It should be noted that the United States often exerted heavy pressure on allies such as the FRG to hold dollars and to moderate their gold purchases, which meant that dollars accumulated abroad to artificially high levels. See Gavin, *Gold, Dollars and Power*, for the view that Washington used monetary coercion to fulfil political and security goals.

13. Bator, 'Lyndon Johnson and Foreign Policy', in Lobel (ed.), *Presidential Judgment*, p. 47; Gavin, *Gold, Dollars and Power*, p. 4.

14. Bator, 'Lyndon Johnson and Foreign Policy', in Lobel (ed.), *Presidential Judgment*, p. 50.

15. Editorial note, *FRUS 1964–1968 VIII*, p. 100. See also David Calleo, 'De Gaulle and the Monetary System: The Golden Rule', in Robert O. Paxton and Nicholas Wahl (eds), *De Gaulle and the United States: A Centennial Appraisal* (Oxford: Berg, 1994), pp. 239–56.

16. Fowler to Johnson, 21 June 1966, *FRUS 1964–1968 VIII*, p. 290.

17. Minutes of meeting of Cabinet Committee on the Balance of Payments, 14 July 1966, *FRUS 1964–1968 VIII*, p. 293.

18. Note 2, *FRUS 1964–1968 VIII*, p. 290.

19. Bator, 'Lyndon Johnson and Foreign Policy', in Lobel (ed.), *Presidential Judgment*, pp. 62–3.
20. Solomon, *The International Monetary System*, p. 81.
21. Johnson to Fowler, 16 June 1965, *FRUS 1964–1968 VIII*, pp. 171–2.
22. Solomon, *The International Monetary System*, p. 82.
23. Current economic developments, 2 August 1967, *FRUS 1964–1968 VIII*, pp. 395–6.
24. Ball to Fowler, 28 July 1965, *FRUS 1964–1968 VIII*, p. 176.
25. Lyndon B. Johnson Presidential Library, Austin, TX (hereafter LBJL), tape WH6508.01, citation 8509, Johnson–Eugene Black telephone conversation, 5 August 1965, 5.50 p.m.
26. LBJL, tape WH6508.02, citation 8510, Johnson–William Martin telephone conversation, 5 August 1965, 11.47 p.m.
27. Roy, 'The Battle for Bretton Woods', p. 37.
28. Fowler to Johnson, 12 November 1967, *FRUS 1964–1968 VIII*, pp. 434–5.
29. Collins, 'The Economic Crisis of 1968', pp. 404–5.
30. Lyndon B. Johnson, *The Vantage Point: Perspectives of the Presidency, 1963–1969* (New York: Holt, Rinehart, Winston, 1971), pp. 316–17.
31. Gavin, *Gold, Dollars and Power*, p. 172.
32. Johnson's meeting with the leadership, 18 November 1967, *FRUS 1964–1968 VIII*, pp. 440–1.
33. Collins, 'The Economic Crisis of 1968', p. 406.
34. Note 6, *FRUS 1964–1968 VIII*, p. 453. Congress removed the gold cover requirement in March 1968. Solomon, *The International Monetary System*, p. 119.
35. Johnson, *The Vantage Point*, p. 317.
36. Report on European balance of payments trip, 7 January 1968, *FRUS 1964–1968 VIII*, p. 496.
37. Collins, 'The Economic Crisis of 1968', p. 407.
38. Rostow to Johnson, 14 March 1968, *FRUS 1964–1968 VIII*, p. 538.
39. Roy, 'The Battle for Bretton Woods', p. 51.
40. Rostow to Johnson, 14 March 1968, *FRUS 1964–1968 VIII*, p. 537.
41. Note 2 (document 189), *FRUS 1964–1968 VIII*, p. 537.
42. Editorial note, *FRUS 1969–1972 III Foreign Economic Policy, 1969–1972; International Monetary Policy, 1969–1972* (2001), p. 389.
43. Johnson, *The Vantage Point*, p. 319.
44. Rostow to Johnson, 2 April 1968, *FRUS 1964–1968 VIII*, pp. 543–4. French hostility to SDR was shown by the fact that Pierre-Paul Schweitzer, Managing Director of the IMF, was said to keep a parrot which he trained to say 'SDR – stick it up your ass'. Denis Healey, *Time of My Life* (London: Penguin, 1990), p. 416.
45. Kissinger to Nixon, 14 October 1969, *FRUS 1969–1972 III*, p. 375.
46. Gavin, *Gold, Dollars and Power*, p. 183.
47. Rostow to Johnson, 15 November 1968, *FRUS 1964–1968 VIII*, p. 573.
48. Gavin, *Gold, Dollars and Power*, pp. 183–4; Embassy Germany to the White House, 21 November 1968, *FRUS 1964–1968 VIII*, p. 592.
49. Diane B. Kunz, 'Cold War Dollar Diplomacy', in Diane B. Kunz (ed.), *The Diplomacy of the Crucial Decade: American Foreign Relations During the 1960s* (New York: Columbia University Press, 1994), p. 84.
50. Johnson, *The Vantage Point*, p. 312.

51. Bator, 'Lyndon Johnson and Foreign Policy', in Lobel (ed.), *Presidential Judgment*, p. 46.
52. Herter to Bundy, 20 July 1965, *FRUS 1964–1968 VIII*, p. 736.
53. Johnson, *The Vantage Point*, p. 311.
54. Ibid., p. 312.
55. Bator to Smith, 19 April 1967, *FRUS 1964–1968 VIII*, p. 890; Bator, 'Lyndon Johnson and Foreign Policy', in Lobel (ed.), *Presidential Judgment*, p. 62; Bator to Smith, 19 April 1967, *FRUS 1964–1968 VIII*, p. 890.
56. Bator to Johnson, 1 May 1967, *FRUS 1964–1968 VIII*, p. 909.
57. Johnson, *The Vantage Point*, p. 313.
58. Bator to Johnson, 13 May 1967, *FRUS 1964–1968 VIII*, p. 928.
59. Thomas Alan Schwartz, *Lyndon Johnson and Europe: In the Shadow of Vietnam* (Cambridge, MA: Harvard University Press, 2003), p. 171.
60. Bator to Johnson, 15 May 1967, *FRUS 1964–1968 VIII*, p. 935.
61. Ibid.
62. Report on the Congressional Briefings, undated, *FRUS 1964–1968 VIII*, p. 941.
63. Enders to Rusk, 16 May 1967, 'General Results of the Kennedy Round', 16 May 1967, *FRUS 1964–1968 VIII*, p. 937.
64. Bator to Johnson, 15 May 1967, *FRUS 1964–1968 VIII*, p. 935.
65. Schwartz, *Lyndon Johnson and Europe*, pp. 171–3.
66. Quoted in Gavin, *Gold, Dollars and Power*, p. 4.
67. Ibid., p. 182.
68. Kunz, 'Cold War Dollar Diplomacy', in Kunz (ed.), *The Diplomacy of the Crucial Decade*, p. 107.
69. Roy, 'The Battle for Bretton Woods', p. 46.
70. Bator, 'Lyndon Johnson and Foreign Policy', in Lobel (ed.), *Presidential Judgment*, p. 62.

Conclusion

This book has sought to provide a fresh account of President Lyndon B. Johnson's conduct of foreign affairs, filling a gap in the literature. It is noted that the President established a White House foreign policy operation responsive to his own needs and inclinations. Although his disinterest towards intelligence reports is not to his credit (he felt that such assessments merely complicated the making of policy), he sought counsel from a wide range of sources for the benefit of hearing different views as well as to legitimise existing policies. Concerns about the United States' international credibility were foremost among the reasons for the escalation of the US commitment in Vietnam in 1965. Historians should seek to judge the decision to 'Americanise' the war on its own terms, in and of itself, rather than in the light of how the war turned out – defeat was not foreordained. In some ways the American military performed adequately in Vietnam, crushing the Tet Offensive of 1968, for example. However, the guerrilla element of the war was not given sufficient attention and by 1968 the death toll had exceeded what in the United States was generally considered to be an acceptable sacrifice.

Britain, the United States' most important ally,[1] provided diplomatic support for the United States' stance in Vietnam but would not provide troops, and the 'dissociation' episode in 1966 showed that even the diplomatic support had its limits. Differences over Vietnam along with the British inability to maintain international defence commitments weakened the high-level Anglo-American relationship, although Britain remained a major ally by virtue of its continued commitment to the NATO theatre. In contrast to London's efforts to preserve a 'special relationship' with Washington, the French sought to assert their independence, as shown by the withdrawal from the NATO command structure in 1966. Anglo-American cooperation facilitated NATO reform in the wake of the withdrawal. The White House opposed Paris's demands for the neutralisation of Southeast Asia on the assumption that such a development would mean the complete communisation of the region. The Administration dealt with de Gaulle in a circumspect manner, minimising the strains and leaving the road clear for improved relations with his successors.

Johnson also had to deal with two challenges to NATO connected with the Federal Republic of Germany (FRG). He acknowledged the reservations of other European states and knew of the deep Congressional scepticism towards the Multilateral Force (MLF) project, which was designed to give Bonn more of a say in the nuclear affairs of the alliance. His conclusion that the MLF was more trouble than it was worth was probably sound, not least because the end of the MLF by 1966 permitted German nuclear aspirations to be fulfilled in the NATO Nuclear Planning Group (NPG), a consultative mechanism instead of a hardware one. The question of the Bonn government's 'offset' of the foreign exchange costs of American troops in the FRG led to the 'trilateral' negotiations of 1966–7, which also included the British. The outcome was a workable, if short-term, offset formula.

Despite difficulties such as the Vietnam War, the mutual dealings of Washington and Moscow saw a range of accords that laid the foundations for superpower détente in the 1970s.[2] Johnson believed that in the nuclear age the superpowers had a special obligation to maintain a stable relationship. The US relationship with China, however, saw less progress than that with the Soviet Union. The tentative American initiatives on matters such as the liberalisation of travel set a precedent, but reasons internal to the Chinese regime along with the impact of the war in Vietnam meant that Beijing was simply not interested in establishing a more cooperative relationship. As such, there was limited scope to exploit the Sino-Soviet 'split' geopolitically, as there was in the 1970s.

The first major dispute in the Middle East with which the Administration had to deal, over the island of Cyprus in 1964, had a distinctly European dimension. The Administration's effort in June 1964 to dissuade Turkey from military intervention on Cyprus was distinctly crude, including as it did the suggestion that the United States might ignore its NATO obligations in the event of Soviet involvement in a Greco-Turkish war. The very suggestion that Washington did not consider its NATO commitment absolutely binding could have aroused a controversy that went well beyond the Cyprus question. One wonders too what mischief Moscow might have made of it. Johnson's refusal, in the face of counsel from Dean Acheson and George Ball, to give Turkey the green light to invade Cyprus and thereby to 'end' the problem reflected the unpredictable consequences of such a move. The President's caution was also clear in 1967, when he strove to restrain the Israelis from launching a pre-emptive attack on Egypt and its allies. The fear was that the United States might become embroiled in a Middle Eastern war, but American influence over Israel had its limits. US policy during the Six-Day War demonstrated a bias towards Tel Aviv, perhaps not unreasonable given that Israel's very existence was at stake.

In the Western Hemisphere, Johnson lacked enthusiasm and ambition for the Alliance for Progress, confining its work mainly to economic modernisation rather than political reform. The Alliance did in fact help to encourage regional economic development. The challenge from Castro's Cuba to the US naval base at Guantánamo early in 1964 saw the President respond firmly and proportionately. The US military intervention in the Dominican Republic the following year was based on an exaggerated though not groundless fear of Castro-inspired communism. The troops were used constructively, to achieve a truce rather than to crush the rebels, and to bring about democratic elections.[3] The Dominican Republic was able to develop a system of constitutional government in large part due to the American intervention.

Although the Administration's prescriptions for reform in the international monetary realm were more piecemeal than visionary, the President and his colleagues handled the economic crisis of 1967–8 in a capable manner. There was success in liberalising international trade among Free World nations through the Kennedy Round of tariff negotiations. While one might question how far the results of these negotiations benefited American trading interests, the talks helped to bolster unity between the United States and its allies in a challenging period.

What general verdict might one reach, then, about President Johnson's handling of foreign affairs? As H. W. Brands and Paul Y. Hammond have intimated,[4] any such assessment needs to consider that Johnson had to operate in an environment in which US dominance was declining. The retreat of European imperialism left many unresolved issues such as the war in Vietnam, where there were limits on what American material power might achieve. Despite its wishes to maintain a 'special relationship' with Washington, Britain was in relative decline and could be counted upon less and less to shoulder global defence burdens. Restiveness in Western Europe found expression in France's efforts to chart a more independent course, and in the FRG's nuclear aspirations. The Soviet Union approached a position of rough nuclear parity by the time Johnson left office, from a position of decisive inferiority at the beginning of the decade. The communist Chinese demonstrated their technological progress when they detonated an atomic bomb in 1964 and a hydrogen bomb in 1968.

In the Middle East, Cyprus was an unresolved postcolonial issue. The growing commitment to Israel – stemming largely from Johnson's political friendships in the United States rather than any foreign policy rationale – fostered tensions in the Middle East without bringing greater control over Tel Aviv's policies. The United States' southern neighbours were less inclined to tolerate American paternalism. The example set by Cuba in 1959 led the Administration to engage in fire-fighting in the Dominican Republic. The United States' balance of payments deficits encouraged de Gaulle to attack the dollar, and although Washington retained the leverage to push through its desired reforms, the Bretton Woods system was far less favourable to American interests than it had been. In 1960 the United States possessed 25.9 per cent of the world's GNP, but by 1970 that figure had fallen to 23 per cent. Although this was nearly double that of the Soviet Union,[5] the Johnson years were a period of declining relative wealth and influence for the United States.

Vietnam, of course, saw the Administration extend American commitments significantly and, whatever the merits of the decision to intervene, was a self-imposed burden. The American war in Vietnam strained bilateral relationships such as those with Britain and France, and intensified Congressional pressure to reduce US military and financial commitments in Europe.[6] The desire to strengthen American 'credibility' by expanding the commitment in the former Indochina did not, for instance, assuage the French fear that the United States was more likely to leave Western Europe undefended rather than risk war with the Soviet Union. Vietnam inhibited progress toward détente with Moscow and was one reason why the Chinese were so ill-disposed to Washington. The US preoccupation with Vietnam probably encouraged Nasser to launch his challenge to Israel in 1967.[7] Vietnam contributed to Johnson's unwillingness to appear soft on communism in the Western Hemisphere. Military spending in Southeast Asia increased the balance of payments deficit and weakened the dollar.

At the same time, the outcome of the war could have been far worse. The Administration's refusal to take the ground war into North Vietnam helped to keep the conflict limited, and there was no sell-out of South Vietnamese interests in the peace negotiations that began in 1968. The very fact that the Administration had engaged in peace talks, however fruitless at this stage, offered an opportunity for President Nixon.[8] There was no outright breach with an ally over Vietnam, and controversy over the war did not prevent other countries cooperating with Washington when it suited them to do so.[9] It has been argued that Johnson's waging of limited war in Southeast Asia permitted him to improve Soviet–American relations, because escalating the war in Vietnam ensured that his domestic opponents could not depict him as an appeaser of communism.[10] There is little evidence, though, that the desire for détente with Moscow played a role in Johnson's escalation of the war in Vietnam, and it was also the case that the American critics of détente could bolster their arguments by pointing to increased Soviet support for Hanoi as the US commitment expanded. Johnson felt that escalating the commitment in Vietnam was a necessity, while East–West détente was merely desirable.

The sustained burden of Vietnam meant that the President's attention to issues such as, for example, the Soviet–American relationship was rather intermittent. There is also the broader issue that any President has far more to contend with than just foreign affairs. Nevertheless, Johnson's guiding hand was evident to some degree, and usually to good effect, in all the foreign and economic policy issues surveyed in this book. During the Kennedy Round talks, for example, he even concerned himself at one point with the tariff on canned hams (tariffs on this product, as well on various other products, deadlocked the negotiations).[11] Johnson had a sound grasp of the international monetary system and all its implications for inter-allied relations as well as for the financial and economic standing of the United States.

While he was not inclined to question the globalist containment policies and the perceived need to stand up to dictators that formed the foundation of the United States' approach to the outside world, his view that the tenets of Bretton Woods were by no means sacrosanct showed that he was not hidebound. He was not a reflexive Cold Warrior, as shown by his commitment to détente with Moscow. The President had the ability to push the agenda, as shown by the pursuit (admittedly overoptimistic) of arms control negotiations in 1968. The question of how to respond to de Gaulle's NATO move in 1966, when figures such as Dean Acheson were agitating for a tough line, was an example of an approach that was inherently Johnson's own and one that demonstrates how he could have a more intuitive and effective grasp of an issue than some of his most sophisticated and prestigious advisers.[12]

Sometimes, such as in the case of Vietnam, Johnson's style of decision-making was drawn out and dithering, probably reflecting the approach he had grown accustomed to while in Congress.[13] He liked to keep his options open as long as he could, but the example of the Dominican Republic showed he could act decisively when he felt it appropriate.

Johnson made good use of his advisory system, weighing up counsel from various formal and informal sources and then implementing his own, usually sensible, preference. Johnson might endorse a suggestion such as that from the State Department early in 1966 to create what turned out to be the NPG.[14] Sometimes, as one would expect, he would reject ideas such as that of taking a tough line towards de Gaulle, and there were times when he overruled his advisers and refrained from taking action in response to major communist actions in Vietnam.[15] He also felt it necessary on occasions to rein in advisers, such as those who were pushing the MLF to the point where doing so was counterproductive.

Johnson demonstrated an evolution in his conduct of foreign policy. It is hard to imagine him indulging in 1968 in the shrill and exaggerated anti-communism of the sort that he used to justify the intervention in the Dominican Republic three years earlier, and his attitudes towards communist China became more mature and sophisticated as time passed.[16] As time went on, too, he was less prone to clumsiness in his personal dealings with foreign diplomats. The failure to prosecute the war in Vietnam more effectively shows that Johnson's aptitude as a military commander was limited, but his general record of success in foreign and economic affairs demonstrates that his skills in the diplomatic realm were more formidable than is generally assumed. He had the acumen, in what amounted to his greatest success, to deal with the challenges to NATO in ways that left the alliance more unified in 1969 than it had been in 1963. President Johnson displayed a sound understanding of the world beyond the shores of the United States and in most instances dealt well with it.

Notes

1. The Federal Republic of Germany was the strongest economic power in Europe and Johnson got along especially well with Chancellor Erhard, but as noted in Chapter Four, Britain had more extensive extra-European connections and was an important collaborator with the United States in nuclear and intelligence matters.
2. John Dumbrell, *President Lyndon Johnson and Soviet Communism* (Manchester: Manchester University Press, 2004), p. 185.
3. Walt W. Rostow, *The Diffusion of Power: An Essay in Recent History* (New York: Macmillan, 1972), p. 527.
4. H. W. Brands, *The Wages of Globalism: Lyndon Johnson and the Limits of American Power* (New York: Oxford University Press, 1995), pp. 256–7; Paul Y. Hammond, *LBJ and the Presidential Management of Foreign Relations* (Austin, TX: University of Texas Press, 1992), p. 211.
5. Paul M. Kennedy, *The Rise and Fall of the Great Powers: Economic Change and Military Conflict from 1500 to 2000* (New York: Random House, 1987), p. 436, table 43. The figure cited above is compared with 25.9 per cent in 1960.

6. Andreas Wenger, 'Crisis and Opportunity: NATO's Transformation and the Multilateralization of Détente, 1966–1968', *Journal of Cold War Studies*, 6, 1 (Winter 2004), p. 31.

7. CIA Board of National Estimates to Helms, *Foreign Relations of the United States* (hereafter FRUS) *1964–1968 XIX Arab-Israeli Crisis and War, 1967* (Washington, DC: USGPO, 2004), p. 151.

8. Harriman memorandum, 14 December 1968, *FRUS 1964–1968 VII Vietnam September 1968–January 1969* (Washington, DC: USGPO, 2003), p. 762.

9. Thomas Alan Schwartz, *Lyndon Johnson and Europe: In the Shadow of Vietnam* (Cambridge, MA: Harvard University Press, 2003), p. 235.

10. Ibid., citing the views of Jack F. Matlock, the former US Ambassador to the Soviet Union, pp. 235–6.

11. Francis Bator, 'Lyndon Johnson and Foreign Policy: The Case of Western Europe and the Soviet Union', in Aaron Lobel (ed.), *Presidential Judgment: Foreign Policy Decision Making in the White House* (Hollis, NH: Puritan Press, 2000), p. 51.

12. Schwartz, *Lyndon Johnson and Europe*, p. 229.

13. Dumbrell, *President Lyndon Johnson and Soviet Communism*, p. 180.

14. Note 2, *FRUS 1964–1968 XIII Western Europe Region* (1995), p. 314.

15. Bator, 'No Good Choices', pp. 311, 312.

16. Lumbers, *Piercing the Bamboo Curtain*, p. 255.

Bibliography

Archival Sources

Lyndon B. Johnson Presidential Library, Austin, Texas.
The National Archives, Kew, Surrey.
US National Archives, College Park, Maryland.

Printed Primary Sources

Association of Diplomatic Studies and Training, Arlington, Virginia, 'Frontline Diplomacy: The US Foreign Affairs Oral History Collection' (CD-ROM).
Beschloss, Michael (ed.), *Reaching for Glory: Lyndon Johnson's Secret White House Tapes, 1964–1965* (New York: Simon and Schuster, 2001).
Beschloss, Michael (ed.), *Taking Charge: The Johnson White House Tapes, 1963–64* (New York: Simon and Schuster, 1997).
US Department of State, *Foreign Relations of the United States 1964–1968* and *1969–1976* series (Washington, DC: USGPO, various years and volumes).

Memoirs and Diaries

Ball, George, *The Past Has Another Pattern: Memoirs* (New York: Norton, 1982).
Benn, Tony, *Out of the Wilderness: Diaries 1963–1967* (London: Hutchinson, 1987).
Brandon, Henry, *Special Relationships: A Foreign Correspondent's Memoirs from Roosevelt to Reagan* (London: Macmillan, 1988).
Clifford, Clark, with Richard Holbrooke, *Counsel to the President: A Memoir* (New York: Random House, 1991).
Healey, Denis, *The Time of My Life* (London: Penguin, 1989).
Humphrey, Hubert, *The Education of a Public Man: My Life and Politics* (London: Weidenfeld and Nicolson, 1976).
Johnson, Lyndon B., *The Vantage Point: Perspectives of the Presidency, 1963–1969* (New York: Holt, Rinehart, Winston, 1971).

Kissinger, Henry A., *The White House Years* (London: Weidenfeld and Nicolson and Michael Joseph, 1979).

Kissinger, Henry A., *Years of Renewal* (London: Weidenfeld and Nicolson, 1999).

McNamara, Robert S., with Brian VanDeMark, *In Retrospect: The Tragedy and Lessons of Vietnam* (New York: Times Books, 1995).

Rostow, Walt W., *The Diffusion of Power: An Essay in Recent History* (New York: Macmillan, 1972).

Rusk, Dean, *As I Saw It: A Secretary of State's Memoirs* (New York: Norton, 1990).

Schlesinger, Arthur Jr, *Journals 1952–2000* (London: Atlantic, 2007).

Wilson, Harold, *The Labour Government, 1964–1970: A Personal Record* (London: Weidenfeld and Nicolson, 1971).

Secondary Sources: Books

Ahlberg, Kristin L., *Transplanting the Great Society: Lyndon Johnson and Food for Peace* (Columbia, MO and London: University of Missouri Press, 2008).

Aid, Matthew M., *The Secret Sentry: The Untold History of the National Security Agency* (New York: Bloomsbury, 2009).

Aldrich, Richard, *The Hidden Hand: Britain, America and Cold War Secret Intelligence* (London: John Murray, 2001).

Andrew, Christopher, *For the President's Eyes Only: Secret Intelligence and the American Presidency from Washington to Bush* (London: HarperCollins, 1995).

Barrett, David M., *Uncertain Warriors: Lyndon Johnson and his Vietnam Advisers* (Lawrence, KS: University Press of Kansas, 1993).

Baylis, John (ed.), *Anglo-American Relations Since 1939* (Manchester: Manchester University Press, 1997).

Beisner, Robert L., *Dean Acheson: A Life in the Cold War* (Oxford and New York: Oxford University Press, 2006).

Berman, Larry, *Lyndon Johnson's War: The Road to Stalemate in Vietnam* (New York: Norton, 1989).

Bill, James A., *George Ball: Behind the Scenes in US Foreign Policy* (New Haven, CT and London: Yale University Press, 1997).

Bird, Kai, *The Color of Truth: McGeorge Bundy and William Bundy: Brothers in Arms* (New York: Touchstone, 1998).

Blackburn, Robert M., *Mercenaries and Lyndon Johnson's 'More Flags': The Hiring of Korean, Filipino and Thai Soldiers in the Vietnam War* (Jefferson, NC and London: McFarland, 1994).

Bozo, Frédéric, *Two Strategies for Europe: De Gaulle, the United States, and the Atlantic Alliance* (Lanham, MD: Rowman and Littlefield, 2001).

Brandon, Henry, *Anatomy of Error: The Secret History of the Vietnam War* (London: André Deutsch, 1970).

Brands, H. W. (ed.), *The Foreign Policies of Lyndon Johnson: Beyond Vietnam* (College Station, TX: Texas A&M University Press, 1999).

211

Brands, H. W., *The Wages of Globalism: Lyndon Johnson and the Limits of American Power* (New York: Oxford University Press, 1995).

Burns, Richard Dean and Joseph M. Siracusa, *The Historical Dictionary of the Kennedy-Johnson Era* (Lanham, MD and Oxford: Scarecrow Press, 2007).

Buzzanco, Robert, *Masters of War: Military Dissent and Politics in the Vietnam Era* (Cambridge: Cambridge University Press, 1997).

Carter, James M., *Inventing Vietnam: The United States and State Building, 1954–1968* (Cambridge: Cambridge University Press, 2008).

Cogan, Charles G., *Forced to Choose: France, the Atlantic Alliance, and NATO: Then and Now* (Westport, CT: Praeger, 1997).

Cohen, Warren, *Dean Rusk* (Totowa, NJ: Cooper Square, 1980).

Cohen, Warren I. and Nancy Bernkopf Tucker (eds), *Lyndon Johnson Confronts the World: American Foreign Policy, 1963–1968* (New York: Columbia University Press, 1994).

Colman, Jonathan, *A 'Special Relationship'? Harold Wilson, Lyndon B. Johnson and Anglo-American Relations 'at the Summit', 1964–68* (Manchester: Manchester University Press, 2004).

Conkin, Paul K., *Big Daddy from the Pedernales: Lyndon Baines Johnson* (Boston: Twayne, 1986).

Cooper, Chester, *The Lost Crusade: America in Vietnam* (New York: Dodd, Mead, 1971).

Costigliola, Frank, *France and the United States: The Cold Alliance since 1945* (New York: Twayne, 1992).

Dallek, Robert, *Flawed Giant: Lyndon Johnson and his Times, 1961–1973* (Oxford and New York: Oxford University Press, 1998).

Daum, Andreas W., Lloyd C. Gardner and Wilfried Mausbach (eds), *America, the Vietnam War and the World: Comparative and International Perspectives* (Cambridge and New York: Cambridge University Press, 2003).

DiLeo, David, *George Ball, Vietnam and the Rethinking of Containment* (Chapel Hill, NC: University of North Carolina Press, 1991).

Divine, Robert A. (ed.), *The Johnson Years, Volume One: Foreign Policy, the Great Society and the White House* (Lawrence, KS: University Press of Kansas, 1981).

Divine, Robert A. (ed.), *The Johnson Years, Volume Two: Vietnam, the Environment, and Science* (Lawrence, KS: University Press of Kansas, 1987).

Divine, Robert A. (ed.), *The Johnson Years, Volume Three: LBJ at Home and Abroad* (Lawrence, KS: University Press of Kansas, 1994).

Dobson, Alan P., *US Economic Statecraft for Survival, 1933–1991* (Abingdon: Routledge, 2002).

Dockrill, Saki, *Britain's Retreat from East of Suez: The Choice between Europe and the World?* (Basingstoke: Palgrave, 2002).

Donaghy, Greg, *Tolerant Allies: Canada and the United States, 1963–1968* (Montreal, London and Rochester, NY: McGill-Queen's University Press, 2002).

Dumbrell, John, *President Lyndon Johnson and Soviet Communism* (Manchester: Manchester University Press, 2004).

Ellis, Sylvia, *Britain, America and the Vietnam War* (Westport, CT: Praeger, 2005).

Ellison, James, *The United States, Britain and the Transatlantic Crisis: Rising to the Gaullist Challenge, 1963–1968* (Basingstoke: Palgrave, 2007).

Foot, Rosemary, *The Practice of Power: US Relations with China Since 1945* (Oxford and New York: Oxford University Press, 1995).

Fry, Joseph A., *Debating Vietnam: Fulbright, Stennis, and their Senate Hearings* (Lanham, MD: Rowman and Littlefield, 2008).

Gardner, Lloyd C., *Pay Any Price: Lyndon Johnson and the Wars for Vietnam* (Chicago: Dee, 1995).

Gardner, Lloyd C. and Ted Gittinger (eds), *International Perspectives on Vietnam* (College Station, TX: Texas A&M University Press, 2000).

Gardner, Lloyd C. and Ted Gittinger (eds), *The Search for Peace in Vietnam* (College Station, TX: Texas A&M University Press, 2004).

Garthoff, Raymond, *Détente and Confrontation: American-Soviet Relations from Nixon to Reagan* (Washington, DC: Brookings, 1994).

Garthoff, Raymond, *A Journey Through the Cold War: A Memoir of Containment and Coexistence* (Washington, DC: Brookings, 2001).

Gavin, Francis J., *Gold, Dollars and Power: The Politics of International Monetary Relations, 1958–1971* (Chapel Hill, NC and London: University of North Carolina Press, 2004).

Geyelin, Philip, *Lyndon B. Johnson and the World* (London: Pall Mall, 1966).

Goodwin, Doris Kearns, *Lyndon B. Johnson and the American Dream* (London: André Deutsch, 1976).

Haftendorn, Helga, *NATO and the Nuclear Revolution: A Crisis of Credibility. 1966–67* (Oxford: Clarendon Press, 1996).

Hammond, Paul, *LBJ and the Presidential Management of Foreign Relations* (Austin, TX: University of Texas Press, 1992).

Hanyok, Robert J., *Spartans in Darkness: American SIGINT and the Indochina War, 1945–1975* (Center for Cryptologic History, National Security Agency, 2002). http://www.nsa.gov/public_info/_files/cryptologic_histories/spartans_in_dark ness.pdf

Herring, George C., *America's Longest War: The United States and Vietnam, 1950–1975*, 2nd edition (New York: McGraw Hill, 1986).

Historical Division, Joint Secretariat, Joint Chiefs of Staff, *The History of the Joint Chiefs of Staff: The Joint Chiefs of Staff and the War in Vietnam, 1960–68 Part I* (FOIA release, 1994).

Hopkins, Michael F., Saul Kelly and John W. Young (eds), *The Washington Embassy: British Ambassadors to the United States 1939–1977* (Basingstoke: Palgrave, 2009).

Hughes, Geraint, *Harold Wilson's Cold War: The Labour Government and East-West Relations, 1964–1970* (Woodbridge and Rochester, NY: Boydell, 2009).

Hunt, Michael H., *Lyndon Johnson's War: America's Cold War Crusade in Vietnam, 1945–1968* (New York: Hill and Wang, 1996).

Jeffreys-Jones, Rhodri, *Cloak and Dollar: A History of American Secret Intelligence* (New Haven, CT: Yale University Press, 2002).

Jeffreys-Jones, Rhodri, *The CIA and American Democracy* (New Haven, CT: Yale University Press, 2003).

Johnson, Paul, *A History of the American People* (London: Weidenfeld and Nicolson, 1997).

Johnson, Thomas R., *American Cryptology During the Cold War 1945–1989 Book II, Centralization Wins, 1960–1972* (National Security Agency, 1995).

Kaiser, David E., *American Tragedy: Kennedy, Johnson and the Origins of the Vietnam War* (Cambridge, MA: Harvard University Press, 2000).

Kattenburg, Paul M., *The Vietnam Trauma in American Foreign Policy, 1945–1975* (New Brunswick, NJ and London: Transaction, 1980).

Kennedy, Paul M., *The Rise and Fall of the Great Powers: Economic Change and Military Conflict from 1500 to 2000* (New York: Random House, 1987).

Kissinger, Henry A., *Diplomacy* (New York: Simon and Schuster, 1994).

Kunz, Diane B. (ed.), *The Diplomacy of the Crucial Decade: American Foreign Relations During the 1960s* (New York: Columbia University Press, 1994).

Kunz, Diane B., *Butter and Guns: America's Cold War Economic Diplomacy* (New York: Free Press, 1997).

Lankford, Nelson K., *The Last American Aristocrat: The Biography of Ambassador David K. E. Bruce* (Boston: Little, Brown, 1996).

Larsen, Stanley Robert and James Lawton Collins Jr, *Allied Participation in Vietnam* (Washington, DC: USGPO, 1975).

Lathrop, Charles E. (ed.), *The Literary Spy: The Ultimate Source for Quotations on Espionage and Intelligence* (New Haven, CT and London: Yale University Press, 2004).

Lenczowski, George, *American Presidents and the Middle East* (Durham, NC: Duke University Press, 1990).

Lind, Michael, *The Necessary War: A Reinterpretation of America's Most Disastrous Military Conflict* (New York: Free Press, 1999).

Logevall, Fredrik, *Choosing War: The Lost Chance for Peace and the Escalation of the War in Vietnam* (Berkeley, CA: University of California Press, 1999).

Lumbers, Michael, *Piercing the Bamboo Curtain: Tentative Bridge-building to China During the Johnson Years* (Manchester: Manchester University Press, 2008).

Lundestad, Geir, *The United States and Western Europe Since 1945* (Oxford: Oxford University Press, 2003).

Macmillan, Margaret, *Seize the Hour: When Nixon Met Mao* (London: John Murray, 2006).

Mak, Dayton and Charles Stuart Kennedy (eds), *American Ambassadors in a Troubled World: Interviews with Senior Diplomats* (Westport, CT and London: Greenwood, 1992).

Mastny, Vojtech, Sven G. Holtsmark and Andreas Wenger (eds), *War Plans and Alliances in the Cold War: Threat Perceptions in the East and West* (Abingdon: Routledge, 2006).

Mayers, David, *The Ambassadors and America's Soviet Policy* (Oxford and New York: Oxford University Press, 1995).

McMahon, Robert J., *The Limits of Empire: The United States and Southeast Asia Since World War II* (New York: Columbia University Press, 1999).

Milne, David, *America's Rasputin: Walt Rostow and the Vietnam War* (New York: Hill and Wang, 2008).

Moyar, Mark, *Triumph Forsaken: The Vietnam War, 1954–1965* (Cambridge and New York: Cambridge University Press, 2006).

Moyar, Mark, *A Question of Command: Counterinsurgency from the Civil War to Iraq* (New Haven, CT and London: Yale University Press, 2009).

Oren, Michael B., *Six Days of War: June 1967 and the Making of the Modern Middle East* (New York: Oxford University Press, 2002).

Paxton, Robert O. and Nicholas Wahl (eds), *De Gaulle and the United States: A Centennial Reappraisal* (Oxford: Berg, 1994).

Petersen, Tore T., *The Decline of the Anglo-American Middle East, 1961–1969* (Brighton: Sussex Academic Press, 2006).

Pickering, Jeffrey, *Britain's Withdrawal from East of Suez: The Politics of Retrenchment* (London: Macmillan, 1998).

Pierre, Andrew J., *Nuclear Politics: The British Experience with an Independent Strategic Force, 1939–1970* (London: Oxford University Press, 1970).

Ponting, Clive, *Breach of Promise: Labour in Power 1964–1970* (London: Hamish Hamilton, 1989).

Preston, Andrew, *The War Council: McGeorge Bundy, the NSC and Vietnam* (Cambridge, MA: Harvard University Press, 2006).

Priest, Andrew, *Kennedy, Johnson and NATO: Britain, America and the Dynamics of Alliance, 1962–68* (London: Routledge, 2006).

Richelson, Jeffrey T., *Spying on the Bomb: American Nuclear Intelligence from Nazi Germany to Iran and North Korea* (New York: Norton, 2006).

Schrafstetter, Susanna and Stephen Twigge, *Avoiding Armageddon: Europe, the United States and the Struggle for Nuclear Nonproliferation, 1945–1970* (Westport, CT: Praeger, 2004).

Schulzinger, Robert D., *A Time for War: The United States and Vietnam, 1945–1975* (New York and Oxford: Oxford University Press, 1997).

Schwartz, Thomas Alan, *Lyndon Johnson and Europe: In the Shadow of Vietnam* (Cambridge, MA: Harvard University Press, 2003).

Sheehan, Neil, Hedrick Smith, E. W. Kenworthy and Fox Butterfield (eds), *The Pentagon Papers: The Secret History of the Vietnam War: The Complete and Unabridged Series as published by the New York Times* (New York: Bantam Books, 1971).

Short, Anthony, *The Origins of the Vietnam War* (London: Longman, 1989).

Siracusa, Joseph M., *Nuclear Weapons: A Very Short Introduction* (Oxford and New York: Oxford University Press, 2008).

Solomon, Robert, *The International Monetary System, 1945–1976* (New York: Harper and Row, 1977).

Stearns, Monteagle, *Entangled Allies: US Policy Towards Greece, Turkey and Cyprus* (New York: Council on Foreign Relations, 1992).

Steinbruner, John D., *The Cybernetic Theory of Decision: New Dimensions of Political Analysis* (Princeton, NJ: Princeton University Press, 1974).

Thornton, Martin, *Times of Heroism, Times of Terror: American Presidents and the Cold War* (Westport, CT and London: Praeger, 2005).

Turner, Stansfield, *Burn Before Reading: Presidents, CIA Directors and Secret Intelligence* (New York: Hyperion, 2005).

Twigge, Stephen and Len Scott, *Planning Armageddon: Britain, the US and the Command of Nuclear Forces, 1945–1964* (Amsterdam: Harwood Academic Press, 2000).

Tyler, Patrick, *A World of Trouble: America in the Middle East* (London: Portobello, 2009).

Uslu, Nasuh, *The Cyprus Question as an Issue of Turkish Foreign Policy and Turkish-American Relations, 1959–2003* (New York: Nova, 2003).

VanDeMark, Brian, *Into the Quagmire: Lyndon Johnson and the Escalation of the Vietnam War* (New York: Oxford University Press, 1991).

Vandiver, Frank E., *Shadows of Vietnam: Lyndon Johnson's Wars* (College Station, TX: Texas A&M University Press, 1997).

Walton, C. Dale, *The Myth of Inevitable US Defeat in Vietnam* (London: Cass, 2002).

Weiner, Tim, *Legacy of Ashes: The History of the CIA* (London: Penguin, 2007).

Winand, Pascaline, *Eisenhower, Kennedy and the United States of Europe* (Basingstoke: Macmillan, 1993).

Woods, Randall B., *LBJ: Architect of American Ambition* (New York: Free Press, 2006).

Yim, Kwan Ha (ed.), *China and the US, 1964–72: From Johnson and Vietnam to Nixon and Détente* (New York: Facts on File, 1972).

Young, John W., *The Labour Governments, 1964–1970: Volume 2: International Policy* (Manchester: Manchester University Press, 2003).

Zeiler, Thomas W., *Dean Rusk: Defending the American Mission Abroad* (Wilmington, DL: Scholarly Resources, 2000).

Zhai, Qiang, *China and the Vietnam Wars, 1950–1975* (Chapel Hill, NC and London: University of North Carolina Press, 2000).

Zimmerman, Hubert, *Money and Security: Troops, Monetary Policy and West Germany's Relations with the United States and Britain, 1950–1971* (Cambridge: Cambridge University Press, 2002).

Secondary Sources: Articles and Book Chapters

Anderson, David L., 'A Question of Political Courage: Lyndon Johnson as War Leader', in Mitchell B. Lerner (ed.), *Looking Back at LBJ: White House Politics in a New Light* (Lawrence, KS: University Press of Kansas, 2005), pp. 101–27.

Anderson, David L., 'The Vietnam War', in Robert D. Schulzinger (ed.), *A Companion to American Foreign Relations* (Malden and Oxford: Blackwell, 2006), pp. 309–29.

Bator, Francis M., 'The Political Economics of International Money', *Foreign Affairs*, 47, 1 (October 1968), pp. 51–67.

Bator, Francis, 'Lyndon Johnson and Foreign Policy: The Case of Western Europe and the Soviet Union', in Aaron Lobel (ed.), *Presidential Judgment: Foreign Policy Decision Making in the White House* (Hollis, NH: Puritan Press, 2000), pp. 41–78.

Bator, Francis, 'No Good Choices: LBJ and the Vietnam/Great Society Connection', *Diplomatic History*, 32, 3 (June 2008), pp. 309–40.

Benvenuti, Andrea, 'The British Military Withdrawal from Southeast Asia and its Impact on Australia's Cold War Security Interests', *Cold War History*, 5, 2 (May 2005), pp. 189–210.

Ben-Zvi, Abraham, 'Influence and Arms: John F. Kennedy, Lyndon B. Johnson and the Politics of Arms Sales to Israel, 1962–1966', *Israel Affairs*, 10, 1 & 2 (January 2004), pp. 29–59.

Boulton, J. W., 'NATO and the MLF', *Journal of Contemporary History*, 7, 3–4 (July–October 1972), pp. 275–94.

Brands, H. W., 'Vietnam and the origins of détente', in Lloyd C. Gardner and Ted Gittinger (eds), *The Search for Peace in Vietnam* (College Station, TX: Texas A&M University Press, 2004), pp. 371–90.

Brands, Hal, 'Non-Proliferation and the Dynamics of the Middle Cold War: The Superpowers, the MLF, and the NPT', *Cold War History*, 7, 3 (August 2007), pp. 389–423.

Brands, Hal, 'Progress Unseen: US Arms Control Policy and the Origins of Détente, 1963–1968', *Diplomatic History*, 30, 2 (April 2006), pp. 253–85.

Brigham, Robert K. and George C. Herring, 'The PENNYSYLVANIA Peace Initiative, June–October 1967', in Lloyd C. Gardner and Ted Gittinger (eds), *The Search for Peace in Vietnam 1964–1968* (College Station, TX: Texas A&M University Press, 2004), pp. 59–72.

Buchan, Alistair, 'The Multilateral Force: a study in alliance politics', *International Affairs*, 40, 4 (1964), pp. 619–37.

Bunch, Clea Lutz, 'Strike at Samu: Jordan, Israel, the United States, and the Origins of the Six-Day War', *Diplomatic History*, 32, 1 (January 2008), pp. 55–76.

Burr, William and Jeffrey T. Richelson, '"Whether to strangle the baby in the cradle": The United States and the Chinese Nuclear Program, 1960–64', *International Security*, 25, 3 (Winter 2000–1), pp. 54–99.

Calleo, David, 'De Gaulle and the Monetary System: The Golden Rule', in Robert O. Paxton and Nicholas Wahl (eds), *De Gaulle and the United States: A Centennial Appraisal* (Oxford: Berg, 1994), pp. 239–56.

Cogan, Charles G., '"How fuzzy can one be?" The American reaction to de Gaulle's proposal for the neutralisation of (South) Vietnam', in Lloyd C.

Gardner and Ted Gittinger (eds), *The Search for Peace in Vietnam* (College Station, TX: Texas A&M University Press, 2004), pp. 144–61.

Collins, Robert M., 'The Economic Crisis of 1968 and the Waning of the American Century', *The American Historical Review*, 101, 2 (April 1996), pp. 396–422.

Colman, Jonathan, 'Harold Wilson, Lyndon B. Johnson and Anglo-American "summit diplomacy", 1964–68', *Journal of Transatlantic Studies*, 1, 2 (Autumn 2003), pp. 131–51.

Colman, Jonathan, 'The London ambassadorship of David K. E. Bruce during the Wilson-Johnson years, 1964–68', *Diplomacy and Statecraft*, 15, 2 (June 2004), pp. 327–52.

Colman, Jonathan, '"Dealing with disillusioned men": The Washington ambassadorship of Sir Patrick Dean, 1965–69', *Contemporary British History*, 21, 2 (June 2007), pp. 247–70.

Colman, Jonathan, '"What Now for Britain?" The State Department's Intelligence Assessment of the "Special Relationship", 7 February 1968', *Diplomacy and Statecraft*, 19, 2 (June 2008), pp. 350–60.

Colman, Jonathan, 'Sir Patrick Dean, 1965–69', in Michael F. Hopkins, Saul Kelly and John W. Young (eds), *British Ambassadors to Washington, 1939–1977* (Basingstoke: Palgrave, 2009), pp. 150–68.

Colman, Jonathan and J. J. Widén, 'The Johnson Administration and the Recruitment of Allies in Vietnam, 1964–68', *History*, 94, 4 (December 2009), pp. 483–504.

Costigliola, Frank, 'Lyndon B. Johnson, Germany, and "the End of the Cold War"', in Warren I. Cohen and Nancy Bernkopf Tucker (eds), *Lyndon Johnson Confronts the World: American Foreign Policy, 1963–1968* (Cambridge: Cambridge University Press, 1994), pp. 173–210.

Dallek, Robert, 'Lyndon Johnson as a World Leader', in H. W. Brands, *Beyond Vietnam: The Foreign Policies of Lyndon Johnson* (College Station, TX: Texas A&M University Press, 1999), pp. 6–18.

Dockrill, Saki, 'Forging the Anglo-American Global Defence Partnership: Harold Wilson, Lyndon Johnson and the Washington summit, December 1964', *Journal of Strategic Studies*, 23, 4 (December 2000), pp. 107–29.

Dumbrell, John, 'The Johnson administration and the British Labour Government: Vietnam, the pound and East of Suez', *Journal of American Studies*, 30 (1996), pp. 211–31.

Dumbrell, John and Sylvia Ellis, 'British involvement in Vietnam peace initiatives, 1966–1967: Marigolds, Sunflowers, and "Kosygin Week"', *Diplomatic History*, 27, 1 (January 2003), pp. 113–49.

Ellison, James, 'Defeating the General: Anglo-American Relations, Europe and the NATO Crisis of 1966', *Cold War History*, 6, 1 (February 2006), pp. 85–111.

Faustmann, Hubert, 'Independence postponed: Cyprus 1959–1960', in Hubert Faustmann and Nicos Peristianis (eds), *Britain in Cyprus: Colonialism and Post-Colonialism* (Mannheim and Mohnesee: Bibliopolis, 2006), pp. 453–72.

Felten, Peter, 'Yankee, Go Home and Take Me With You: Lyndon Johnson and the Dominican Republic', in H. W. Brands (ed.), *The Foreign Policies of Lyndon Johnson: Beyond Vietnam* (College Station, TX: Texas A&M University Press, 1999), pp. 98–144.

Fielding, Jeremy, 'Coping with decline: US policy towards the British defence reviews of 1966', *Diplomatic History*, 22, 4 (Fall 1999), pp. 633–56.

Friedman, Max Paul, 'Retiring the Puppets, Bringing Latin America Back In: Recent Scholarship on United States-Latin American Relations', *Diplomatic History*, 27, 5 (November 2003), pp. 621–36.

Gardner, Lloyd, 'Lyndon Johnson and de Gaulle', in Robert O. Paxton and Nicholas Wahl (eds), *De Gaulle and the United States* (Oxford: Berg, 1994), pp. 257–78.

Garson, Robert, 'Lyndon B. Johnson and the China Enigma', *Journal of Contemporary History*, 32, 1 (1997), pp. 63–80.

Hahn, Peter L., 'An Ominous Moment: Lyndon Johnson and the Six-Day War', in Mitchell B. Lerner (ed.), *Looking Back at LBJ: White House Politics in a New Light* (Lawrence, KS: University Press of Kansas, 2005), pp. 78–100.

Harrison, Benjamin T. and Christopher L. Mosher, 'John T. McNaughton and Vietnam: The Early Years as Assistant Secretary of Defense, 1964–1965', *History*, 92, 308 (October 2007), pp. 496–514.

Heinrichs, Waldo, 'Lyndon B. Johnson: Change and Continuity', in Warren I. Cohen and Nancy Bernkopf Tucker (eds), *Lyndon Johnson Confronts the World: American Foreign Policy 1963–1968* (Cambridge: Cambridge University Press, 1994), pp. 9–30.

Heuer, Richards J., 'Five Paths to Judgment', in H. Bradford Westerfield (ed.), *Inside CIA's Private World: Declassified Articles from the Agency's Internal Journal, 1955–1992* (New Haven, CT and London: Yale University Press, 1995), pp. 379–414.

Hopkins, Michael F., 'David Ormsby-Gore, Lord Harlech, 1961–65', in Michael F. Hopkins, Saul Kelly and John W. Young (eds), *British Ambassadors to Washington, 1939–1977* (Basingstoke: Palgrave, 2009), pp. 130–49.

Hughes, Geraint, 'A "Missed Opportunity" for Peace? Harold Wilson, British Diplomacy and the *Sunflower* Initiative to End the Vietnam War', *Diplomacy and Statecraft*, 4, 3 (2003), pp. 106–30.

Humphrey, David C., 'Tuesday Lunch at the White House: A Preliminary Assessment', *Diplomatic History*, 8, 1 (Winter 1984), pp. 81–102.

Humphrey, David C., 'NSC Meetings During the Johnson Presidency', *Diplomatic History*, 18, 1 (Winter 1994), pp. 29–45.

Jones, Matthew, '"Groping toward coexistence": US China Policy During the Johnson Years', *Diplomacy and Statecraft*, 12, 3 (2001), pp. 175–90.

Joseph, Joseph J., 'The Political Context and Consequences of the London and Zurich Agreements', in Hubert Faustmann and Nicos Peristianis (eds), *Britain in Cyprus: Colonialism and Post-Colonialism* (Mannheim and Mohnesee: Bibliopolis, 2006), pp. 413–30.

219

Kaplan, Lawrence, 'McNamara, Vietnam, and the Defense of Europe', in Vojtech Mastny, Sven G. Holtsmark and Andreas Wenger (eds), *War Plans and Alliances in the Cold War: Threat Perceptions in the East and West* (Abingdon: Routledge, 2006), pp. 286–300.

Kunz, Diane B., 'Lyndon Johnson's dollar diplomacy', *History Today*, 42 (April 1992), pp. 45–51.

Kunz, Diane B., 'Cold War Dollar Diplomacy: The Other Side of Containment', in Diane B. Kunz (ed.), *The Diplomacy of the Crucial Decade: American Foreign Relations During the 1960s* (New York: Columbia University Press, 1994), pp. 80–115.

Kunz, Diane B., '"Somewhat mixed-up together": Anglo-American defence and financial policy during the 1960s', *Journal of Commonwealth and Imperial History*, 27, 2 (May 1999), pp. 213–32.

Lazarorowitz, Arlene, 'Different Approaches to a Regional Search for Balance: The Johnson Administration, the State Department, and the Middle East, 1964–67', *Diplomatic History*, 32, 1 (January 2008), pp. 25–54.

Lerner, Mitchell B., 'Introduction: Lyndon Johnson in History and Memory', in Mitchell B. Lerner (ed.), *Looking Back at LBJ: White House Politics in a New Light* (Lawrence, KS: University Press of Kansas, 2005), pp. 1–19.

Lerner, Mitchell, '"Trying to Find the Guy Who Invited Them": Lyndon Johnson, Bridge Building and the End of the Prague Spring', *Diplomatic History*, 32, 1 (January 2008), pp. 77–103.

Little, Douglas, 'A Fool's Errand: America and the Middle East', in Diane B. Kunz (ed.), *The Diplomacy of the Crucial Decade: American Foreign Relations During the 1960s* (New York: Columbia University Press, 1994), pp. 283–319.

Little, Douglas, 'Choosing Sides: Lyndon Johnson and the Middle East', in Robert A. Divine (ed.), *The Johnson Years: LBJ at Home and Abroad* (Lawrence, KS: University Press of Kansas, 1994), pp. 150–97.

Logevall, Fredrik, 'De Gaulle, Neutralization and American Involvement in Vietnam, 1963–1965', *The Pacific Historical Review*, 61, 1 (February 1992), pp. 69–102.

Lumbers, Michael, 'The Irony of Vietnam: The Johnson Administration's Tentative Bridge-Building to China, 1965–1966', *Journal of Cold War Studies*, 6, 3 (Summer 2004), pp. 68–114.

Lumbers, Michael, '"Staying out of this Chinese muddle": The Johnson Administration's Response to the Cultural Revolution', *Diplomatic History*, 31, 2 (April 2007), pp. 259–94.

Martin, Garrett, 'Playing the China Card? Revisiting France's Recognition of Communist China', *Journal of Cold War Studies*, 10, 1 (Winter 2008), pp. 52–80.

Parker, Robert B., 'The June 1967 War: What Color was the Light?', *Middle East Journal*, 46 (1992), pp. 177–97.

Plischke, Elmer, 'Lyndon Johnson as Diplomat-in-Chief', in Bernard J. Firestone and Robert C. Vogt (eds), *Lyndon Baines Johnson and the Uses of Power* (New York: Greenwood, 1988), pp. 257–86.

Prados, John, 'Prague Spring and SALT: Arms Limitation Setbacks in 1968', in H. W. Brands (ed.), *The Foreign Policies of Lyndon Johnson: Beyond Vietnam* (College Station, TX: Texas A&M University Press, 1999), pp. 19–36.

Prados, John, 'Feature Review: Looking for the Real Lyndon' (review of Beschloss (ed.), *Reaching for Glory*), *Diplomatic History*, 27, 5 (November 2003), pp. 751–6.

Rabe, Stephen G., 'US Relations with Latin-America, 1961 to the Present: A Historiographic Review', in Robert D. Schulzinger (ed.), *A Companion to American Foreign Relations* (Oxford: Blackwell, 2006), pp. 387–403.

Rivas, Darlene, 'United States-Latin American Relations, 1942–1960', in Robert D. Schulzinger (ed.), *A Companion to American Foreign Relations* (Oxford: Blackwell, 2006), pp. 230–54.

Roy, Rajarshi, 'The Battle for Bretton Woods: America, Britain and the International Financial Crisis of October 1967–March 1968', *Cold War History*, 2, 2 (January 2002), pp. 33–60.

Schandler, Herbert Y., 'The Pentagon and Peace Negotiations after March 31, 1968', in Lloyd C. Gardner and Ted Gittinger (eds), *The Search for Peace in Vietnam* (College Station, TX: Texas A&M University Press, 2004), pp. 321–54.

Schulzinger, Robert D., '"It's Easy to Win a War on Paper": The United States and Vietnam' in Diane B. Kunz (ed.), *The Diplomacy of the Crucial Decade: American Foreign Relations During the 1960s* (New York: Columbia University Press, 1994), pp. 183–219.

Suri, Jeremi, 'Lyndon Johnson and the Global Disruption of 1968', in Mitchell B. Lerner (ed.), *Looking Back at LBJ: White House Politics in a New Light* (Lawrence, KS: University Press of Kansas, 2005), pp. 53–77.

Torikata, Youko, 'Reexamining de Gaulle's Peace Initiative on the Vietnam War', *Diplomatic History*, 31, 5 (November 2007), pp. 909–38.

Tucker, Nancy Bernkopf, 'Lyndon B. Johnson: A Final Reckoning', in Warren I. Cohen and Nancy Bernkopf Tucker (eds), *Lyndon Johnson Confronts the World: American Foreign Policy 1963–1968* (Cambridge: Cambridge University Press, 1994), pp. 311–20.

Vaisse, Maurice, 'De Gaulle and the Vietnam war', in Lloyd C. Gardner and Ted Gittinger (eds), *The Search for Peace in Vietnam* (College Station, TX: Texas A&M University Press, 2004), pp. 162–5.

Vanke, Jeffrey W., 'De Gaulle's Atomic Defence Policy in 1963', *Cold War History*, 1, 2 (January 2001), pp. 119–26.

Waldron, Arthur, 'From Nonexistent to Almost Normal: US-China Relations in the 1960s', in Diane B. Kunz (ed.), *The Diplomacy of the Crucial Decade: American Foreign Relations During the 1960s* (New York: Columbia University Press, 1994), pp. 219–50.

Walker III, William O., 'The Struggle for the Americas: The Johnson Administration and Cuba', in H. W. Brands (ed.), *The Foreign Policies of Lyndon Johnson: Beyond Vietnam* (College Station, TX: Texas A&M University Press, 1999), pp. 61–97.

Wenger, Andreas, 'Crisis and Opportunity: NATO's Transformation and the Multilateralization of Détente, 1966–1968', *Journal of Cold War Studies*, 6, 1 (Winter 2004), p. 37.

Widén, J. J. and Jonathan Colman, 'Lyndon B. Johnson, Alec Douglas-Home, Europe and the NATO Multilateral Force, 1963–64', *Journal of Transatlantic Studies*, 5, 1 (2007), pp. 179–99.

Wilson, Harold, 'How a Prime Minister and an Ambassador Almost Stopped the Vietnam War', *The Diplomatist*, 35, 4 (April 1979), pp. 30–2.

Woods, Randall B., 'Beyond Vietnam: The Foreign Policies of the Kennedy-Johnson Administrations', in Robert D. Schulzinger (ed.), *A Companion to American Foreign Relations* (Malden and Oxford: Blackwell, 2006), pp. 330–74.

Woods, Randall B., 'Conflicted Hegemon: LBJ and the Dominican Republic', *Diplomatic History*, 32, 5 (November 2008), pp. 749–66.

Woods, Randall B., 'The Politics of Idealism: Lyndon Johnson, Civil Rights, and Vietnam', *Diplomatic History*, 31, 1 (January 2007), pp. 1–18.

Young, John W., 'Britain and "LBJ's War", 1964–68', *Cold War History*, 2, 3 (2002), pp. 63–92.

Zimmerman, Hubert, 'Who paid for America's War? Vietnam and the International Monetary System, 1960–1975', in Andreas W. Daum, Lloyd C. Gardner and Wilfried Mausbach (eds), *America, the Vietnam War and the World: Comparative and International Perspectives* (Cambridge: Cambridge University Press, 2003), pp. 151–74.

Index